JOHNNY'S CASH & CHARLEY'S PRIDE

LASTING LEGENDS AND UNTOLD ADVENTURES IN COUNTRY MUSIC

BY PETER COOPER

FOREWORD BY PETER GURALNICK

Text © 2017 by Peter Cooper

Illustration © 2017 by Julie Sola

Publisher: Paul McGahren
Editorial Director: Matthew Teague
Copy Editor: Kerri Grzybicki
Design: Lindsay Hess
Illustration: Julie Sola
Indexer: Jay Kreider

Artwork for the following images was adapted from photos provided by Stacie Huckeba:
David Olney; Lloyd Green; Merle Haggard; Peter Cooper

Spring House Press
3613 Brush Hill Court
Nashville, TN 37216
ISBN: 978-1-940611-70-9

Library of Congress Control Number: 2017934493

Printed in the United States of America

First Printing: April 2017

Portions of the chapters about Tom T. Hall and Merle Haggard appeared in *American Songwriter* magazine. Portions of the Kris Kristofferson chapter appeared in the Texas A&M University Press book *Pickers & Poets: The Ruthlessly Poetic Singer-Songwriters of Texas*.

For a list that contains names used in *Johnny's Cash & Charley's Pride* that may be registered with the United States Copyright Office, please see page 251.

To learn more about Spring House Press books, or to find a retailer near you, email info@springhousepress.com or visit us at www.springhousepress.com.

JOHNNY'S CASH & CHARLEY'S PRIDE

LASTING LEGENDS AND UNTOLD ADVENTURES IN COUNTRY MUSIC

BY PETER COOPER
FOREWORD BY PETER GURALNICK

SPRING HOUSE PRESS

For Tim Ghianni, John Lane, Ellen Pryor, Todd Snider,
and Deno Trakas, who encouraged without provocation.

RABBITS AND SONGWRITERS

(Inspired by *Johnny's Cash & Charley's Pride*)

People from all over the world
From all walks of life
Come to Nashville—Music City
Believing in music
The way children believe in magic
Most do not make it and go home
Others
Not accepting failure
Live under bridges
Where they laugh at people
Who do not believe
That rabbits live in hats

—TOM T. HALL,
Country Music Hall of Famer

CONTENTS

FOREWORD

By Peter Guralnick

Peter Cooper has always been in the mix. Who else do you know who would begin a career in music journalism focusing not just on musicians of the moment but loudly championing the resourcefulness and originality of such otherwise unsung artists as Pink Anderson, a medicine show entertainer and street singer from Spartanburg, South Carolina, where Peter began writing for a living in his early twenties? That's how I originally met Peter, through his first book, *Hub City Music Makers* (1997), a remarkable chronicle of the many contributions, both well- and little-known, that Spartanburg artists like The Marshall Tucker Band and, yes, Pink Anderson have made to the American musical landscape.

Peter's new book, a chronicle of his peripatetic travels since arriving in Nashville in 2000 to cover the country music scene, is even more remarkable for its ongoing determination to perpetuate that same mix of fame and obscurity, with little regard for the advantages or disadvantages of either. Peter has always

> **Peter has always celebrated both intimacy and authenticity, two qualities that don't always get along.**

celebrated both intimacy and authenticity, two qualities that don't always get along. A confident chronicler, and perhaps as a result the recipient of many confidences, he has added appreciably to the luster and mystery of such well-burnished legends as Merle Haggard and George Jones that you may *think* you're already thoroughly familiar with (you'll soon discover you're not)—but wait'll you read his accounts of lesser-known and multigenerational figures like Tommy Collins and singer-songwriter David Olney and . . . well, all I can say is you're in for a treat.

Whoever he is writing about, Peter has always celebrated the virtues of individualism, idealism, and existential wit. A familiar of such Falstaffian figures as "Cowboy" Jack Clement and Merle Kilgore, Peter offers brilliant, and *funny*, portrayals of their magnificent eccentricities without ever showing a hint of condescension—and without ever failing to suggest the depths of perception, insight, and regret that may well lie underneath. The overall tale that he tells, however divagacious it may be (and it *is* divagacious), is at its heart a gloriously romantic story, written in the same cool-breezy manner that Cowboy brought to his tragically truncated, unpublished memoir, which offered as a credo, "When all else fails, get lucky. But don't forget to say your prayers, and always be a true believer."

There are gems on every page. Here is David Olney musing on the perils of the search for fortune and fame: "Here's the thing. Not a lot of people like my shit. But the people that do—I'm the only place they can get it. If they don't come hear me, they're not going to get the shit they like. I've got a monopoly on my shit." Or listen to Don Light, one of the most inspired thinkers, aphorists, and multi-taskers you're ever likely to meet (he was at one time or another drummer on the Grand Ole Opry, head of the Nashville office of *Billboard*, manager/discoverer of Jimmy Buffet, originator of the concept of professional

> **"Remember, boys, we're in the fun business. If we're not having fun, we're not doing our jobs."**
> **—Jack Clement**

booking in gospel music, and in his later life champion of nouveau bluegrass). "I've never had an original idea," he declared with typical (and unwarranted) self-deprecation. "What I've been able to do is see something working in one area and realize it could be applied to another area. If you can find a need and fill it, you've probably got a job." Where else can you get a more succinct definition of the music business (or any other business, for that matter) than that?

For me Don Light is the heart of this book. But so is Jack Clement with his own freshly minted adages ("Remember, boys, we're in the fun business. If we're not having fun, we're not doing our jobs") and Shakespearean allusions, not to mention virtuosic philosopher and steel guitarist Lloyd

Green. They are, from my point of view, the book's emotional core. But I don't know. If I were to stick with that, what would I do with Jimmy Martin, the King of Bluegrass, or Earl Scruggs' business-minded wife, Louise, or the late, lamented Ann Soyars, early champion of Chris Stapleton and self-described as "the 'Short Bitch' at the door" of Nashville's own bluegrass capital of the world, the Station Inn? Or how could I leave out Chris Stapleton, for that matter, or Taylor Swift (yes, Taylor Swift—definitely), or Kris Kristofferson? The answer is, I couldn't. And you will have your own preferences, to be sure. So take your pick. But you don't really have to linger on it too long in this far-ranging and lightly treading book. If you don't like what you're reading on this page, or you're hungering for something more, don't worry—it's just around the corner.

In the end Peter defines both his own and his book's intentions best. "I was writing about connection, longing, regret, and pain," he declares, with reference to a story on Guy Clark. "I was doing so with a chuckle line, but it was a chuckle line that got to something deeper." Or, perhaps even more to the point: "I am here to say that objectivity is the mortal enemy. Objectivity is dispassionate. And we're in the passion business."

Or listen to what Don Light used to say whenever he wanted to bestow what he considered to be the supreme compliment. "You know, our little community could really use more individuals like that," he would declare, with reference to someone he was convinced was inclined to measure the world in broader terms than their own. I'm sure he said it to Peter Cooper on more than one occasion. He certainly said it to me *about* Peter. And it's true.

—Peter Guralnick

INTRODUCTION:
THE COWBOY

If I had Johnny's Cash and Charley's Pride
I wouldn't have a Buck Owen on my car
—Cowboy Jack Clement

We should probably start with the Cowboy.

He's the one you should have met.

We all called him a genius. He neither confirmed nor denied.

"I ain't saying I'm a genius," he'd parry. "But you've got to be pretty smart to get all them people saying that on cue."

A bullshit artist, sure, but with emphasis on the "artist" part of that linguistic equation.

He discovered Charley Pride, Jerry Lee Lewis, and Don Williams.

He wrote songs recorded by Johnny Cash, Dolly Parton, Ray Charles, Porter Wagoner, Jerry Garcia, John Prine, and a bunch of others.

He owned the world's smartest cat, and had the world's greatest accordion player living in his backyard.

He ran the Cowboy Arms Hotel & Recording Spa, Nashville's first great home studio, where Cash, Townes Van Zandt, Alison Krauss, Nanci Griffith, John Hartford, and a bunch of others recorded and cavorted.

He engineered the "Million Dollar Quartet" sessions at Sun Records in Memphis, capturing the jovial interactions of Cash, Jerry Lee, Carl Perkins, and Elvis Presley.

He watched his house—the one with the studio, and hundreds of priceless master tapes . . . and the photo of him in his Marine days, saluting Princess Elizabeth . . . and the Gibson guitar with the scuff marks from Elvis' belt buckle . . . burn down. He just stood there out in the yard, wearing his Elvis Presley bathrobe. Singer and dear friend Marshall Chapman heard the furious sirens and joined Cowboy out there in the yard, grimacing at the leaping flames. First thing he said to her was, "Wanna buy a house?"

Cowboy Jack Clement. Everybody called him "Cowboy" even though he wore comfortable shoes and was frightened around ponies.

"They'll kick you and bite you, and step on your toes," he sang. "Some cowboys hate horses, and I'm one of those."

There's a documentary film about him. It's called *Shakespeare Was a Big George Jones Fan: Jack Clement's Home Movies.* He liked making home movies, and he'd get his friends to star in little skits for him. He also blew a cool million one time, making a horror film called *Dear Dead Delilah.* Later, he admitted that he probably should have written a script, or at least should have had someone else write one.

> **Everybody called him "Cowboy" even though he wore comfortable shoes and was frightened around ponies.**

Cowboy name-checked Shakespeare in one of his songs, and he often quoted the Bard. His devotion was neither blind nor complete, though. He'd rattle off the "To be or not to be" line, and the one about "the slings and arrows of outrageous fortune," but he couldn't go all in on "Be all my sins remembered."

"Don't hand me all this shit about all my sins remembered," he'd say. "I want my sins forgot."

He was Nashville's Polka King. When asked how he got that title, he'd say, "I just started calling myself that, and nobody argued."

He drank vodka and smoked what I'm told was the best dope in town.

He arranged the horns and played the guitar on Johnny Cash's "Ring of Fire."

He owned the Dipsy Doodle Construction Company.

For a brief while, he owned Summer Records. Company motto: "Summer hits, and some are not. Hope you like the ones we got."

He was an Arthur Murray dance instructor, and he got the gig in spite of having no knowledge of how to dance. He learned, though, and he'd dance in the recording studio with a wine bottle on top of his head, if the music was going well and there was a wine bottle handy. Turns out there was always a wine bottle handy, though the music didn't always go well.

He was Waylon Jennings' brother-in-law for awhile, and he produced what Waylon said was the best album of his career: 1975's *Dreaming My Dreams*.

For decades, whenever any writer, picker, or dime store philosopher came to Nashville, they'd quickly find their way to Cowboy's place, at 3405 Belmont Boulevard. You couldn't miss it: There was a swimming pool there, and a bunch of cars parked in the circular driveway, and any manner of things going on inside. Somebody would be building a ukulele, somebody would be making a movie or a record, and Cowboy would either be in the middle of it all or he'd be by himself in his office, listening via the speaker system he'd set up.

In the 1970s, a Texas songwriter named Eric Taylor—a brilliant and occasionally wayward soul—visited the Cowboy, in hopes of getting a publishing deal. See, Cowboy published songs, too. He published one of George Jones' biggies, "She Thinks I Still Care." And he published songs for Eric's friend Townes Van Zandt.

Eric sat down and played a song called "Joseph Cross" for Cowboy. "Joseph Cross" is seven minutes of poetry, myth, and wonder. It's about the treatment of Native Americans, which Eric just calls "terrorism."

"His name was Joseph Cross, and he was raised by the mission," Eric sings. "Just one of a hundred Indian boys that wouldn't tie his shoes."

So, Eric played "Joseph Cross" for Cowboy, whereupon Cowboy asked Eric, "Boy, do you know where you are?"

Eric said he thought he knew where he was.

Cowboy asked again, "Boy, do you know where you are?"

Eric looked confused, so Cowboy talked some more.

"Boy, I'd heard your music before you got here. I like you, my wife likes you, and my girlfriend likes you, too. But if I'm not mistaken, you just played me a seven-minute song about an Indian. Is that right?"

Eric agreed that he'd just played a seven-minute song about an Indian.

"If you don't know where you are, I'll tell you. You're in Nashville By God Tennessee. I couldn't sell a seven-minute song here if it was about screwing."

Eric decided to go on back to Texas after that.

Cowboy discovered Charley Pride, an African-American country singer, back in 1965. This was the still-segregated American South, but Cowboy heard what he considered obvious talent, and there were no seven-minute songs about Indians. Actually, Cowboy gave Pride some of his own songs, and told him that if he wanted to make records, he could learn those songs on his trip to see his dad in Mississippi.

"Five or six days later, Charley came back . . . and I had a session set up at RCA Studio B, and we went in and did it," Cowboy said. "I paid for it, and . . . well, then I had the only Charley Pride record in town. I had this office with these big speakers, and I'd get people in there and play Charley's record. Loud, man. Like, really loud. I'd play that record and then I'd show 'em his picture. That was fun."

After hearing the Cowboy sing, it's hard to miss his impact on Charley Pride's vocal phrasing. See, singing isn't just about hitting a note in tune and on time. It's also the way you sing the note . . . how long you hold it, whether you let it tail off into another note or stop abruptly, and how you inflect the thing. We all sing the same notes, after all. And Cowboy was the king of phrasing. He'd let you know it, too, and if you disagreed and wanted to be stubborn about it, you'd find yourself at an impasse.

"I had my ideas about things, songs, and phrasing, and so on, and I was right a lot of the time," he said. "You've got to remember, most singers are insecure. We all know that, right? And a lot of 'em are not too bright. Singers are a pain in the ass, if you want to know the truth about it. Most of 'em. Well, all of 'em."

Cowboy could be a pain in the ass, too. Sam Phillips at Sun Records fired him in 1958 for being just that, though the men remained close friends throughout Sam's life, and Cowboy sang at Phillips' funeral. In Peter Guralnick's *Lost Highway: Journeys and Arrivals of American Musicians* (which I read again every six months, and which I believe to be the quintessential book about American roots music, though I'm glad I didn't tell you that until after you bought my book), Cowboy's protege and good buddy, Dickey Lee, says, "We would go into the studio feeling like heroes, and Jack wouldn't pay much attention to us. While we were recording he would be sitting there reading a comic book or something, and it really deflated me."

When Guralnick asked Jack about that, Cowboy said it's best to keep singers on the edge of anger:

"Singers sing their best when they're thinking of anything but the song. You see, I got 'em so they think I like mistakes. Then if they think I like 'em, they won't give 'em to me. You've got to use two or three kinds of reverse psychology in this game."

The Cowboy was in his late forties when he made his first solo album, *All I Want To Do In Life*, in 1978. That one didn't set the world on fire, a fact that did not devastate.

"I don't remember it being any huge letdown," he told me. "It took a few months before you realized you ain't gonna outdo Elvis or something, and by that time I was off into something else."

That "something else" involved holing up at the Cowboy Arms and letting the rest of the world either go by or drop in.

And a lot of us dropped in: The cast of characters there on Belmont Avenue was so constantly surprising that it dulled surprise. Bono from the rock band U2 came by, and persuaded Jack to co-produce some songs for U2's 1988 *Rattle and Hum* album. The actor Dennis Quaid came by, seeking tips when he was getting set to play Jerry Lee Lewis in a movie. Johnny Cash was there a lot, as were a bunch of recording artists and musicians who recorded at the Spa: The music made there preceded and anticipated what is now called "Americana." There's a professional trade organization now that's devoted to Americana Music. It should probably be called Cowboy Music, except

> **"I tried to keep it where when you hear it you can see things. You can visualize circuses and drinking carrot juice, things like that."**
> **—Cowboy Jack Clement**

that would give people the wrong idea and make them think there were boots and horses involved, and the Cowboy hated boots and horses.

Cowboy made another album of his own in 2004. It was good, too. Again, the phrasing. And the song-craft. And the whimsy.

"I think it's entertaining," he told me. "I tried to keep it where when you hear it you can see things. You can visualize circuses and drinking carrot juice, things like that."

He was in his seventies when album number two, *Guess Things Happen That Way*, came out. But he was ready to roll with it.

"I've always thought if I really wanted to I could cut a hit record," he said. "Well, I want to now. Go on the road and chase girls. Get me a bus. Go to Hollywood and find Salma Hayek."

Cowboy was serious. He had a thing for Salma Hayek.

Cowboy liked rules, so long as he was the one coming up with them. Here are his ten rules for songwriters: Nashville's Cowboy Commandments.

1. *Remember that experts are often wrong.*
2. *Experts tend to be narrow and opinionated.*
3. *Experts don't buy records.*
4. *There's nothing wrong with waltzes, if they're played right.*
5. *A good song gets better with age.*
6. *Reveal some of yourself with most of your songs.*
7. *Don't get stuck on one song too long. Work on other songs as you go.*
8. *Learn to grow from setbacks, delays, and getting your feelings hurt.*
9. *Write the worst song you can think of.*
10. *Write the best song you can think of.*

He also had rules for recording sessions. The first time I saw these rules, they were hanging up in Johnny Cash's personal studio. I've found many of these work well in life situations that have nothing to do with recording music.

1. *Be alert.*
2. *Be on time.*
3. *Don't bring or invite anyone.*
4. *Don't talk about your troubles.*
5. *Don't mention the words "earphones," "headphones," "cans," "earmuffs," or the like. (See, Cowboy preferred recording with all players in the same room, listening to the sound of the room rather than listening through headphones.)*
6. *Be quiet when the Cowboy is speaking.*
7. *Don't be timid or shy with your playing.*
8. *Have a good day.*
9. *Listen.*
10. *Remember that it only takes three minutes to cut a hit record.*

I was at the Cowboy Arms Hotel & Recording Spa one day when Cowboy and producer Don Was were working in conjunction with a young and mighty string band called Old Crow Medicine Show, a group that has since joined the Grand Ole Opry.

The Crow boys are one of several new-century country music artists who have achieved great success without the aid of contemporary country radio: They sold a million copies of their song "Wagon Wheel," even though the terrestrial FM stations ignored it. Good for them. They also have a deep respect—a reverence, even—for country music-makers who came before them. They didn't have any problem with Jack's Rule #6: "Be quiet when the Cowboy is speaking."

But the studio can be a tense place, even when it is the studio belonging to a man who long ago gave up the notion of tension as a creative motivator. Cowboy sensed tension that day, to the point that he raised his arms, demanded and received attention, and spoke his mind:

"Remember, boys, we're in the fun business," Jack said. "If we're not having fun, we're not doing our jobs."

The Cowboy died in 2013. Liver cancer. He was 82, and by then had been elected into the Country Music Hall of Fame. I had to write his obituary for the Nashville newspaper.

"Whimsical maverick Jack Clement—singer, producer, ringleader, writer of classic songs, discoverer of stars, and member of the Country Music Hall of Fame—died this morning at his Nashville home," I wrote.

And I quoted Kris Kristofferson saying Cowboy was one of his favorite people on the planet, and "An amazing character." And I mentioned Cowboy's insistence on informality, and his demand of nothing short of joy.

And I got the Princess Elizabeth thing in there, and the Polka King designation, and some of Jack's production philosophy: "I wasn't trying to get reality, you know? I was trying to make it sound better than reality."

"Clement never joined the world," I wrote. "He danced through it, drank through it, sang through it, made it prettier and more interesting, and gave it further dimension. He caused its inhabitants to laugh and whistle and wonder and arch eyebrows."

It's a good thing people who read a newspaper can't watch you while you write your stories, though I suppose some might have been impressed by my ability to type and cry at the very same time.

Before he died, Jack recorded a final album, one that was released posthumously on I.R.S. Records, as *For Once and For All.* David Ferguson and Matt Sweeney produced it, and a bunch of Cowboy's admirers—Emmylou Harris, Vince Gill, Gillian Welch, Jim Lauderdale, Dierks Bentley, and Dan Auerbach, among them—lined up for guest appearances.

John Grady at I.R.S. asked me to write the liner notes, and I quickly agreed. I was all set to do it, when Cowboy intervened and transmitted them through me. Nice of him to do, and I still cashed the check from the record company. Anyway, here are the Cowboy's words, sent through me to you.

I must have been eight or nine.

I'd be lying in my little bed with the window open, and out the window I could hear girls singing "You Are My Sunshine." They sang it so pretty, and I envisioned them as being beautiful. It's great to be in a sealed place and not have to sweat, but you can miss something good when you don't have those windows open.

So, maybe keep your windows open more often. And sometimes in a really tough situation, ask yourself, "What would the smartest man in the world do in a case like this?" Because he might just wait it out, hole up for awhile, and let the rest of the world either go by or drop in.

I wish you'd dropped in to my place while I was around. We had good times there. We laughed and sang, smiled and smoked, right up until the end. Which wasn't really the end, as it turns out, though this is my final earthly album. We recorded it upstairs at the Cowboy Arms Hotel & Recording Spa. That was my place. You should have dropped in, but maybe it's better that you didn't. It sounds better when you listen this way. We weren't trying to get reality, you know? We were trying to make it sound better than reality. A lot of times, it did.

Don't ever sit and try to figure out all of the answers. You don't have to. I already figured some of them out. Remember that experts are often wrong, and that there's nothing wrong with waltzes if they're played right. Learn to grow from setbacks, delays and getting your feelings hurt. If you're a songwriter, reveal some of yourself with most of your songs. If you're a musician, be alert, on time, listen and have a good day. If you're a singer, don't be such a pain in the ass.

No matter who you are, remember that whatever may be wrong with the world, at least it has some good things to eat. Oh, and remember that we're in the fun business. If we're not having fun, we're not doing our jobs.

As Shakespeare must have said at one time or another, "I could have said that better if I had wanted to."

Aloha,
Cowboy Jack Clement

-S Spot
east nashville

~Blue bird
cafe , to hear
songwriters playing
acoustic guitar

★ station Inn
402 12th
Avenue South
→ good for live
country music
- dresses bertty
went there

Songs to listen to :

1) For once & For All~ ~~produced~~ recorded by
Jacke Clement
produced by
David Ferguson &
Matt Sweeney
1 other cowboy
admirers

-Me My Gang -Rascal
Flatts
-John Prine - Souvenirs

2) Wagon Wheel - Crow boys
All cowboy
3) I want To Do in LIFE - Jack
clements
1st solo
4) Dreaming My Dreams album
- produced by 1978.
Cowboy Jack clements
- Waylon Jennings = singer

5) She Thinks I still care
by George Jones cowboy
produced by Jack clement

6) Joseph Cross - Eric Taylor

7) Corfelio Clark - montazuma Hall

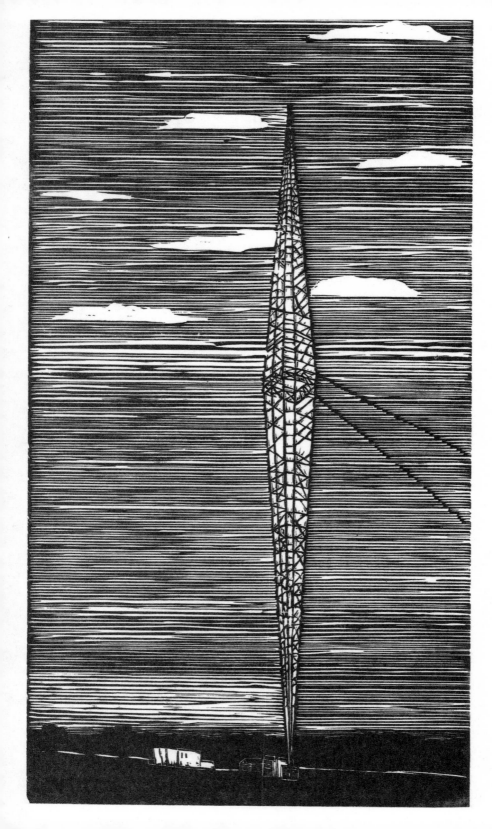

BEGINNINGS

The Music City of Nashville rests atop an 808 foot rhomboid spire, located beside I-65 in the southern suburb of Brentwood.

If you don't know what a rhomboid is, it's an oblique-angled parallelogram. If you don't know what a spire is, it's a tapering conical or pyramidal structure. If you want to know what a rhomboid spire looks like, drive twelve miles south from Nashville on I-65 and look to your left. You'll see the WSM radio tower, and it's a rhomboid spire. I didn't know that until I read a book by Craig Havighurst called *Air Castle of the South: WSM and the Making of Music City*. The tower is only a couple of feet wide at its base, and then it gets fatter in the middle, and then it tapers skinny at the top. Rhomboid spire, apparently.

Anyway, if you're twelve miles south of Nashville and someone asks you why the town became Music City, you can point to that rhomboid spire, better known as the WSM radio tower.

Without it, Nashville is Charlotte, or Cincinnati, or some other place. And Charlotte or Cincinnati or some other place might be Music City.

In November of 1928, the federal government of the United States of America dictated that WSM would be a "clear channel" station. That meant that no other radio station could exist at 650 AM. With no interference, and with the erection of the tower in 1932, the WSM signal could be heard, especially at night, in most parts of America, and on up into Canada.

That meant that an Iowa farmer could tune in to WSM for emergency weather updates and such, which is why the government decided it was important to establish these "clear channel" stations. But it also meant that hillbilly musicians could play live on WSM AM 650 and be heard by a national audience. That kind of thing was impossible in Charlotte or in Cincinnati.

In 1925, George D. Hay began broadcasting a "barn dance" featuring local musicians over WSM's airwaves. On December 10, 1927, he changed that barn dance's name to the "Grand Ole Opry." In less than a year's time, that local "Opry" wasn't local. It was nationwide, via clear channel. Musicians could play the Opry on Saturday night, and hype their tour stops in other towns. If you were playing the Opry on a Saturday in 1938, and playing a Florence, South Carolina schoolhouse the following Wednesday, you knew that some folks in Florence would be listening to your Opry show, and would buy tickets to see you once you told them you were coming their way.

With the clear channel Opry, there was a reason for musicians to come to Nashville. With the clear channel Opry, there was a reason for songwriters to write for those musicians. With the clear channel Opry, there was a reason for publishers to hire songwriters to write for those musicians. And we would need recording studios, to make the records that people would buy after they heard the Saturday night music beamed in from Nashville.

Nashville had the music, the Opry, the rhomboid spire, and the federal government on its side.

There were radio barn dances in other cities. There was hillbilly music made in plenty of other places. But Nashville had the music, the Opry, the rhomboid spire, and the federal government on its side.

Sorry, Cincinnati. You'll always have that weird cinnamon chili you cook, and the tainted legacy of baseball hit king Pete Rose.

Nashville is known as the home of country music. Nearly three hundred miles to the east is Bristol, the border town on the Tennessee/Virginia line that bills itself as "The Birthplace of Country Music."

Now, country music was not born in Bristol, and certainly was not born in Nashville. The roots of country music are in the British Isles and in Africa. Fiddle music from Ireland arrived in the American South via immigrants. The sound of the banjo arrived, as Ketch Secor of string band Old Crow Medicine Show often notes, in the minds of African slaves who played a banjo predecessor before being taken against their wills to America. In the American South, the fiddle met the banjo, and the music that we have come to call "country" was born.

Country music was not born in Bristol or Nashville, and neither was it first recorded in Bristol or Nashville. A fiddler named Eck Robertson (nobody's named Eck these days, are they?) went to the annual Old Confederate Soldiers' Reunion in Richmond, Virginia, in 1922, and after the reunion he and Henry C. Gilliland headed to New York City and auditioned and recorded for the Victor Talking Machine Company. When we listen today to Eck Robertson's fiddle on "Sallie Gooden," recorded on July 1, 1922, we hear sounds that clearly fit into the country music continuum.

But Bristol isn't just blowing smoke. It is a crucial contributor to the rise of country music, having hosted the recording sessions that Johnny Cash always called the most important in country music history.

In 1927, record companies were really in the furniture business. They were selling large "talking machines," living room centerpiece "hardware" that played the "software" that we now call "records." Or maybe we call them "files" now, or something like that. You know the drill. Anyway, the folks at the talking machine companies figured out that if they were going to sell talking machines to folks in various parts of America, they were going to need to have software that was representative of the kind of musics popular in various parts of America. It made sense to sell polka music to folks in Cleveland and Wisconsin. It made sense to sell hillbilly music to people in Appalachia.

Trouble was, it was hard to get hillbillies to head up to recording centers like New York, and sometimes even tough to get them to head down to recording centers like Atlanta. Nashville was not a recording center at all, at this point.

So, the Victor Talking Machine Company wound up sending a producer named Ralph Peer down to the border town of Bristol in 1927, to record as many viable southern artists as he could in hot July and August. Peer spread the word of a cattle call audition/session via a newspaper article in the days prior to the session, and then he set up a temporary recording studio in the Taylor-Christian Hat Company building, on the Tennessee side of State Street. The Virginia side of that street, with the state border in the middle, would have to sit and watch in silence, disgust, and, we'd like to think, some level of admiration.

On the last day of July, The Carter Family left their homes in aptly named Poor Valley, Virginia, to take the 32-or-so mile trip to Bristol to meet Mr. Peer. The Carter Family was the plaintive lead singer, Sara Carter, and her husband, A.P. Carter. The most important element of the band may have been Maybelle Carter, Sara's sister-in-law and the first guitar hero of country music. Maybelle

But at the end of July in 1927, the Carters weren't important or notable. They were different, though: They were a group performing hillbilly music with a female lead singer.

would eventually become known as "Mother Maybelle," and her guitar style became known as "The Carter Scratch." The Carter Scratch involved playing melody notes on the lower-toned strings and frailing chords on the high-pitched strings. It is the basis for the way most acoustic guitarists today approach the instrument, whether or not they've ever heard of Mother Maybelle Carter.

But at the end of July in 1927, the Carters weren't important or notable. They were different, though: They were a group performing hillbilly music with a female lead singer. That was different enough to give record companies pause, in that day. A.P. was once told that with voices like theirs, and guitar talent like Maybelle's, they shouldn't have to be poor. That was enough for him to cling to any distant possibility, and, to be sure, the 32 miles from Poor Valley to Bristol was a distance. It took the Carters all day to drive there in Maybelle's husband's Essex automobile, and they had to ford the Holston River, and to repair a couple of blown tires. Maybelle was eighteen years old, and eight months pregnant. No telling how many stops the Carters had to make.

When they got to Bristol, they found fitful sleep.

The next morning, the Carters got up and started tuning their instruments. Today, electronic implements allow for easy tuning. In 1927, not so much. And these Carters were poor people, from Poor Valley, with cheap instruments. Sara's autoharp had so many strings, and all of them had to be in tune with Maybelle's little guitar.

When the Carters weren't tuning, they were dressing, in their best Sunday clothes. They prepared to arrive in style.

"What confidence the trio had mustered took a shot when they got to the old hat warehouse downtown," wrote Mark Zwonitzer and Charles Hirschberg in the brilliant book, *Will You Miss Me When I'm Gone: The Carter Family & Their Legacy in American Music*. The Carters saw the other hopeful musicians gathered around, milling about, and they felt shame.

"Years later, A.P. confessed to a friend that he'd been so shaken when they arrived that they decided to go around to the alley and climb the fire escape," wrote Zwonitzer and Hirshberg. "They didn't want to walk through that crowd and let everybody get a look at their country clothes."

But they made it up to the warehouse loft, where they saw the recording machine. Sara's daughter, Gladys, and her baby, Joe, were ushered into the corner by Anita Glander Peer, Ralph's wife. On a little Stella guitar, Maybelle started playing a song, and Sara began singing, with accompaniment from Maybelle and A.P.

My heart is sad and I'm in sorrow
For the only one I love
When shall I see him, oh, no, never
'Til we meet in heaven above

The song was "Bury Me Under the Weeping Willow," and it was stirring. Anita Glander Peer began feeding baby Joe Carter ice cream, in hopes of keeping him quiet through the session. The Carters recorded three more songs that night, and Ralph Peer invited them back the next morning. A.P. didn't show that next day, but Sara and Maybelle recorded two more. Then they, Joe, Gladys, and A.P. got in Eck's Essex automobile to drive back to Poor Valley, with $300 that they'd earned from singing and playing.

And then, nothing much happened, at least at first. But in early 1928, the Victor company released one of the songs the Carter's had sung in Bristol, one called "Single Girl."

Single girl, oh single girl, she goes to the store and buys
Oh, goes to the store and buys
Married girl, oh, married girl
She rocks the cradle and cries

That one caught on, and soon there was something called a royalty check, delivered to Poor Valley. And there was news that Ralph Peer wanted the Carters to come to the Victor Recording Studio in Camden, New Jersey, to make more recordings. In May of 1928, they did just that. One of the resulting recordings, "Wildwood Flower," is an enduring anthem of country music. And the Carter Family is known as country music's first family. The Carters' harmonies are templates, models for the way that people sing together. And Maybelle's guitar rings clear and true across decades of Carter recordings, rising above those harmonies.

How did it rise above those harmonies? Well, that was a tough deal, since guitars in the 1920s tended to be tiny and quiet, suited for parlors rather than concert halls. Maybelle's guitar needed to be heard above the singing, and above Sara's autoharp. To do that at the Bristol sessions, Maybelle had to lean way into the microphone and play extra-hard: an unnatural hassle. Luckily, the Gibson guitar company began making a large guitar in 1922, one called an L-5, that was twice as loud as any other guitar on the market. Unluckily, in 1928, that guitar cost $275, which equates to about $4,000 in today's economy. That was huge money. Maybelle could have erected a seven-room Dutch Colonial home on her Poor Valley lot for that, and then she could have built two more homes for good measure.

But the guitar was important, and she bought it. She loved it. She kept it throughout her life, even in the 1960s when she had to work at a nursing home to make ends meet: Being important and beloved doesn't mean being wealthy. She could have sold the L-5 and provided herself significant comfort, but she would not have been comfortable without it.

Maybelle Carter died in 1978. By then, she'd been immortalized in the Nitty Gritty Dirt Band's recording of another Carter standard, "Will the

Circle Be Unbroken." She was among the many guests on the a Dirt Band album that sold millions of copies. It was the biggest commercial success of Maybelle's life, and Nitty Gritty Dirt Band member John McEuen went to her Madison, Tennessee home to present her with her first-ever "gold" record, in commemoration of the album's extraordinary popularity.

The words, "Will the Circle Be Unbroken" are the wraparound inscription on the walls of the Country Music Hall of Fame's rotunda, above the plaques of each Hall of Famer. One plaque signifies that Maybelle, Sara, and A.P. Carter made history with their music. On the third floor of the Country Music Hall of Fame and Museum, Maybelle's L-5 sits in a display case that identifies the Gibson as a "Precious Jewel" of American music.

"His is a thousand and one tongues yet singularly his own," wrote Bob Dylan, about Jimmie Rodgers. "His is the voice in the wilderness of your head . . . Only in turning up the volume can we determine our own destiny."

"The sun's not yellow, it's chicken," wrote Bob Dylan, but that wasn't about Jimmie Rodgers. I don't really know what that was about.

Tim McGraw had a hit song called "Live Like You Were Dying." It was written by Craig Wiseman and Tim Nichols. The deal with that song was that a man was told by a doctor that he was on the outs, and he responded by doing all the things that he'd always meant to do. Riding a bull, skydiving, climbing mountains, etc. As it turns out in the song, he gets a reprieve, but he tells others that he's glad he got the chance to live like he was dying.

Meridian, Mississippi-born Jimmie Rodgers didn't get a reprieve, but he lived like he was dying. He contracted tuberculosis in 1924, at age 27. At the time, he was a drifter who hung around train yards. He thought to himself, "What do I want to do with the short rest of my life?" He answered himself, "Sing." And that's what he did.

When he was 29, he heard about the all-call recording sessions Ralph Peer was putting on in Bristol. He recorded for Peer on August 4, 1927, and he made enough of an impression to be allowed to record for Victor that November, up in Camden, New Jersey. On November 30, 1927, Rodgers walked into Camden's Trinity Baptist Church and sang a rather un-churchly song that became known as "Blue Yodel No. 1 (T for Texas)."

"I'm gonna shoot poor Thelma, just to see her jump and fall," he sang, and those words have been repeated in versions by Johnny Cash, the Everly Brothers, Lynyrd Skynyrd, Waylon Jennings, and hundreds of others. It wasn't Rodgers' lyricism that secured his legacy, though, and many of his lines were strung together from blues and folk songs he'd heard during his rambling days. In "Blue Yodel No. 1," at one point he sings "I'm going where the water tastes like cherry wine," and then he says, as a kind of blues aside, "Aw, sing 'em, boy, sing 'em," even though he's the only one singing. In any case, the magic wasn't in the lyrics, it was in the voice, and in the way he delivered his songs with a mash of African-American blues and Swiss yodeling.

"Jimmie was alive in a way that others were not and are not," Dylan wrote of the man sometimes called "The Singing Brakeman." "His message is all between the lines, and he delivers it like nectar that can drill through steel."

Rodgers recorded twelve more blue yodels and more than one hundred songs before his death in May of 1933, not even six years after he first recorded. In that brief time, he established himself as the "Father of Country Music," but his influence goes far beyond even that anointed designation.

"It's a shame . . . that people think of Jimmie Rodgers as the root of just one thing, when he was a root for so many things," is how Phil Everly of the Everly Brothers put it to author and music scholar Barry Mazor, whose *Meeting Jimmie Rodgers* is an artfully dense, illuminating study of Rodgers' impact on decades of musicians, including the Beatles' George Harrison. If you've impacted a Beatle and Bob Dylan, you've done pretty well for yourself. If you can do that while also forging a musical path that leads to a creation that came to be called "country music," your name is Jimmie Rodgers, and you've been gone from this world since 1933. Anytime we hear up-tempo country music, with flair and braggadocio, there's a way to trace it back to Rodgers. But the up-tempo stuff isn't his only mark: Bono, of rock band U2, recorded a gorgeous, ephemeral ballad of Rodgers' called "Dreaming with Tears in My Eyes."

Jimmie Rodgers did a lot of dreaming with tears in his eyes. He dreamed that a frail rounder, stricken with tuberculosis, could be a national hero who recorded with Louis Armstrong, who made the women scream, and who in many ways remains present and contemporary. But those dreams weren't enough to mitigate his certain sorrow.

"When it rained down sorrow, it rained all over me," he sang. "'Cause my body rattles like a train on that old S.P./ I've got the T.B. blues."

In the end, the music transcends. At least that's what we like to think. Jimmie Rodgers wasn't sure about that transcendence bit.

"Lord, that graveyard is a lonesome place," he sang. "They put you on your back, throw that mud down on your face/ I've got the T.B. blues."

Country music's most famous show is the Grand Ole Opry, the longest-running radio show in American history.

And its first star was DeFord Bailey, a black man in the segregated South.

The Opry began in 1925 as the WSM Barn Dance. It featured everything from string bands and singer-guitarists to military bands during its early years. One day in the autumn of 1927, Bailey was booked to play on "Judge" George D. Hay's WSM radio show. Back then, WSM featured a variety of music, some of it piped in from other cities. This particular day, Hay waited for NBC's *Music Appreciation Hour* show to end, and he heard conductor Walter Damrosch say that there was no place in the classics for realism.

When he took to the airwaves, Hay boasted that his barn dance would present nothing but realism: "It will be down to earth, for the earthy," he said, in words preserved in historian Charles Wolfe's fine book, *A Good Natured Riot: The Birth of the Grand Ole Opry*.

DeFord Bailey was a master of musical realism. He had been a sickly child who spent lots of time in his bedroom, listening to fox chases, train whistles, and other sounds from outside the home, and he learned to mimic those sounds on his harmonica. The roar of a locomotive, the baying of hounds, the yelps of foxes . . . he could recreate all of that by sending breaths of air into the reeds of his little Hohner harmonica, and he could amplify the sounds with a handmade megaphone. People loved it. They were charmed.

When Bailey went on Hay's show that day—after the conclusion of the *Music Appreciation Hour* that was clearly unappreciated by Hay—he played "Pan American Blues," a harmonica solo that mimicked the sounds of the train that rolled past the WSM radio tower.

And Judge Hay explained, "For the past hour we have been listening to the music taken largely from the Grand Opera, but from now on we will present the Grand Ole Opry."

Thus, DeFord Bailey became the first musician heard on the show known thereafter as the "The Grand Ole Opry."

Bailey was a crowd-pleaser, and he was one of the biggest stars of the early Opry, judging from audience response and from letters sent to him via WSM.

He performed every Saturday night for the first thirteen years of the Grand Ole Opry.

Bailey toured with Roy Acuff, Bill Monroe, and others, and he seemed to have found a permanent place as an Opry member. In the early 1940s, however, Judge Hay fired Bailey from the Opry, almost certainly acting on instructions from WSM management. "They turned me loose to root hog or die," Bailey said later.

The firing was in part due to a dispute over whether Bailey would continue to play his most famous songs, which were licensed for public performance through performing rights organization ASCAP (American Society of Composers, Authors, and Publishers.)

At this point, in 1941, radio's contract with ASCAP—which let radio stations broadcast any songs licensed by ASCAP-affiliated songwriters and publishers in return for annual fees—had expired, and no station could broadcast an ASCAP-licensed song without incurring heavy fines. Therefore, Opry officials were asking the show's performers to play songs that could be licensed (at less expense) through the rival performance licensing organization BMI.

Lots of technical words in that paragraph you just skimmed, frustratedly. Basically, DeFord Bailey wanted to play the songs that made him famous, which is the same thing every Opry member has done, through history. In the second decade of the twenty-first century, Opry member Little Jimmy Dickens often said from the stage, "Here's my latest hit. It's from 1965."

The Opry brass claimed they wanted Bailey to learn new songs that could be licensed through BMI, and that was true enough, on the surface. But by 1941, segregation in the South was something that was being both challenged and defended. The storm of change was far away, but the winds were perceptible. The idea of a black man playing on the radio and touring with white musicians in 1927 seemed interesting. The reality of a black man playing on the radio and toured with white musicians in 1941 seemed like a social statement.

Bailey wouldn't play ball, feeling (justifiably) that his audiences wanted to hear his most popular songs. Five years after he fired Bailey, Judge Hay wrote a book called *A Story of the Grand Ole Opry*. In that book, he wrote, "Like some members of his race, and other races, DeFord was lazy . . . He knew about a dozen

Bailey quit playing music professionally. He shined shoes on a corner near what became Nashville's "Music Row,"

numbers, which he put on the air and recorded for a major company, but he refused to learn any more."

Hay also referred to Bailey as "a little crippled colored boy," and a "mascot," and claimed that when Bailey was fired, he replied, "I knowed it was comin', Judge, I knowed it was comin'."

After being let go, Bailey quit playing music professionally. He shined shoes on a corner near what became Nashville's "Music Row," the town's recording and music business center.

The sign at his shop read:

Stop here,
Get your shoes shined quick,
Boston slick,
Dust won't stick,
Stop here.
Get yours shined quick.
You're next.

Bailey would occasionally play harmonica for interested folks who had stopped by for a shoe shine. But he wouldn't play music gigs, even if they offered more than a week's shoe-shining wages for so doing. His reasoning was that he was one of Nashville's top musical acts when he was fired, and he knew what Nashville's top acts were making for appearances in the years after WSM dropped him. So, he wasn't going to play unless he was offered the kind of money that others were making. He occasionally made exceptions to his rule, appearing a few times on the Opry.

Bailey lived his final years in a public housing complex at the corner of 12th Avenue South and Edgehill Avenue. If you drive past there today, you'll see two big statues of polar bears throwing snowballs at each other, and you'll see a smaller historic marker, noting that this was where DeFord Bailey lived and worked. He died in 1982, at age 82, thinking that his mark on country music had been largely forgotten. A year later, Nashville mayor Richard Fulton declared "DeFord Bailey Day," and the metropolitan government passed a resolution that held three truths to be irrefutable and evident: That "Mr. Bailey was the first musician to perform on the Grand Ole Opry"; that he "performed for the first recording session ever held in Nashville" (on October 2, 1928); and that he "made major contributions to country music and to the Nashville community."

"DeFord Bailey Day" was June 23, 1983, and on that day the late harmonica wizard received a proper tombstone. At the celebration of that stone, early Opry stars (and Country Music Hall of Fame members) praised Bailey in speeches, asserting that he should be a member of country music's Hall of Fame. But it wasn't until 22 years later that Bailey became a Hall of Famer.

Bailey's story is at once troubling and inspiring, sad and triumphant. Late in his life, he befriended a young Metropolitan Development and Housing Agency employee named David Morton, and in time he convinced Morton to write his biography.

"I want you to tell the world about this black man," Bailey told Morton. "He ain't no fool. Just let people know what I am . . . I take the bitter with the sweet. Every day is Sunday with me. I'm happy go lucky. Amen!"

My own beginnings as a chronicler of country songs and songsters are rooted in the spectacular acoustic music I heard as a teenager.

On my fifteenth birthday, my dad and stepmother took me to hear a band called the Seldom Scene. The Seldom Scene's name was a misnomer if you lived in the Washington, DC area in the 1980s, as they played a club called the Birchmere each Thursday night.

The Seldom Scene was a bluegrass band, but they played songs from diverse sources: The Stanley Brothers, Bob Dylan, Eric Clapton, Gram

Parsons, and many others. Upon hearing them, I loved them, immediately. I asked what kind of music they played and was told, "bluegrass." I decided I must love bluegrass music, and was disheartened when I went to my first bluegrass festival and found out that not everyone was as great as the Seldom Scene.

Many Thursdays, I got to the Birchmere four hours before the show, which was two hours before the doors opened. I'd do that so I could be the first person in line, which meant I could have the seat of my choice . . . which meant I could sit in the front row, in a seat just underneath the part of the stage where Mike Auldridge would stand and play the dobro.

> **The dobro was a clattering instrument that was sometimes used as a comedy prop.**

Though I didn't know this then, Mike was the first elegant dobro player. The dobro is a square-necked guitar, with a resonator plate that looks like a hubcap in the face of the thing. The resonator plate amplifies the sound, which is already pretty loud and live, thanks to the picks the player wears, and the metal bar that dobroists move across the metal strings. Historically, the dobro was a clattering instrument that was sometimes used as a comedy prop. It was hard to play in tune, and was used for rambunctious clamor rather than for beauty. Mike Auldridge changed all that. He found nuanced ways to play the dobro, and he preferred beauty over aggression. He was a buttoned-down guy, who ironed his blue jeans. I'd sit in the front row and stare up at the crease in those jeans, then look up as multi-colored lights ricocheted off the dobro's resonator plate.

I loved it. And I began to view music as one big football game, where you pulled for your favorites and rooted against everyone else. At the time, there was a dobro player in Nashville named Jerry Douglas who was getting credit for reinventing the instrument. Douglas had studied at Auldridge's feet, and I was dismayed to see the student getting credit for things the teacher had imparted.

One night, at a set break, I walked into the bathroom at the Birchmere. There, washing his hands, was Mike Auldridge.

I was seventeen years old, and didn't know what to say. But here I was, face to face with a hero.

I said, "Mr. Auldridge, I don't know why people keep talking about Jerry Douglas, because you are the greatest dobro player in the world."

Mike looked at me crossly, wiped his hands, and said, "You need to LISTEN to Jerry Douglas."

I received the lesson like it was a sucker punch, but it was true and right. Musicians aren't sports teams. There is no score to keep. No one has to arm-wrestle about good, better, and best. Since then, I've taken care not to place my heroes in some kind of hypothetical and unnecessary competition. Freed from that competition, we can all go in search of our own, unique voice, and if we find it then the world can hear something it has never heard before.

I wound up recording with Mike Auldridge, and came to treasure his friendship and his wisdom. He was something special. The day he died, I was in a hospital in Columbia, South Carolina, visiting my father after he'd had a stroke. The stroke deal worked out okay, but at the time things were touch-and-go. I had to write an obituary for Mike from the hospital, and send it in to the *Tennessean* newspaper. I called Jerry Douglas, who was effusive in his praise for Mike, and I wrote his comments into the obituary.

My dad got better that day. What was fearful became positive and confident. I left that night, hoping to get halfway to my Nashville home.

I made it to the northwest side of Atlanta, listening to Jerry Douglas the whole way.

I started writing about music at twenty-two.

I was still in college, because I'd taken one year off from my studies to play bad guitar and sing through my nose on the streets of San Francisco.

My English professor, John Lane, called me and said he was sick with pneumonia. He asked if I would drive an hour north from Spartanburg, South Carolina to Asheville, North Carolina, to review a Guy Clark show for a weekly magazine called *Mountain X-Press*.

John had been assigned the review, but was too sick to go. I'd never published any stories, but my professor said I was the only person in Spartanburg who knew every word to all of Guy Clark's songs.

That was true, by the way.

Guy Clark was amazing. He wrote a song that began, "I'd play the 'Red River Valley' and he'd sit in the kitchen and cry/ Run his fingers through seventy years of living, and wonder 'Lord, has every well I drilled run dry?'/ We was friends, me and this old man."

See, I still know every word to all of Guy Clark's songs.

Anyway, John Lane said I could get into the show at no charge.

So off I went, to write about whether or not Guy Clark—already a legendary songwriter in his fifties, known for remarkable emotional specificity and clarity of language—was any good. Hey, free ticket.

I got to Asheville and watched and listened as Guy sang genius song after genius song, with his son, Travis, accompanying on bass.

Halfway through the library-quiet show, there came a disruption.

And I knew the disrupter.

He was Ashley Fly, a friend of mine.

He was from Spartanburg, and he had grown emotional watching Guy Clark sing songs with his son, Travis, on bass.

A lump came to Ashley's throat, and he said, way too out loud, "I wish Guy Clark was my daddy."

Then he said it again, and then one more time.

"I wish Guy Clark was my daddy."

I made a note.

When I wrote the review, I didn't lead with biographical facts about Guy, or with a measured appraisal of the show's highs and lows.

I led with Ashley Fly, and with, "I wish Guy Clark was my daddy."

In doing so, I was avoiding writing what everyone else wrote: That Guy Clark is a renowned veteran of American song who delivers rhyming truths with whiskeyed gravitas.

I was writing about connection, longing, regret, and pain. I was doing so with a chuckle line, but it

> **A lump came to Ashley's throat, and he said, way too out loud, "I wish Guy Clark was my daddy."**

was a chuckle line that got to something deeper: Guy Clark's presence is such that he can stand on a stage, sing a song called "Desperadoes Waiting for a Train," and make a grown man weep over the tyranny of lineage.

When I turned the story in, the editor called me and asked, "Is there really an Ashley Fly?" I said, "Yes, I can give you his number." Then he said, "Did that thing with the crying and the wishing Guy Clark was his daddy really happen?" I said, "Yes, you can ask anyone who was there." Then he asked if

I'd be interested in writing more reviews, in going to more shows for free, and in sometimes getting CDs sent to me in the mail. I said, "Let me think, yes." And then he sent me a check for $25 dollars.

In late September of 2000, I was six months into my tenure as a music writer for the *Tennessean* newspaper in Nashville.

It was a dream job that involved talking to the most creative, interesting people in the world, and writing down the creative and interesting things they said.

Then I just had to turn stories into an editor named Tim Ghianni, who loved Guy Clark and Kris Kristofferson as much as I did.

At that point, I got to meet Johnny Cash.

And I was freaking out a little bit. I'm not starstruck under normal circumstances. But this was Johnny Cash.

I didn't know what to do.

So I did something I'd never done before.

I said to Cash, "Before we start talking, I just want to tell you, 'Thank you.' Thank you for all the hours of my life that were better because they were spent in the company of your music. I'm a huge fan, and I thank you."

And Cash said, "Well, Peter, I'm a fan of yours, so I want to thank you. The newspaper hits my driveway every day, and June and I read it in the morning over coffee. I read everything you write."

Immediately, I was ten feet tall.

Johnny Cash reads all my stuff.

Then I shrunk eight feet down from ten.

Johnny Cash reads all my stuff.

All my stuff.

Stuff I write on deadline . . . stuff I just can't nail . . . stuff where I am writing over my head . . . stuff where I am unduly judgmental . . . stuff where I am overly kind.

All my stuff.

Johnny Cash.

Writer's block ensued.

AN ASIDE: **A TENDER LIE**

In the 1970s, Dave Roe was an electric bass player in Hawaii, specializing in jazz and pop. Enamored of country music, he moved to Nashville in 1980 and wound up landing some high-profile country gigs, touring and recording with Grand Ole Opry legend Charlie Louvin, premiere guitarist (and Burt Reynolds sidekick in the *Smokey and the Bandit* movies) Jerry Reed, and others.

In 1992, Dave got a call from his friend Hugh Waddell, a Johnny Cash confidante.

The bass gig in Cash's band had opened up, and Hugh told Cash that Dave Roe was the best rockabilly-style upright bass player in Nashville. Cash needed an upright bass—it's the enormous instrument that looks like a fiddle on steroids, and it's quite difficult to play—for the portions of his concerts when he would go back to the sound he employed at Sun Studio in Memphis in the 1950s. Playing an electric bass and playing an upright bass are two very different exercises: It's like the difference between driving a tank and flying a plane.

Now, Hugh Waddell knew he was telling a bit of a stretcher by saying that Dave Roe was the best rockabilly-style upright bass player in Nashville. What he didn't know was that Dave had never played an upright bass, and never played rockabilly music.

Dave took the gig, borrowed an upright bass, and tried to amount to something passable. Cash didn't rehearse, and didn't do sound checks, so he wouldn't hear Dave's upright playing until the middle of his first concert.

In the show, Dave wasn't awful, but neither was he good. And he certainly wasn't up to the level of the other aces in Cash's band.

After the show, Cash said, "Dave, you don't play upright, do you?"

Dave allowed as to how he didn't. He apologized, and said he appreciated the once-in-a-lifetime chance to play with the great Johnny Cash.

And then he stood in astonishment as Cash didn't fire him.

"In six months, I need to look back at you and know that you are the right guy for the job," Cash told him.

Over those months, Roe took lessons, working to gain entry-level upright bass skills so that he could do a job that dozens of virtuoso players in town would crawl across cut glass to do.

In time, he willed himself not only to decency, but to a place as a master of the instrument. He became the best rockabilly-style upright bass player in Nashville, and he stayed with Cash until the Man in Black's retirement.

CHAPTER 2

INNOVATION BEGAT TRADITION

DeFord Bailey was on Nashville's very first recording session, but it's not true that the entertainment world soon began descending (or ascending?) upon Nashville as soon as they heard his sweet and fine harmonica.

Truth is, the Nashville recording scene was dry for a long time. The first hit recorded in Music City was "Near You," by Francis Craig and His Orchestra. It was a pop hit, cut (in Nashville, "cut" is a good term, meaning "recorded for posterity") in 1947. It was a number one–seller that stayed on top of the pop chart for seventeen consecutive weeks. That set a chart record that lasted until 2009, and "Near You" was the top song of the year for 1947. It also became a country hit in 1977, when George Jones and Tammy Wynette took it to the top of the country charts.

Prior to 1947, musicians were more apt to record in New York, Atlanta, Charlotte, Cincinnati, and other cities than they were likely to come to Nashville. This was true in spite of the fact that loads of artists who would later be considered essential to the country music story were staying in town each weekend to play on the Grand Ole Opry.

One of those musicians was Roy Acuff, who became known as "The King of Country Music." He was an early Opry star, and he sang loud and strong, and when that wasn't enough he balanced a fiddle bow on his nose, right there in front of God and everyone. His biggest hits were "Wabash

Cannonball" and "Great Speckle Bird" (also called "The Great Speckled Bird," and other things), and he played those most every time he performed on the Opry. And, mind you, he performed on the Opry for more than a half-century, up until his death in 1992. One of my prize possessions is Acuff's final tube of Super Poligrip Dental Adhesive Cream, with extra holding formula and fresh mint taste. But I won't tell you the name of the *New York Times* best-selling author who gave it to me.

All tradition is rooted in innovation.

Many people consider Ernest Tubb to be a traditional country artist, but his "traditional" sound was created by adding an electric guitar to what had been a largely acoustic soundscape. Bill Monroe's "traditional" bluegrass sound was created by the addition of his own percussive mandolin chunks, keening tenor voice, and dazzling lead playing, in addition to Earl Scruggs's fleet-fingered banjo stylings and Lester Flatt's rock-solid rhythm guitar licks. Today's country performers are highly influenced by the rock, pop, and hip-hop they heard growing up. That's not heretical, that's natural. Ah, but isn't there beauty and timelessness to be found by reaching back to the music's sources? Well, sure. But we're not here to throw stones at musicians who seek to marry country music with emerging trends and technologies, because that's exactly what Ernest Tubb and Bill Monroe did.

Why all this talk about Ernest Tubb? Well, he's a good one to talk about. Interesting guy, and hugely important in the development of country music. Ernest Tubb grew up in Texas, and by his mid-teens he was working hard to sing exactly like Jimmie Rodgers. That meant a whole lot of yodeling, and it also meant that he wasn't doing much to separate himself from the pack: A generation of young men were trying to sing exactly like Jimmie Rodgers. Tubb was playing Texas clubs, doing the not-quite-Jimmie-Rodgers thing, when he noticed that his throat kept hurting. He wound up having to go to a hospital and get a tonsillectomy. No big deal, right? Wrong. The history of country music hinges on this tonsillectomy.

When Tubb went in for the operation, he was a yodeler. When the tonsillectomy was done, Tubb found his voice to resemble nothing approaching Jimmie Rodgers's fluid, playful, bluesy flights. It no longer soared. It was a low and growling rumble.

Dang.

Wait, hold on . . . .

Tubb's tonsil-free throat was incapable of replicating Rodgers or of sounding like any other popular singer. Which meant that suddenly he was completely and utterly distinctive. If you've ever heard Ernest Tubb sing, whether live, on record, or on TV, you know what he sounds like. If you've never heard him sing and then all of a sudden you do, you ask, "What is that?" The answer returns, "That's Ernest Tubb."

Technically, Tubb's voice was much poorer for the transition. But we're not here for technical assessment. Ernest Tubb was a superstar in large part because of his tonsil-free growl. Tubb said that people felt free to enjoy themselves and sing along with him, because his voice

> **When Tubb went in for the operation, he was a yodeler. When the tonsillectomy was done, ... [his voice] was a low and growling rumble.**

wasn't intimidating to them. When he set that voice to a band that featured an electric guitar and a steel guitar, the music could be heard above any barroom din. With the success of songs like 1941's "Walking the Floor Over You," Tubb became known as the "Texas Troubadour." He became a major star on the Grand Ole Opry, and he toured to hundreds of show dates each year, right up until his death in 1984.

When Tubb joined the Opry on January 16, 1943, it was held at Nashville's War Memorial Auditorium, on Legislative Plaza, downtown. Some people assume that the Opry was held at the Ryman Auditorium from its inception until it moved to the Grand Ole Opry House at Opryland in 1974. But in its early years, the Opry had several homes. First, it was held in WSM studios in the National Life and Accident Insurance Company Building at 7th Avenue North and Union Street, also downtown. In 1934, it moved to what is now called the Belcourt Theatre in Hillsboro Village. In 1936, it moved to 410 Fatherland Street in East Nashville, to a place called the Dixie Tabernacle. In 1939, it moved to War Memorial Auditorium, before finding a longtime home at the Ryman, beginning in June 1943. Today, it is held at the Opry House out on Briley Parkway, except during winter months, when it returns to the Ryman.

Tubb augmented his Opry and touring income by opening up a record shop at 720 Commerce Street in 1947. Since 1951, The Ernest Tubb Record Shop has been a fixture on Lower Broadway, at 417 Broadway. That's an important address: Each Saturday night when the Opry ended at the Ryman, the Ernest Tubb Record Shop would host something called The Midnight Jamboree, except when it was called The Midnite Jamboree. Country folks aren't always sticklers for spelling. In any case, that Jamboree was broadcast on WSM AM radio, and it became the second longest-running music show on American radio. The first, as I've told you, was the Grand Ole Opry.

All of this, thanks to a botched tonsillectomy.

Early country music wasn't called country music.

It was sometimes called "race music," sometimes called "folk music," and sometimes called "hillbilly music," though early Ernest Tubb hated the "hillbilly" term, thinking it a denigration.

He started telling record companies, "Don't let's call it 'hillbilly,' let's call it something else.'"

Eventually, the term became "country & western," and then that was shortened to just "country." If anyone today says they like "country & western" music, they probably don't.

Tubb wasn't the only one who didn't like the word "hillbilly." Another was the first female manager and booking agent in Nashville music history, a no-nonsense, certified tough cookie named Louise Scruggs.

If anyone today says they like "country & western" music, they probably don't.

Scruggs had a flat, hard telephone voice, which was developed out of necessity: She wanted members of the boys' club that was the professional music world of the fifties and sixties to understand that she meant business. She had always meant business, by the way: As a young girl, her favorite toy was a typewriter.

Louise was married to Earl Scruggs, one of only a couple of people to change the world with a banjo, and Louise made business decisions concerning the career of Earl's duo with Lester Flatt. Most people called that duo "Flatt & Scruggs," though they sometimes went by "Lester Flatt and Earl Scruggs," and sometimes by "Lester Flatt, Earl Scruggs, and the Foggy Mountain Boys." Louise usually just called them "Earl and Flatt," though that one never made a poster print.

One day, the phone rang at the Scruggs home at 201 Donna Drive in Madison, Tennessee. Well, actually, the phone rang every single day at the Scruggs home at 201 Donna Drive in Madison, because the house also served as the Flatt & Scruggs office. But on this particular day, in 1962, the fellow on the other end of the phone that rang on Donna Drive was calling from Los Angeles, from the offices of CBS television. The conversation went something like this:

Louise Scruggs: (In disaffected voice) "Hello."

CBS guy: (In excited, radio-ish voice that sounds as if he might swallow his tongue) "Mrs. Scruggs, this is Elmer Poofenfleck, from CBS television in Los Angeles, California."

LS: (In a voice that is the essence of unimpressed) "What do you want?"

CBS: (In still-excited, though now a little nervous voice) "We want to have Lester Flatt and Earl Scruggs perform the theme song for what we think will be a breakout hit comedy, *The Beverly Hillbillies!*"

LS: (In a voice of certainty: "Certain" was actually Mrs. Scruggs's maiden name.) "No."

CBS: (In a voice of confusion) "What do you mean?"

LS: (In agitated voice) "I mean, 'No.'"

CBS: (In 13-year-old, Peter Brady-ish voice) "Why would you not want to take part in this? It's an amazing opportunity. This is network television."

LS: (Slowly, and louder now) "Because I don't like the word 'hillbillies.' People called my family that when I was growing up, and they did not mean it kindly."

So the CBS guy had his work cut out for him. He eventually convinced Louise to agree to allow CBS to fly to Nashville with a pilot episode, screen it at a local theater for Louise, Earl, Lester and Lester's wife, Gladys, and decide whether the show was a put-down of country people. Only after all of that would Louise let Flatt & Scruggs music be heard in millions of homes: *The Beverly Hillbillies* wound up running on CBS for nine seasons, and it twice ranked as the number-one series of the year.

For viewers, the show's theme song, "The Ballad of Jed Clampett," was a window into the rollicking pleasures of bluegrass, and the placement of a regional music into a national context was invaluable in growing an audience base for Flatt & Scruggs, and for many other artists.

Good thing Louise's business sense overrode her squeamish reaction to the word "hillbillies." She was an impressive person, Louise. And she was often motivated to bring the music to non-traditional audiences.

"When you analyze it down, it comes under the heading of management," Earl Scruggs told me. "Louise had a plan for us. She wanted to get us into the colleges with the younger set, the age group that was buying records . . . You do that and you start selling records and it gets attention."

Others realized Louise's acumen, and they'd call on her for advice. One such occasion came when folk queen Joan Baez was coming to Nashville for the first time, in the early 1960s. Baez was slated to play a show at Vanderbilt University, which fashioned itself as "The Harvard of the South." At the time, there was very real tension between the country musicians who populated the Grand Ole Opry each weekend and the blue bloods who populated Nashville's moneyed west side. Vanderbilt tended to side with the west siders.

"The guy that was putting the concert on called me and said, 'I've got Joan Baez booked in there, and I don't know how to advertise it,'" Louise recalled. "He said, 'Could you help me make some decisions?' Baez was known as 'protest' or whatever, and he didn't know how she'd be accepted."

Louise walked the man through some advertising processes, and gave him advice about putting on a show with Joan Baez, who her husband respected, admired, and had worked with.

"I talked to him about it, tried to help him out," she said. "In one of our conversations, I said, 'Why don't you book Flatt & Scruggs over at Vanderbilt?' He said, 'Oh, we'd never have a Grand Ole Opry act here at Vanderbilt.' I said, 'Really, why?' He said, 'Well, it's not our kind of music.' Part of this town hated the Opry, hated country music, and didn't want anything to do with it. But I thought, 'Don't tell me I can't book *Flatt & Scruggs at Vanderbilt University*.'"

With that, Louise Scruggs went to work.

"Sometimes it takes something to get you to jump the gully or whatever, and that did it for her," Earl said.

In 1964, Flatt & Scruggs played Vanderbilt's Neely Auditorium, and the concert was recorded. The concert was then released on a Columbia Records album called *Flatt & Scruggs—Recorded Live at Vanderbilt University*.

"We splashed 'Recorded Live at Vanderbilt' across the front of the record," Louise said. "I wanted the whole world to see that you can put country music in Vanderbilt University: It says so right here on the album cover."

Earl Scruggs was a genial revolutionary. He is one of the commanding figures in popular music history, though he would never have asserted that on his own. He was a quiet guy, and an argument-loser. I was at his house to interview him once, when he sat down on his couch and was quickly joined by his beagle dog, Bonnie.

Louise Scruggs soon came in the room, looked at him, and said, "Earl."

He looked a little somber, and questioned, "Louise?"

She said, more tartly, "Earl."

He said, defeatedly, "She ain't hurtin' nothing."

Louise's glare bore down on the banjo man.

"Earl."

"Okay," he said, and led the dog off the couch and out into the yard.

Earl Scruggs re-imagined the banjo.

As a boy in Boiling Springs, North Carolina—which was near Shelby—he had a hard time of it. His father died when Earl was young, and he took to playing his dad's banjo on long, lonely afternoons. Flustered with his inability to keep up with complex fiddle tunes, he began playing banjo with a thumb and two fingers, rather than the usual thumb-plus-one style that most banjo players employed.

There were a few other players in Earl's region of the world who played with a thumb and two fingers, including Spartanburg, South Carolina's Don Reno. But Scruggs' playing was different, and infused with bluesy authority.

I asked Earl if he could remember when it was that he realized he was doing something different than what other people were doing.

He said he could remember, precisely.

He said it was when he was a teenager, working at the Lily Mills in Shelby, making sewing thread.

"On Saturdays, I would work second shift, from 2 p.m. to 10 p.m.," he said. "I was a spare hand, which meant you didn't know from day to day what you'd be doing. It might be the spool room, might not be."

At dinner break, Earl would pull out his banjo.

"Me and Grady Wilkie would sit in the backseat of my '36 Chevy and play music" he said. "He'd play guitar and I'd play banjo until they'd motion us to come back into the mill. That's when I finally realized that what I was doing was of interest to other people. They'd stand around and watch us pick. One of them hadn't heard nothing like that before, and he took his hat off, threw it down on the ground, and said, 'Hot damn!' That's the only time I run into a guy that when he got excited would throw his hat down and dance on it . . . That's hard on a hat."

Earl wound up coming to Nashville in 1945, to play with a guy named Lost John Miller. One night, he visited the Grand Ole Opry, and Bill Monroe was playing.

Monroe had just gotten rid of a banjo player, one that played in the thumb-and-index-finger style that Monroe found less than satisfying. Suffice to say, Monroe was happy not to have a banjo around.

But some of Monroe's Blue Grass Boys heard Scruggs playing, and they told Monroe he needed to hear this kid. Eventually, he acquiesced, and was mightily impressed by Scruggs' "fancy banjo."

He offered Scruggs a job, and, after some negotiation and consternation, Earl Scruggs joined the Blue Grass Boys. On December 8, 1945, Scruggs made his debut with Monroe on the Opry, and the sound was an immediate sensation. People went absolutely bonkers. It sounded like a magic trick to them. Soon, at the Opry, they'd introduce, "Bill and Earl, with that fancy banjo," and the place would go nuts. Every significant banjo player from that point forward started by figuring out how to pick in Earl's style.

It's called "Scruggs-style" banjo, now.

And the sound the Blue Grass Boys played that night is called "bluegrass." It's considered a traditional music, though it was born of innovation.

AN ASIDE: **BLUE MEETS NEW**

Bill Monroe is considered the "Father of Bluegrass."

Bluegrass music—an un-amplified form of country music that is heavy on instrumental virtuosity and stacked harmonies—was created in December of 1945, when fleet-fingered banjo player Earl Scruggs joined Monroe's Blue Grass Boys band at the Grand Ole Opry. Since then, bluegrass "traditionalists" have sought to replicate the sound of that original bluegrass band. And bluegrass progressives have sought to expand the music's boundaries.

One progressive form of bluegrass featured jazzy sequences and jammy excursions. This kind of bluegrass came to be called "Newgrass," named after the inventive band New Grass Revival. The Revival sometimes shared festival stages with Monroe and his Blue Grass Boys, and those occasions made for intriguing cultural and musical collisions. New Grass Revival mandolin player Sam Bush recalled one such occasion:

"In 1976, we were at a festival in Martinsville, Virginia, and Bill didn't have a banjo player," Bush said. "Our banjo player, Courtney Johnson, was standing with Bill's fiddler, Kenny Baker, and Monroe walked up. To Bill, in front of Courtney, Kenny said, 'Courtney's a good banjo player. Let's get him to play with us.'

"Bill said, 'No sir.'

"Kenny said, 'Courtney's a good banjo man.'

"'No sir, I won't have it.'

"See, Kenny was putting him on the spot.

"The third time Kenny asked, Bill said to Courtney, 'What is it you call that music you play?'

"Courtney said, 'Newgrass, sir.'

"Bill said, 'Oh yes, I hate that.'"

CHAPTER 3

A MEMPHIS FLASH, A NASHVILLE SOUND

Elvis Presley was making $40 a week back in 1954, driving a truck for Crown Electric in Memphis. He was driving supplies out to industrial building sites. He was eighteen years old, and had a chance to maybe train to be an electrician at Crown Electric. He was a weird-looking kid, and he lived with his parents in a little apartment complex. He had longish hair, or at least it seemed longish in those days. Every Friday, he brought most of his $40 paycheck home to his father, taking out a few bucks for himself: enough for gas and a movie ticket or two.

He wanted to be a singer, though, and he kept coming by this place called Sun Records at 706 Union Ave. He'd chat up the secretary and ask her about recording. He even recorded a little demo record of the song "My Happiness" as a present for his mother, and the guy who owned Sun, Sam Phillips, heard his voice and wound up thinking there was something interesting about it. Sam had also heard a song called "Without You" that was a pop ballad, and he thought the song was odd but endearing, kind of like that shy kid who kept stopping by to talk to the secretary, Marion Keisker.

Sam wound up asking the secretary for that kid's name, and she called to see if this young Elvis Presley could come in to sing "It Wouldn't Be the Same Without You." And he did, and it was pretty awful. The boy sounded nervous. He couldn't relax, and a singer who can't relax is of little practical use.

So, it was back to the Crown Electric truck for Elvis, but Sam did think enough of him to set him up for a practice session and informal audition with a country guitar player named Scotty Moore. They set the audition for the Fourth of July, after lunch, at Scotty's house on Belz Street.

Elvis showed up that 100 degree afternoon wearing a white shirt, white shoes, and pink pants with a black stripe down the legs. He and Scotty talked for awhile and started playing, and then Scotty had his wife call for bass player Bill Black to come over. They played for more than an hour, and Scotty wound up calling Sam Phillips and reporting that the kid knew a lot of songs and had good timing and a good voice. In turn, Sam called Elvis and invited him back to Sun for a recorded audition the next night.

On July 5, Elvis drove the Crown Electric truck during working hours. Then he met up with Scotty, Bill, and Sam at 706 Union, around 7 p.m.

At Sun, they labored through some pop and country songs, arriving at nothing in the way of excellence, excitement, or distinction. Multiple takes of an Ernest Tubb song called "I Love You Because" were unsuccessful. Sam started drumming his fingers on the recording console. No two takes were the same, and no one take was ever right.

Late that night, they took a break that felt like evening's end. Everybody had to work the next day, and they weren't any closer to a finished recording than they had been at the start of this endeavor. All of a sudden, Elvis started banging his guitar and clowning around with an old blues song that had been recorded by Arthur "Big Boy" Crudup. The song was "That's All Right, Mama," and as soon as Bill Black heard it, he started playing frenetic bass. Then Scotty joined in with some Chet Atkins–inspired guitar licks. Sam was in the studio control room, where he had been tending to some menial task, but he saw the men up and animated, and he poked his head out of the control room door and asked, "What are y'all doing?"

"Just foolin' around," was Scotty's answer, but it was a lie.

What they were doing was changing the way people talked, dressed, thought, and sounded.

This was, we now know, a big damn deal.

Sam turned on some microphones and moved them around, and then he mashed the tape machine's "record" button.

And in that moment, without any of our protagonists realizing what they'd done, the entire world changed.

Scotty recalled later that Sam heard the playback and said, "Man, that's good. It's different," and that someone then asked, "Yeah, what is it?"

No one knew the answer to that one, but Bill said, "Damn, if we get that played, they might run us out of town."

From today's perspective, "That's All Right, Mama" doesn't sound revolutionary. But Bill Black knew in the moment that it was a challenge to staid pop music, and to the segregated South.

There's lots of discussion about just what was the first rock 'n' roll record. Some people say it was a 1951's "Rocket '88," credited to Jackie Brenston and His Delta Cats. Others point to Bill Haley and the Comets' 1953 cut on "Crazy Man, Crazy," or Haley's April 1954 recording of "Rock Around the Clock."

I won't posit that "That's All Right, Mama" was the first rock 'n' roll record, but it was the first culture-shifting rock 'n' roll record made in the the South. It was a game-changer: a white southern boy singing black music. Since then, lots of folks have said, "Country and blues had a baby, and called it rock 'n' roll."

They didn't call it that in July of 1954, though, and the men had a conundrum on their hands: In order to put a song out on the market as a "single," they had to have something for the other side of the vinyl '45. A single was really a double, and since they'd just created something unique and atypical, it was tough to know what the other side of the record should sound like.

> **"That's All Right, Mama" was a challenge to staid pop music, and to the segregated South.**

Two nights later, in another accident, they figured it out.

Flailing away at Sun on July 7, Bill Black started slapping his bass and singing a song in a high falsetto voice. The song was one the men all knew from listening to the Grand Ole Opry on Saturdays. It was "Blue Moon of Kentucky," a song Bill Monroe and his Blue Grass Boys often trotted onto the Opry stage. Monroe did it as a slow and earnest waltz on the Opry, and on his 1946 recording. But Bill was singing it as an up-tempo raver, and Elvis and Bill quickly joined in.

Sam heard this commotion, stuck his head out the door, and said, "Hey, that's the one!"

Then they went to work. Sam employed a pronounced echo effect called "slapback" that made the whole thing more exhilarating, and at some point he said to the three, "That's fine, now. Hell, that's different. That's a pop song now, nearly."

Elvis and Scotty and Bill just laughed, as the world shifted on its axis.

Radio used to be more fun.

Memphis radio in the 1950s, in particular, was a gas.

A big reason for that was a WHBQ disc jockey named Dewey Phillips, who answered to "Daddy-O Dewey" and had a six-nights-a-week show called Red, Hot and Blue. Dewey was no blood relation to Sun Records' Sam Phillips, but they each believed in radical independence, and they each sought what Sam described as "perfect imperfection."

When Sam was having trouble in the studio with someone who seemed tentative or inauthentic, he would often advise them to "Dig down real deep and pull it out of your asshole."

These were wild men who rejected musical, social, and racial categories.

Sam hated the status quo. Once, he praised Marty Stuart for production on an album that was, in Sam's words, "Not just unusual, but unusually unusual."

Dewey's elliptical on-air patter was a Memphis wonder. Out of nowhere, he'd ask, "Anybody wanna buy a duck?" On behalf of sponsor Falstaff beer, he'd say, "If you can't drink it, freeze it and eat it. If you can't do that, open up a cotton-picking rib and pour it in."

These were wild men who rejected musical, social, and racial categories.

Today's air personalities (that's what they're called now . . . disc jockeys became air personalities, like stewardesses became flight attendants) most often have no say in what music is played on their stations, even during shows they are hosting. There are some exceptions to that, and one of the grandest may be heard on weeknights, on Nashville's WSM, AM-650. That's the same station that gave us the Opry, which made Nashville a country music mecca.

WSM's weeknight air personality is Eddie Stubbs, who ranks as one of the most knowledgable and impassioned country music advocates on the planet. Eddie's shows find him playing deep catalogue cuts, talking about the players who made the music, conducting marvelous interviews, and simultaneously entertaining and educating everyone who listens.

That said, Stubbs is nothing like Dewey Phillips. Stubbs is a sober traditionalist. Dewey was a tipsy anarchist, and Sam often took test pressings of new Sun records—called acetates—to play for Dewey, who would play them on the air and gauge listener reaction. If it didn't cause a stir, Sam might never put the record out. If it raised a ruckus, Sam would get a bunch of them pressed up and sent out.

Sam took an acetate of Elvis's first recording to Dewey, and played it for him, excitedly. The men drank beer (presumably Falstaff) and listened, over and over, for a couple of hours. Dewey listened intently, but somberly. He didn't make any promises as to whether he'd put it on the air, and he asked Sam to let him think about it overnight. He seemed to understand that it was something very different, even groundbreaking.

The next morning, Dewey called Sam and, according to Scotty Moore's memoir, "told him it was the damnedest record he had ever heard. He asked for a copy to play on Red, Hot and Blue."

That July night, Elvis went to a movie. Dewey played "That's All Right, Mama" repeatedly on his program, talking up this brand new voice. Memphis was, of course, deeply segregated, but Dewey's listeners were white and black, rich and poor. You can segregate lots of things, but the radio isn't one of them. Anyone with a transistor unit could hear Daddy-O Dewey blather about buying a duck and play an unruly mix of country, blues, pop, and R&B.

"Dewey had no color," said R&B great Rufus Thomas, who meant that as a compliment.

As audience response grew ardent, Dewey called the Presley home, looking for Elvis. He was, of course, at the movies, but Dewey told his mother, Gladys, "Mrs. Presley, you just get that cotton-picking son of yours down here to the studio. I played that record of his, and them birdbrain phones haven't stopped ringing since."

Mrs. Presley found her boy, and he headed to Dewey's studio at the Chisca Hotel, more than a little scared and shaken. He started the day as a truck driver, and now here he was, a star on the most popular radio show in Memphis, Tennessee.

"Sit down, I'm gonna interview you," Dewey told Elvis, who had no idea that the microphone was already hot. Dewey's first question was about where Elvis had gone to high school.

He asked the question for two reasons. The first was to establish that Elvis was a Memphis kid. The second was to establish Elvis's color: black kids didn't go to Humes High School.

The interview was over before Elvis knew it had begun, but things had changed. Elvis was a local celebrity, and that celebrity soon spread from the Memphis airwaves to the whole wide world.

See, radio used to be more fun.

So, I just spent a lot of words telling you about the big bang of rock 'n' roll, and this book is about country music. Was that a misstep?

Wait, don't answer.

I've already written these words, and I can't hear you.

Also, it wasn't a misstep.

That Memphis development impacted many things that have happened in the world since 1954, but they specifically impacted country music and country music-makers.

At first, the country music establishment considered whether Elvis should come into the fold. He played on package shows with various country artists, and on October 2, 1954, he played the Grand Ole Opry. Response was not aggressively positive, though, and he was never invited back to the show. Opry officials could have welcomed him, but they didn't, and he left the Ryman Auditorium (where the Opry was held) feeling unwanted by the country music mainstream.

Had he felt welcomed, he could have brought untold ticket-buying fans to the Opry. As it stood, he went his own way, and many of the listeners who had enjoyed country music decided that they more enjoyed Elvis Presley and this new sound that came to be called rock 'n' roll.

Some nights, the formerly packed Ryman was only drawing about 700 fans to its 2,100 seat Opry shows. And country music went into a dark and deep commercial decline. Ernest Tubb pondered going back to Texas and taking a straight job. And young artists like Buddy Holly who might previously have gone into country music decided they would be rock 'n' rollers instead.

At first, country music record labels and artists responded with imitation. But they weren't good imitators. As it turned out, having middle-aged hillbilly singers like Webb Pierce attempt to replicate rock 'n' roll by singing songs like the laughable "Teenage Boogie" (Webb couldn't even properly pronounce "boogie," instead singing

> **He went his own way, and many of the listeners who had enjoyed country music decided that they more enjoyed Elvis Presley and this new sound that came to be called rock 'n' roll.**

"t-boogie") didn't reel in the teenagers drawn in by Elvis Presley's swiveling hips and sinewy grooves. George Jones, Little Jimmy Dickens, and others tried replicating rock 'n' roll, to little avail (Though you may want to search out Dickens' "Hole in My Pocket" if you like scorching electric guitars: Hank Garland and Grady Martin, who Chet Atkins called the greatest guitar players in Nashville history, play starring roles).

By 1956, the youngsters who had grown up on early 1950s country stars Hank Williams, Lefty Frizzell, Carl Smith, and Ernest Tubb had shifted their attention and their record-buying dollars to Elvis, Chuck Berry, and other rockers. And clumsy attempts at replication didn't sway their allegiances.

What to do?

In fewer than ten days in the fall of 1956, Capitol Records producer Ken Nelson figured it out.

One of Nelson's artists was a fresh-faced, 28-year-old, Alabama-reared singer who went by the stage name of Sonny James. Nelson found a song called "Young Love" that wasn't about drinking or trains or mommas or other traditional country themes. This one was about teenage romance: "Young love, first love/ Filled with deep devotion."

Ken Nelson decided to record the song without fiddle, banjo, or steel guitar, but with a big, sugary backing chorus. In the studio on that day before Halloween, it sounded like a pop song, though James' heart of dixie drawl offered some regional flavor.

James was skeptical of the new sound, and he asked his producer, "Are you sure, Ken?"

Ken was sure. And, as it turned out, Ken was right. By February, "Young Love" topped country and pop charts.

On November 7 of 1956, Nelson was producing a session on another Capitol artist, Ferlin Husky. "Ferlin Husky" was not a stage name: He'd tried recording for a time under the monicker "Terry Preston," but that didn't work out so well. In 1952, as Terry Preston, he'd recorded a song called "Gone" that didn't kick up any commercial stir. A year later, his father told him he'd never be a hit singer until he started using his real name. And after some middling successes in 1955, he found himself in late 1956, still in search of a big hit.

Nelson had a plan for "Gone" that was similar to what he'd enacted with "Young Love": Remove traditional elements, and replace them with a pop-ready soundscape. Husky was fine with that, but he wanted to take things even further afield. He told me in 2009 that he essentially took control of the session.

"We had the Jordanaires on there as the backing vocal group, and Grady Martin on vibes, and a ton of people in the studio," he said. "Ken Nelson got upset. He said, 'If one more person comes through those doors, the session is off.' And then here comes Miss Millie Kirkham to sing the soprano vocal part. He said, 'You're going to cost me my job.' In the middle of the song, I stopped the band and sung this 'Ohhhhh' part, and Ken said, 'What in the world are you doing?' I said, 'I'm making a hit record.' And that's what we did."

They did, indeed. When "Young Love" topped the pop charts in February, "Gone" was right behind it. "Gone" topped the *Billboard* country singles chart for two-and-a-half months, and became a major star.

"For a while there, I was all the way across that radio dial," he said. "Elvis Presley opened shows that I headlined, and I got a star on the Hollywood Walk of Fame."

That's what it did for Ferlin Husky. But what the success of "Gone" and "Young Love" did for the rest of Nashville was to offer a new model for making music that makes money.

Author and historian Rich Kienzle wrote liner notes to a compilation of Husky's enduring works. He asserts that "Young Love" and "Gone" "demonstrated what became the ultimate goal for Nashville producers: A country hit that could 'cross over' to pop success."

Soon, producers Chet Atkins and Owen Bradley were making similar musical choices on works by Marty Robbins, Jim Reeves, Patsy Cline, Eddy Arnold, Skeeter Davis, and others. The lush (detractors will say "slick") recordings that resulted are now grouped under the term, "The Nashville Sound."

"The Nashville Sound" doesn't mean "music that comes from Nashville." It refers specifically to the records made in the late 1950s and throughout the 1960s that charmed pop audiences and sometimes irritated traditionalists, but that revived country music's sales. There were string sections instead of fiddles, the tempos tended to lope, and the vocals were more likely to whisper than to bellow.

Some of my favorite Nashville Sound recordings are Connie Smith's "Once, a Day," Jim Reeves' "He'll Have to Go," the Browns' "The Three Bells," and Skeeter Davis's "The End of the World." Those are killer, but the trouble with the Nashville Sound was that it could get samey and saccharine. Whatever its failings, Nashville's country music industry needed something to save it, and the Nashville Sound provided a way to survive.

Chet Atkins sometimes wondered whether the Nashville Sound went too far towards pop, and he was conflicted about his role in developing—some would say "perfecting"—this style of record-making. When asked just what the Nashville Sound was, Chet would grab some change from his pocket, jangle it in his hand, and say, "It's the sound of money."

After Sam Phillips sold his recording contract to RCA, Elvis Presley began recording in Nashville. He wound up cutting

> **"The Nashville Sound" doesn't mean "music that comes from Nashville." It refers specifically to the records made in the late 1950s and throughout the 1960s that charmed pop audiences and sometimes irritated traditionalists, but that revived country music's sales.**

more than 250 songs at the Music Row studio now known as RCA Studio B, and the musicians on his rock 'n' roll sessions were the same players who graced thousands of country sessions. Musicians like Harold Bradley, Hank Garland, Grady Martin, Bob Moore, Buddy Harman, and Chet Atkins routinely began their day with Nashville Sound recordings and ended their evening with lengthy Presley sessions.

Rock and pop acts including the Everly Brothers, Brenda Lee, and Roy Orbison also recorded on Music Row, and when Bob Dylan arrived in 1966 to record his epic *Blonde on Blonde* album, the floodgates opened. The late 1960s brought Joan Baez, the Byrds, and Gordon Lightfoot. In the 1970s, Paul McCartney came to Nashville to record, and Neil Young cut his biggest hit, "Heart of Gold," at Quad Studios along Music Row. In the new century, rock acts Jack White, The Black Keys, and Kings of Leon have made homes in Nashville properties and music in Nashville studios. Nashville is not Country Music City. It is an ecumenical Music City.

AN ASIDE: CASH IS THE REAL KING

When Elvis came to the Grand Ole Opry in 1954, lots of people were dismissive of him. On tour with various country acts, he was sometimes ridiculed by those he saw as heroes: One night, while touring with harmony duo The Louvin Brothers, he told the Louvins backstage that he loved their music. Ira Louvin, one of the most gifted singers in country music history, made a nasty comment back to Elvis, essentially saying, "If you love this music, why are you singing the shit you sing."

Ira's words were, by the way, much uglier than my paraphrase.

And Ira knew exactly why Elvis was singing what he was singing. Audiences loved it. The records were selling. And Elvis was on his way to becoming the biggest solo artist in the world.

In Nashville, folks figured that Bill Monroe would view Elvis's cover of his "Blue Moon of Kentucky" with aggressive negativity. After all, Monroe held grudges against musicians who played bluegrass—the music he is credited with inventing—because in his mind they were using his own sounds against him, competitively. What would he feel about a brash young rock 'n' roller taking his waltz-time ballad, turning it into a rave-up, and using it to achieve a popularity that threatened the commercial future of country music itself?

Someone found Monroe backstage at the Opry one night and asked him about "Blue Moon of Kentucky," saying, "I'll bet you just hate that, don't you, Mr. Monroe?"

Monroe paused and said, "No, I like it a lot."

Puzzled, his inquisitor said, "Really?"

Monroe looked him in the eye and said, "Them's powerful checks."

CHAPTER 4

KRIS KRISTOFFERSON, THE GOING UP

In the introduction to this book, I wrote that Cowboy Jack Clement is the one you should have met.

In truth, there are a bunch of them you should have met. Maybe you met some of them. I hope so. I know I'm better off for knowing them. When I moved to Nashville, I was told by well-meaning people, "Never meet your heroes: They're bound to disappoint you."

I know what those well-meaning people meant by that. At fourteen, I went to the Cracker Jack Old Timers baseball game and met an idol: Warren Spahn, the winningest left-handed pitcher in Major League Baseball history. I asked noble, graceful icon Warren Spahn for an autograph, and mean, beak-nosed old man Warren Spahn cursed at me—loud enough to silence a crowd—and refused.

What, then, if the people who had created the music that intrigued and sustained me, and that undergirds the city of Nashville, were assholes like Warren Spahn?

I quickly found that it was simply impossible for such a thing to be true.

The music-makers I most often admire are songwriters, and it isn't possible to write intelligent, empathetic songs about human beings without being an intelligent, empathetic person who cares about human beings.

Can't be done.

You can write such songs and then mask your humanity with substances and circumstances, but underneath it you are a smart and caring person.

You can win 363 baseball games and be a bullying twerp. But you can't write truth and beauty without seeking and finding such things.

In Nashville, the people I admired enough to have been able to crumble my spirit and enthusiasm turned out to be righteous enough to bolster these things.

I relate this to you for a couple of reasons, and I suppose one of them is to humble-brag about knowing Johnny Cash, Tom T. Hall, Emmylou Harris, Kris Kristofferson, and John Prine. But the other is to tell you that you don't need to worry that the person who writes songs that move you and inspire you and make you feel deep and great things is somehow pulling the wool over your eyes, or tricking you into feeling something that they themselves don't feel.

You can't write truth and beauty without seeking and finding such things.

Kristofferson met Cowboy Jack Clement on his first night in Nashville.

He recognized the Cowboy as some Tennessee-warped version of Shakespeare's Falstaff, only truer of heart.

In short order, he met Johnny Cash, and then Tom T. Hall. And he came to think that if he could never rise to their station, he could stay in Nashville and write about them. He'd been all over the world by this point, and these were the wisest, most fascinating, most absurd, and most brilliant creative forces he'd ever considered.

Things came easy for Kristofferson, and that's something that plagued him. He was never much for easy, but easy adored him. In his young life, he was a Golden Gloves boxer, a college football player, a published writer, a competitive wrestler, an Army Ranger, a Rhodes Scholar, and many other lofty things. Yet he craved both desperation and accomplishment, or perhaps he craved the kind of accomplishment that can only spring from desperation.

He threw himself into worlds of bruised-hearted trouble, of excess and alcohol and worry and peril. That everything all worked out in the end is one measure of the man.

"All alone all the way on your own/ Who's to say that you've thrown it away for a song?" he once sang. Well, plenty of people said that about him. His mother, for one, but only for awhile. Born into a solid, traditional, well-to-do family and raised to think about honor, duty, justice, excellence, and other such things, Kristofferson's personal turning point came in 1965, when he gave up an appointment to teach at West Point in order to head to Nashville, to drink and laugh, howl, scuffle, and learn to write songs. Soon, his mother sent him a letter informing him that he was essentially disowned and disavowed for his lousy decision-making. He was already a Rhodes scholar, a military man, a prose writer who had been published in *Atlantic Monthly*, a husband . . . and the first thing he did when he got to Nashville was to buy a motorcycle.

"I was dangerous enough in a car," he said. "I did a lot of drinking in those days."

This is all stuff of myth and adulation. Most of us know how the story ends: Kristofferson writes "Me & Bobby McGee," "Sunday Morning Coming Down," "For the Good Times," "Help Me Make It Through the Night" and a slew of other master-works, alters the possibilities and expectations for Nashville songwriting, becomes a movie star, reconnects with his loving mother, makes controversial political stances (for freedom, justice, human rights, and other apparently divisive ideals), joins Hank Williams and Johnny Cash as a member of the Country Music Hall of Fame, and sleeps in fancy hotel rooms. All good, all true. Those are the facts, and the triumphs.

But it was holy hell to get there, and it could have gone the other way. Overwhelming talent and empathetic humanity were his constants. Turns out that those were the winning numbers, but he could easily have wrecked on the way to cash the lottery ticket. Again, Kristofferson was never much for easy.

"Was it bitter then, with our backs against the wall?" he wrote, in a song old friend Willie Nelson later reprised. "Were we better men than we'd ever been before?"

Yes, it was probably bitter. And probably yes to the last part, too.

Kris Kristofferson made the newspaper one time for punching someone out. In the photo, a teenaged Kristofferson's right hand pounded the chin of a Golden Gloves boxing opponent, temporarily but grotesquely smashing the boy's face out of its customary, face-like configuration. The fight ended there, which was not long after it began.

In the next fight, Kristofferson was thoroughly beaten down by a better opponent. He realized after that one that the shame wasn't in the losing.

"The thing that was embarrassing was that I gave up," he told documentary producer Paul Joyce. "I thought, 'If this guy can beat me, I'll never be the champion.' I just took the beating."

It was decades after that before Kristofferson gave up on anything else, and by then all he ceded were bottles of whiskey and other mind-clouders. Though he was a child who knew substantial privilege, he sought to out-work others rather than to dazzle them with charm or footwork. Under-sized and under-quick, he made his small college football team and played through multiple concussions. He loved the game, living for competition as much as for football itself. His competitive inclinations extended into summer jobs as well: He still beams a little in remembering that the superintendent of his construction crew once told him he was the best man on the job.

"I took pride in being the best laborer, the guy that could dig the ditches the fastest," he said. "I think something, maybe my parents or maybe something inside me, made me want to do the tough stuff, to work up in Alaska fighting forest fires or on the railroad as a gandy dancer. And in California on road construction. Part of it was that I wanted to be a writer, and I figured that, like Jack London or something, I had to get out and live. I know that's why I ran in front of the bulls in Pamplona. I did it every day that whole week at the Fiesta de San Fermin, and they got closer and closer, until they finally ran around me the last day."

One of the ironies of Kristofferson's life has been that the acceptance of his parents' teachings and examples led him to veer from the road to traditional accomplishment that they'd plotted for him.

Father Henry was sturdy and driven, a major general who served in World War II and in Korea, worked as a commercial airlines manager and pilot after he retired from duty and gave his son "a sense of living up to who I should be." "He was the shining best at everything he did," was how Kristofferson wrote about his father in "The Heart," a song that recalled advice from his dad including "You'll feel better if you take it like a man."

And Kristofferson's mother, Mary Ann, helped inspire in him a sense of social justice that would pervade his creative works.

"When I was growing up down in Brownsville, Texas, the racial issue wasn't between blacks and whites," he said. "It was Mexicans that there was prejudice against, and my mother made sure we knew that was wrong. One example I remember of it is when a Mexican from Brownsville won the Medal of Honor and they had a parade for him, and we were the only Anglos at the parade."

Kristofferson would later get used to the feeling of being among the only Anglos at the parade. Sometimes, he'd get his own parades together, and people would call it career suicide: The crowd would arrive to hear "Help Me Make It Through the Night" and he'd hit them with "Sandinista, may the soldiers disappear," or the one in support of Jesse Jackson, or the one in which he ponders what his military-grade father's reaction would be to a newfangled army "killing babies in the name of freedom."

The formative scenery shifted from Brownsville to San Mateo, California, where Kristofferson graduated high school in 1954. He went to college at Pomona, his mother's alma mater, though his decision was based neither on family ties nor academics. He wanted to play football, and he was good enough to play at Pomona but not at a bigger school.

"I was pretty slow, but I was small," is his assessment today.

At the college, he immersed himself in military studies through the ROTC, following in the footsteps of his father and of his military officer grandfathers. Still, Pomona's prime mark on Kristofferson would come in the form of Dr. Frederick Sontag, a writing instructor who pushed him to apply for the Rhodes scholarship.

When he arrived in London, Kristofferson was acknowledged as a writer, as a talent. He was creating short stories that were good, and that got published. In London, he worked on a novel. He was dabbling in music, crafting songs and even recording a session for the ill-titled Top Rank Records as "Kris Carson."

Kristofferson's main man at Oxford was long-dead writer William Blake, who had a riff about how anyone who refuses spiritual acts in favor of worldly desires and the need for natural bread will be pursued by sorrow and desperation through life and by shame and confusion for eternity.

Some people take that to mean we shouldn't hesitate to fill the collection plate even when the car payment is coming due. But Kristofferson was beginning to think that writing and creativity just might be spiritual acts.

Maybe he was put here to create, and if that was indeed the case then maybe the suppression of creativity was as sinful . . . maybe more sinful . . . than any much-chastised natural act. Sorrow and desperation didn't scare him, but eternal shame and confusion seemed too heavy a load. Then again, maybe William Blake didn't know any more about the grand scheme than the rest of us.

In 1960, Kristofferson earned his master's degree from Oxford. Then he went back home to California, got reacquainted with his high school sweetheart, got married, joined the Army, and learned to fly helicopters. He was still excelling, but creativity pulled at him. He'd come up with funny songs to entertain his fellow soldiers, setting ribald words to the melodies of familiar hits. He'd always loved Hank Williams—though his parents had never understood the attraction—but he wasn't sure that country songwriting as it stood back then was worth a life's full attention.

"I was more interested in being Faulkner, Hemingway . . . a serious writer," he said.

That's when a serious writer came along. Bob Dylan was a riddle-speaking prophet whose words struck Kristofferson as being elevated enough to make writing songs seem a worthwhile avocation.

"The direction Dylan was pointing in made it a respectable ambition, a respectable thing to do," he said. "I still didn't know I was going to do it, though. I didn't know that I could."

That was about the time when he unsuccessfully volunteered for Vietnam. He tried to go fight, but was turned down. Kristofferson's colonel at division headquarters in Germany sent a telegram to the Pentagon to find out the reasons behind the denial, and word came back that the military had deemed it inappropriate for Kristofferson to fight in Vietnam because he was going to be assigned to teach literature at the Academy, at West Point, a long damn way from rival Vietcong. Safety. Relief. Honor. Terror.

"I went to West Point and got briefed about what might be expected of me, which looked pretty frightening," he said. "The guy said the cadets would come into class in a semi-rectangle around you. They'd be at attention. I'd say 'Seat' and they'd sit down. And then I'd have had to turn in a lesson plan 24 hours before that, about what I'd be doing that day in class. It sounded like hell to me."

So by the time Kristofferson visited Nashville in 1965, he was looking for a way out of hell. He was there through the kindness of Marijohn Wilkin, a respected Nashville songwriter and publisher who had penned hits like "Long Black Veil" and "Waterloo" and who was related to Kristofferson's platoon leader. She'd agreed to show the commissioned West Point teacher around if he ever got to Nashville, and he did, and she did.

If Kris Kristofferson could time-warp back to any time in his life, it might be those first two weeks in Nashville. He spent the first night at a bar called the Professional Club with Cowboy Jack Clement—a songwriter, an idea man, a dreamer, and a reckless soul. The next morning, the cowboy and the still-in-uniform soldier were in Clement's office when Rusty Kershaw came in to try to sell the rights to a song called "Louisiana Man." Cowboy should have bought it, but he didn't.

Then the odd couple headed down to the

> ## Kristofferson's radical decision to abandon both pedigree and security was cemented backstage at the Grand Ole Opry, when he met an emaciated, wild-eyed panther named Johnny Cash.

Gulch beside 11th Ave., where trains moved in and out of Music City.

"He had a thing about trains," Kristofferson said. "He talked about how he'd get onto a train and ride from Nashville to New Orleans and back. Just ride down, come back."

It became quickly clear that Nashville was a town without lesson plans. Kristofferson's radical decision to abandon both pedigree and security was cemented backstage at the Grand Ole Opry, when he met an emaciated, wild-eyed panther named Johnny Cash.

"He shook my hand, and it was electric," Kristofferson said. He'd told the story hundreds of times, and yet the words still spill with a sense of wonder. "Backstage at the Opry, breathing the same air that Hank Williams breathed, it all felt enchanted. I told Marijohn when she drove me back to the hotel the last night I was there, 'I'm coming back to Nashville, and I'm going to write for you.'"

Wilkin hadn't offered to employ the young, close-clipped Army man. If she had wanted him, she would have told him so. He wasn't even very good yet. She had spent two weeks trying to be nice to her cousin's military friend and had instead aided and abetted what appeared to be a frightfully poor change of direction.

"When I told her, I remember that her head went right to the steering wheel," he said. "She said, 'Oh, my God.' That's exactly what she said, 'Oh, my God.'"

Everybody in Kristofferson's army company went to Vietnam. He met up with them in '65, at Fort Campbell in Kentucky, as they were getting ready to head oversees. Kristofferson tried to enlist Mel Tillis for the trip to see his old buddies, but Tillis' wife wouldn't let him go. Something about a bottle of vodka that Kristofferson dropped on the Tillis' steps.

So Kris traveled alone, blew a tire just outside of the base and rolled the car about 300 yards. When some fellows came to survey the wreck, they found the car upside down and figured the driver was dead.

"It scared 'em when I yelled at them," he said. But they pushed the car over, some MPs came, and a drunken but persuasive Kristofferson told the police he wanted to go see the guys in his unit that were on their way to Vietnam. He was taken directly to a runway where his friends sat on a plane that was about to take off. He ran up the steps to the plane and thought, "I might as well go with them." His car was trashed, his wife would be angry, and his talent had not yet overwhelmed his new hometown to the point where any real possibilities were emerging.

"God looks after fools and songwriters," he said. "They made me get off that plane, and I laid down on the floor at that little guardhouse where you go into Fort Campbell. I called back to Linebaugh's Restaurant in Nashville, 'cause songwriters hung out there and I knew one of them would come get me, and a friend finally came and picked me up. Had I gone to Vietnam, I have no doubt that if I didn't get killed over there then I would have done something in the name of duty that I would have had a hard time living with later. I didn't know that at the time, but I know that now."

The letter from home arrived soon after Kristofferson's move to Nashville. He was disowned, was the gist of the thing. His mother could not accept such a foolish and selfish turn of events, even if Marijohn Wilkin's Bighorn Publishing was offering a small weekly stipend. Train-loving Jack Clement told his buddy Johnny Cash about the letter, and Cash was impressed with the struggling writer's gumption.

Kristofferson lived along Music Row, right down the street from the Tally Ho Tavern that he would immortalize in "The Silver Tongued Devil." At the Tally Ho, the owner would let you get drunk, but he wouldn't let you arrive that way. The place was located on a corner, and it had a seating area in the back and a standard bar up front. A wino walked in soused one night, was quickly thrown out, stumbled around the corner, turned right, saw the back seating area and found his way into a chair. The owner saw him there and hollered "I told you to get the hell out of here!" The drunk stammered, "Damn, do you own every bar on this block?"

On many nights, Kristofferson's life wasn't far removed from that drunk's.

Columbia banned him from working during a Johnny Cash session, but Cash insisted that the janitor be present. Cash had a soft spot for the young man.

As he entered his 30s, he figured total immersion into Nashville's blurry wildlife was the only way to learn to create. He and his wife broke up with frequency and then with permanence. He could not provide adequately for his children, one of whose health conditions required medical attention and money.

He worked as a bartender and worked more famously as a janitor at Columbia studios, where some of the musicians grumbled about his late arrivals. Seems he seldom got to the studio early enough to make a pot of coffee before the 10 a.m. sessions began. Some at Columbia also faulted Kristofferson's opportunistic streak: He'd try to talk to artists about cutting one of his songs. At one point, Columbia banned him from working during a Johnny Cash session, but Cash insisted that the janitor be present. Cash had a soft spot for the young man. Something about a letter from home.

In 1966, Dave Dudley recorded Kristofferson's "Viet Nam Blues," and took it into country's top 20. Then the Nashville newbie's luck ran dry. Billy Sherrill produced a single on Kristofferson as an artist in 1967, but it failed to draw any flies. Searching for a way to earn some money, Kristofferson took jobs flying helicopters around the oil rigs in the Gulf of Mexico.

"I remember in 1967, taking my daughter, Tracy, into the Tally Ho, to say goodbye to the people in there that knew her," he said. "Somebody saw us and said, 'Look, here comes Critter and the kid.' Some people called me Critter. Not long after that I wrote a song called 'Jody and the Kid.' When I was working in the Gulf, I wrote songs all the time. I was flying for hours without anything to think about except for the songs. I'm surprised they didn't all come out with the same rhythm of the blades."

He began to seriously consider getting back into the Army and going to Vietnam. Friends in the service talked him out of it. "These were veterans of Korea," he said. "They told me, 'You must be out of your mind. This is the most screwed-up thing we've ever been involved with.'"

Somewhere in there, hope began to poke its way through the desperate times and booze clouds. Billy Walker recorded Kristofferson's "From the Bottle to the Bottom," and wisened, well-established Tom Hall (soon to be Tom T. Hall) heard the song on the Tootsie's Orchid Lounge jukebox and was impressed enough to speak kindly about the song to its writer.

At a point when money and hope were in short supply, publisher and record mogul Fred Foster signed Kristofferson on the basis of four songs: "Jody and the Kid," "To Beat the Devil," "Duvalier's Dream," and "Best of All Possible Worlds." Foster told the writer that he'd sign him on the condition that Kristofferson would do an album for Foster's Monument Records. Kristofferson deferred, saying, "I sing like a fucking frog." Foster shot back, "Yeah, but a frog that can communicate."

In hindsight, all these developments are signs of the genre-shaking, culture-tweaking successes that would soon come. At the time, they were merely straws at which to grasp. Kristofferson would walk an empty Music Row on Sunday mornings, impatient for the bars to open at noon and knowing that his musical aspirations had led to the dissolution of relationships with his mother and with his wife. In a bachelor's apartment, he wrote lines that spoke to his condition and that would later be received by millions.

"On the Sunday morning sidewalk/ Wishing, Lord, that I was stoned/ 'Cause there's something in a Sunday/ Makes a body feel alone."

In another instance, depleted by his strains to pay the bills and at the same time remain creative, he confessed to Fred Foster that he thought he had run out of songs. Foster offered some extra money to ease the evident financial distress, and he offered an idea to combat Kristofferson's writer's block. Write a song called "Me and Bobby McKee," Foster advised. McKee was a secretary in Foster's office building, and the repeating hard E sounds made for a good title.

Back in a chopper, flying this time around Baton Rouge, Kristofferson was thinking of the rhythm to a Mickey Newbury song called "Why You Been Gone So Long" when he began working on "Me and Bobby McGee."

"When it came together was when the lines finally came about 'With them windshield wipers slapping time/ And Bobby clapping hands we finally sang up every song that driver knew,'" he said.

Helicopters and hard times provided for one more now-epic moment, the day Kristofferson determined that the great Johnny Cash was going to take notice of more than his mother's letter of dismissal. Kristofferson had been giving tapes of his songs to Cash for a couple of years, and Cash would put the tapes in a pile with all the other tapes he got from all the other would-be writers, and then he'd throw the tapes into Old Hickory Lake. Convinced that Cash would like his stuff if he would take the time to listen, Kristofferson took a tape with him in a National Guard helicopter and flew the machine onto Cash's lawn.

"I could have damaged the house or the helicopter, and I could have gotten into trouble with the Guard, or John could have shot me out of the sky," Kristofferson said. "It could have gone real wrong."

It didn't go wrong. Cash wound up cutting a stunning version of "Sunday Morning Coming Down," and the two began a friendship of mutual respect and admiration that would last throughout Cash's life and that would result in Kristofferson's appearances on Cash's taste-making ABC television show.

The down side is that Kristofferson has spent a few minutes in nearly every one of his thousands of interviews talking about the flying-onto-Cash's-yard stunt. And Cash's interviews about the thing gave people the wrong idea.

"Johnny always said I got out of the helicopter with a beer in one hand and a tape in the other," Kristofferson said. "I wouldn't have been able to fly while holding all that. It was damn hard to fly a helicopter in those days."

Roger Miller was a big deal. Still is, really. Maybe more so now in death, when he's larger than life. Back then he was just . . . life, though his was considerably more frenetic than most. And back then he took an interest in Kristofferson. He took an interest in the Bobby McGee song, particularly, though he was well pleased with the Miller-esque "Best of All Possible Worlds" and the ruminative "Darby's Castle" as well. In 1969, he recorded all of those, and in that same year Johnny Cash brought Kristofferson up to sing at the Newport Folk Festival, and in that same year Ray Stevens recorded "Sunday Morning Coming Down." And after that things got good and weird and lucrative for Kris Kristofferson. Decades later, Tim Carroll would write that Nashville is a five-year-town. Kristofferson got in just under the wire. The helicopter trick was neither shame nor salvation.

In the spring of 1970, Kris Kristofferson released his first album. It was called *Kristofferson*, and, in terms of dollars earned, it wasn't any kind of table-thumping smash. The songs contained on that album, though, spoke to people. "For The Good Times" hit No. 1 for Ray Price and "Sunday Morning Coming Down" hit No. 1 for Johnny Cash. "For The Good Times" wound up as the Country Music Association's song of the year and "Sunday Morning Coming Down" wound up as the Academy of Country Music Association's song of the year. No matter what organization was doing the tallying, Kristofferson went from nonentity to relative affluence. And then people started to want to hear the way the author sang the songs that were on the radio. Turned out he sang them like a frog, but like a frog that could communicate.

Kris Kristofferson's songs changed things. Some people point to the way he used sex as part of the storyline, the "Shake it loose and let it fall" deal. That was part of it, but all of that was in service of the songs. Mostly, what he did was to transform reality through poetry and melody. Or to transform poetry and melody through reality. It was not altogether different than what Hank Williams tried, and lots of people will swear it's just as memorable. Kristofferson, Tom T. Hall, Mickey Newbury, John Hartford, and some others transformed country songwriting in the same way that Dylan transformed rock 'n' roll song-craft. Nashville-based country songs became literate, layered, and respectable.

And other folks began to cut those songs, too. Kristofferson's friend and companion Janis Joplin cut the hell out of "Me and Bobby McGee," and then she died, and after that the song became a hit, and Kristofferson still found the thing tough to hear. He loved the way she did it, but his nerves were raw and frayed, and he couldn't think about her without getting sad.

His career as a performer took off quickly, with a festival performance at the Isle of Wight coming just weeks after he began performing with his band in clubs. Kristofferson brought his band to Europe for the festival show, and he found himself far from the star attraction.

"They were throwing shit at me, but I kept singing," he said. "I told 'em, 'I brought this band over here at my own expense. They told me to do an hour, and I'm going to do an hour, in spite of anything but rifle fire.'"

Right then, band member Billy Swan got Kristofferson's attention and reprimanded, "Don't say 'Rifle fire!'"

For Kristofferson, the early 1970s should have been nothing but fun, yet they were laced with regret. He reconnected with his mother, but love affairs went awry. And there was the lingering notion that perhaps the payoff wasn't worth the struggle, or that the going up wasn't worth the coming down. He knew his victories were made possible by what others would call wildness, irresponsibility, and selfishness. If Blake was correct, and if he was called to create, then he was alright. If not, then he was doing something far worse than not living up to his parents' plans: He was not living up to their ideals.

He had built himself a myth, with the drunken nights and the helicopter rides and all such as that. And he was writing things like, "He's a pilgrim and a preacher and a problem when he's stoned/ He's a walkin' contradiction, partly truth and partly fiction/ Takin' every wrong direction on his lonely way back home."

"Of course I was writing about myself," he said.

The second marriage was an all-star affair, as Kristofferson hooked up with glamorous singer Rita Coolidge. The two will forever be recalled as one of Nashville's power couples. Onstage, they were augmented by Funky

Donnie Fritts, Stephen Bruton, Billy Swan (Yes, the same fellow who did "I Can Help"), and others. Offstage, they were beautiful people surrounded by what appeared for all the world to be beautiful circumstances. The husband was good in the movies, where he exuded a combination of handsomeness and believability that was more truth than fiction. The wife was a fine singer and a lovely lady, and they seemed perfect. Trouble is, nothing is perfect. It's all a walking contradiction of some sort. And the marriage didn't last.

In the bitter wake of things, Kristofferson was outraged by the reaction of the people around him, by the ways that friends would turn away.

"Hey, goddamn you, he was your brother," he wrote and sang, talking to the people who were supposed to be close to him. "Turn on your father, sister, mother, brother he was your friend/ Don't you condemn him, leave it to strangers."

Much is made of Kristofferson's politics, of his attention to justice and compassion and fairness. But there is no greater example of such things than the remainder of "Maybe You Heard," a divorce song in which he finds as much fault with those who shun his ex-bride as with those who blame him for the bust-up.

"You used to love her," he sings. "Don't you condemn her, leave it to strangers."

Fame isn't inherently interesting, though Kris Kristofferson made it seem so. After writing a batch of songs with enough intelligence, sensuality and emotion to alter the course of country music, he moved to California, starred in movies, and wrote more songs with intelligence, sensuality, and emotion.

He was a fine big-screen actor. Lord, he'd lived enough to play so many parts from memory: Sinner, sage, fool, drunkard, hard-ass, villain, and martyr. He sometimes invested himself so fully in his characters as to swirl creativity and reality. Those swirls came at the detriment of his own life, though they usually bolstered the believability and impact of whatever film he was working on at the time.

As for the songwriting, his mastery knew few bounds. And the writing led to a performing career that found him playing major halls throughout the 1970s. He was a revered writer, a sex symbol, a movie star, and other things to which men aspire, mostly because of the way women react to them. And then he went and got political . . . back to being the only Anglo at the parade. He became a riddle-speaking prophet who released albums with names like *Repossessed* and *Third World Warrior*. It

> **It bugged him, and still bugs him, that the more he spoke out the more he was called "irrelevant."**

bugged him, and still bugs him, that the more he spoke out the more he was called "irrelevant."

"I was trying, and I'm still trying, to live up to my responsibilities as a human being," he said. "If you're given the tools to be a creative person, would you use them right?"

There's that Blake riff about eternal shame and confusion. Kristofferson never forgot that one.

Not once in the 21st century was Kris Kristofferson called "irrelevant." His legacy is secured in part by the things he did to put that legacy in question: Toughened by alcohol fire, broadened by his acting experiences, hardened by the passing of decades, and illuminated by the performers whose art he's supported (John Prine, Steve Goodman, Todd Snider, etc.) in much the same way that Cash nurtured Kristofferson's art. Blasts of creativity from decades ago now begin to take on a timeless quality, and a Country Music Hall of Fame plaque now hangs in Nashville as a reminder of the transformative nature of Kristofferson's contributions. "Every true thing we wrote on the wind is still singing," is a good way to put it, which is why he put it that way.

Kristofferson's remained a contradicted soul. He willingly took every wrong direction along the way, and while the results of those wanderings are unassailable, there was a substantial toll. Pride and embarrassment held hands through his memories, and he was given to fits of bleak depression.

"I have lived with the dark, with the 'black dog' they call him," he said. "It never leaves totally. You fight it off with family, friends, and your work."

In 1983, he married for the last and best time, to the former Lisa Meyers. He spent his 70s writing lines like "Am I young enough to believe in revolution," and acting in ways that made such questions easier to answer than they were to conceive. Kristofferson believed in revolution, in art, in justice, in words, in actions, in love, in mercy, in excellence, in sorrow, and in redemption.

Kristofferson wrote his music's epitaph early on, in 1971, on the back cover of his second album, *The Silver Tongued Devil and I*.

"Call these echoes of the going-ups and the coming downs, walking pneumonia and run-of-the-mill madness, colored with guilt, pride, and a vague sense of despair," he wrote.

That's as good a description as any for the pleas, prayers, and shouts that ring loud enough to drown out guitars, snare strikes, bass rumbles, or helicopter blades of any era.

But then there are the lines that ring from his songs and inform his life:

"The going up was worth the coming down."
"We'll take our own chances and pay our own dues."
"Dreaming was as easy as believing it was never going to end."
"If you can't find nobody else then help yourself to me."
"Freedom's just another word for nothing left to lose."
"You have lived up to your name."
"Let me go on loving and believing, 'til it's over."
"So help me, Jesus, I know what I am."

In January of 2014, Kris Kristofferson understood that he was facing dementia. Old friends looked like old friends, but, often, he couldn't call their names. This was an everyday frustration. He'd been fighting memory loss for the past decade, spending airplane time on word puzzles because he'd heard that kind of thing might help. Finally, he agreed to use a teleprompter when playing shows: his melodies never wavered, but the lyrics could fly away if they weren't there in front of him.

On January 26 of that year, Kristofferson agreed to appear on live television, at the Grammy Awards, singing a medley of hits with old friends Willie Nelson and Merle Haggard, and with contemporary country star Blake Shelton. A couple of days prior to the live show, he rehearsed the performance at Los Angeles' Staples Center. Just after the rehearsal, he pulled me aside:

"The good thing about my brain being so messed up is that I feel kinda high all the time," he said. "Of course, come to think of it, I *did* just get off of Willie's bus."

Two years later, he and Lisa were back in Nashville at the Bridgestone Arena, for a multi-artist tribute called "The Life & Songs of Kris Kristofferson." Kris sang a few songs, aided by the prompter, but the bulk of the evening found him and Lisa sitting side-stage as Alison Krauss, Emmylou Harris, Willie Nelson, and others sang Kristofferson songs.

Just before the show, I told Kris that I hoped he could enjoy the show, in the moment. I told him that the whole night would be his friends singing songs they loved, for a person they loved.

He smiled and said, "I just hope I can remember it happened when it's over."

Two hours after the show was done, he didn't remember it.

But during the concert, he sat and smiled, slapping his thigh and beaming as he heard his songs' shining brilliance, as if for the first time.

AN ASIDE: WELCOME TO NASHVILLE

Tom T. Hall wasn't always Tom T. Hall.

He used to be just Tom Hall.

The "T" was added as a showbiz affectation, after he got a record deal.

One night in 1965, the pre-T Tom Hall was drinking at a place called the Nine-O-One Club.

He ordered another beer, and a necklace-wearing fellow brought the beer over to him.

"Are you Tom Hall?" the voice growled.

"Yes, sir, I am."

"I'm Kris Kristofferson. I like your songwriting. I'm trying to write myself."

Hall welcomed him: "Good to see you, it's a hairy-legged town."

CHAPTER
5

MERLE HAGGARD AND DAVID OLNEY, WISE MEN

Merle Haggard is on the short list anytime talk turns to the most significant singer-songwriters in music history, in any genre, and anytime anyone talks about the greatest artists in country music.

His history is staggering.

Kris Kristofferson liked to say that Haggard was the most successfully rehabilitated prisoner in the history of the American penal system. He went from San Quentin State Prison to the White House. At the former, he got hassled. At the latter, President Obama put a Kennedy Center Honor medallion around his neck.

Haggard grew up in and around Bakersfield, California, which was a musical hotbed. His dad died when Merle was nine years old, and his teen years were wayward.

"I turned 21 in prison doing life without parole," he sang. "No one could steer me right, but Mama tried."

The parts about turning 21 in prison and his Mama trying were true. So was the part about no one being able to steer him right. The "life without parole" part wasn't autobiographical, though in prison he met men in that situation, and men on death row.

At one point, Merle Haggard went to prison for stupidity. He and at least one other partner-in-crime thought it was 3 a.m., and they knew for certain that they were poor and desperate. They found a restaurant to rip off, and Merle took a crowbar to the screen of the restaurant's back door. Haggard was prying at the lock when the door came open and he heard a voice say, "What are you boys doing? Why don't you boys come around to the front door like everybody else?"

In Merle's autobiography, he wrote, "What we hadn't realized was that it wasn't 3 a.m. at all. Hell, it was barely 10, and the place was still open with several customers inside. Drunk as I was, I figured right away we'd made a slight miscalculation."

At San Quentin, he saw Johnny Cash perform for the prisoners. Cash was in lousy, hoarse, amphetamine-dogged voice, but his conviction and charisma moved Haggard like nothing else. When Haggard got out of prison and entered the music business, he confessed to Cash that he had been a convict, and he said he feared public disapproval if the news ever got out. Cash advised him to come clean, and he took Cash's advice, speaking about his incarceration and writing songs that addressed his rambling early years.

When Haggard signed a record deal with Capitol, he entered into a period of intense creativity. In the first nine years of his career, he recorded thirty albums, peppered with songs that are now classics.

I'm going to repeat that: Thirty albums in nine years.

Today's star-level artists release one album every two years. In the first nine years of Luke Bryan's career, he released five full-length studio albums. Taylor Swift, same thing. Brad Paisley released six in his first nine years. Wait, his first nine-and-a-half years.

Haggard released thirty, and they weren't of the "two hits and a bunch of filler" variety.

They were real-deal Merle Haggard albums.

Merle remained voraciously creative throughout his life. He'd endure divorces, setbacks, cancer, and hard habits, writing and singing his way through all of it. And the songs weren't just therapeutic for Haggard, they gave voice to the emotions of millions of people. He became known as "The Poet of the Common Man," though he himself was an uncommon man.

Haggard wrote a major hit in 1969 called "Okie From Muskogee." The song was taken as a repudiation of the counter-culture, with lines slagging "hippies" with "long and shaggy" hair, and war protesters with "beads and roman sandals." The song's first line was, "We don't smoke marijuana in

Muskogee," ironic since Haggard became the second most notorious (or victorious) pot-smoker in country music, just behind his pal Willie Nelson.

"It's a character study," he said. "It was the photograph that I took of the way things looked through the eyes of a fool."

Turns out, Haggard said, he was that fool.

"I was just as dumb as a rock at about that time, and most of America was under the same assumptions I was . . . If you use that song now, it's a really good snapshot of how dumb we were in the past. They had me fooled, too. I've become educated."

Yeah, but don't people take a reversal of opinion as a sign of weakness, or of lack of conviction?

"I think one of the bigger mistakes politicians do is to get embarrassed when somebody catches them changing their opinion," he said. "God, what if they learned the truth since they expressed themselves in the past? I've learned the truth since I wrote that song . . . It's a different song now. I'm different now."

Haggard's early songs came with a jutted chin and a pin to prick. Later on, he was more likely to trade on optimism.

> **If the sound, the band, and the audience were all good, he'd stay up there for hours, locking eyes with people in the seats, and playfully jousting with his band.**

A Haggard concert could be absolute magic, or it could be something far less. He died in 2016 and last took a set list onstage with him in 1969. If he was dealing with squealing monitors, an inattentive crowd, or players that favored hot licks over depth of emotion, he'd jump offstage the minute he'd fulfilled his contractual obligation. Over the years, there were a lot of 55-minute-long Merle Haggard shows. But if the sound, the band, and the audience were all good, he'd stay up there for hours, locking eyes with people in the seats, and playfully jousting with his band, the Strangers.

I asked him once about those comfortable nights, when he seemed at home on well-lit stages, just like he would have been in his living room. I asked if it had always been that way for him.

"I used to have some of that . . . I guess you'd call it 'stage fright,'" he said. "Then I got to thinking about it. I finally realized that stage fright is nothing more than the fear of people paying attention to you . . . and, they don't do that . . . They're too wrapped up in their own fucking shit."

David Olney is the kind of Nashville songwriter who other Nashville songwriters either praise for being a wondrous original or curse for being a wondrous original.

Olney doesn't write like other people. He wrote a song called "Titanic," a rhyming love story, from the iceberg's point of view. He wrote a song called "Jerusalem Tomorrow," a spoken-word epic in the voice of a Bible-times religious huckster ("I'd hire a kid to say he was lame, then I'd touch him and make him walk again/ Then I'd pull some magic trick, I'd pretend to heal the sick") who joins up with Jesus Christ. One time, Emmylou Harris told a great songwriter named Kieran Kane that she needed some songs for an upcoming album. Kieran made her a tape that had "Jerusalem Tomorrow" on it. He could have loaded the tape up with his own songs. But he couldn't bear to have "Jerusalem Tomorrow" go unheard.

> **"Okay, so the greatest female voice of our time is recording my song . . . and it's a spoken-word."**
> **—David Olney**

Of course, Emmylou recorded "Jerusalem Tomorrow." And Olney had a nuanced reaction.

"I hear that Emmylou Harris, the greatest female voice of our time, is recording one of my songs," he said, one hotel room night. "So it's, 'Great. What song?' I hear back, 'Jerusalem Tomorrow.' Okay, so the greatest female voice of our time is recording my song . . . and it's a spoken-word."

No worries, as Emmylou also recorded a version of a melodic Olney song called "Deeper Well." That's part of her *Wrecking Ball* album, which came out in 1995 and became a touchstone for what is now called Americana music.

Oh, Olney has another one called "1917," a World War 1 song, told from the point of view of a French prostitute. It's so good, I can't bear to tell you about it. Emmylou recorded that one, too, with help from duo partner Linda Ronstadt.

I used to get angry about music.

Angry about music is a dumb, dumb way to be. If you're angry about music, you should re-direct your anger towards something else. Try being angry about hunger, poverty, war, or Duke University's basketball team. All are more valid targets than music. People who are angry about music think, as I once did, that the reason David Olney isn't a big radio star is because of the people who are big radio stars. They think that musical acumen is quantifiable, and that fame and riches are rewards that should be based on their perception of greatness.

That perception is incredibly stupid.

In the first place, music is helpful to different people for different reasons. Some of my favorite times with music are when I am alone in a car, driving around and listening to the somber and searing folk songs of a doomed Texas troubadour named Townes Van Zandt. I love Townes, and Steve Earle once said that Townes was the greatest songwriter in America and that Steve would gladly stand up with his boots on Bob Dylan's coffee table and proclaim that fact.

But, you want to clear a party? Put on an album of Townes Van Zandt's called *Live at the Old Quarter*. You want to pump up a party? Put on some vapid celebration of carnal acquisitions. And you know who goes to parties? People go to parties. And if they go to a party and dance to a vapid celebration of carnal acquisitions, they're likely to buy a copy of the vapid celebration in question, so they can remember that party when they're on their way to their job in sales or marketing. Come February, the vapid celebration of carnal acquisitions will win a Grammy, and Townes Van Zandt will still be lying dead in the cold, hard ground.

I've never made a list of my ten favorite country and Americana albums.

Perhaps I'll make one here, in no particular order (and the list will change ten minutes from now, but still . . .

Emmylou Harris, *Pieces of the Sky*
Tom T. Hall, *In Search of a Song*
Charley Pride, *Recorded Live at Panther Hall*
Guy Clark, *Old No. 1*
John Hartford, *Mark Twang*
John Prine, *John Prine*
Townes Van Zandt, *Live at the Old Quarter*

Nanci Griffith, *Last of the True Believers*
Merle Haggard, *Serving 190 Proof*
Waylon Jennings, *Dreaming My Dreams*

Again, that list will change in a minute, and I'm already wondering what kind of idiot would leave George Jones, Willie Nelson, and Mickey Newbury off such a list. I'm giving myself a pass on Hank Williams, Jimmie Rodgers, Patsy Cline, and the Carter Family by saying that they existed before the album was really a thing, and it's cheating to put Greatest Hits collections on this.

All that said, my point is that at one moment in time I legitimately listed those ten albums as my favorite in this music. And that none of them won Grammy awards or were blockbuster commercial successes. None of the above musicians reaped remarkable fiscal rewards from efforts that I, after a half-lifetime of studying into country music, believe to be the best of the best.

So, don't get mad about music, or treat music like it's a football game where you cheer for the uniforms and live by the scoreboard.

Don't be like I once was.

All that ended for me one night in Spartanburg, South Carolina, when David Olney was on my back porch.

It was the part of late at night that is actually early in the morning, and then it was the part of early in the morning that is closer to the crack of dawn. David and I were talking about life and music, and I was griping about whatever vapid celebration of carnal acquisitions was the feel good hit of that summer.

David said, "Do you ever read Shakespeare?"

I said, "Yeah."

David said, "I've been re-reading Shakespeare, all summer. And . . . I suck. I suck."

I was worried about what was on the radio.

David was considering the greatness of Shakespeare, and bemoaning that his own work wasn't measuring up to the Bard.

Another time, David played an ill-attended concert.

I was there, among the ill-attendees.

The show was in a crappy bar, with a ballgame showing on the television. Patrons' attentions were divided between the ballgame and the music, and there weren't many patrons' attentions to divide.

David played with intensity, even ferocity, for three hours.

I've seen him play maybe fifty times, and I'd put this show in the top five. It was incredible.

After the concert (but before the ballgame was over), I said, "Dave, that was something special."

He said, "Yeah, it was a good one."

I said, "It must have been hard, what with the ballgame and the lack of people and the divided attentions and everything."

He said, "I learned a long time ago, it's twice as hard to do the songs wrong. I like to take it easy on myself."

Yet another time, David played a moderately-attended concert.

I was there, among the moderate attendees.

The show took place in the early spring, when people were doing their taxes and such. Maybe some folks who would have come out to the show were stuck at home crunching numbers and filling out forms.

David played what I and other moderates thought of as a tremendous show.

And when it was over, he walked over to the table where he sold CDs and other merchandise, and accepted apologies.

This is a common thing for those of us who hold acoustic guitars and sing to dozens of people: When the show is over, the people who took the time and trouble to come, and paid money at the door, will apologize to you on behalf of the millions of people who did not take the time or trouble to come and pay money at the door.

Blows my mind.

"Dave, great show," this guy said. "I'm sorry there weren't more people here."

"Well, word of my fame may not have spread to this part of the country," David said.

"Yeah, but you're great."

"Well, I agree. I'm pretty good. But the thing is, not a lot of people like my shit."

This stopped the guy in his tracks.

After a pause, Olney said, "But here's the thing . . . I think there may be forty or fifty people in most decent towns that like my shit. And some of them are married or have people that are obligated to come along . . . And if forty people in a town like my shit and sixty people come out to my show, and some of them buy CDs . . . I can make a living at this."

> **"Not a lot of people like my shit. But the people that do . . . I'm the only place they can get it. If they don't come hear me, they're not going to get the shit they like. I've got a monopoly on my shit."**
> **—David Olney**

The guy nodded.

"And here's the other thing," David said. "Not a lot of people like my shit. But the people that do . . . I'm the only place they can get it. If they don't come hear me, they're not going to get the shit they like. I've got a monopoly on my shit."

More nods, less comprehending.

"You know Britney Spears?" Dave asked.

The guy said he didn't know her.

"But you know who she is, right?"

Yes, the guy knew who she was. She was a provocatively dressed pop star who lip-synched her songs while performing intricate dance moves that often involved writhing around poles.

"Well, when she fills out her tax forms . . . in the place where they ask you to list your occupation . . . she and I write the exact same thing."

AN ASIDE: **MORE ADVICE**

I was out of sorts, drained from the plane ride and the wait for the rental car, sapped by the Houston heat, and taxed by the traffic on the way to Wymer, Texas, home of marvelous songwriter Eric Taylor.

When I got to the farmhouse, I parked and pulled a heavy bag and a Martin guitar from the car. Hands full, I struggled with the gate latch and bumbled into the yard. The dogs—two big dogs—heard the clamor. They darted from the house, barking, menacing.

I remember the noise. The low growls. The scratching of hounds' nails on my guitar case. And then, suddenly, the slap of the screen door and the commanding admonition.

"Dogs, get down!" yelled Eric. "Peter, don't be tentative around those dogs! Don't be tentative! . . . About anything! . . . Fucking ever!"

STORYTELLING

Let me tell you what I learned in journalism school.

Nothing.

Didn't go. Didn't take a class. But I'm told that part of what is taught, and I've heard editors mention this, is that we must be objective.

As a music writer—and I would suggest this is true of the vast majority of writers—I am here to say that objectivity is the mortal enemy. Now, for sure, you need a good bullshit detector, and you shouldn't rant, and you shouldn't cheerlead.

But objectivity is dispassionate.

And we're in the passion business.

We're trying to make people feel something different than what they felt before they read our words.

The only way I've found to do this is to feel something before I write my words, and to feel something while I'm writing.

Who would I be to be objective about George Jones, or Emmylou Harris, or Ray Charles, or Tom T. Hall? How could I be objective about music, which is inherently subjective?

Objective about people? How? And why?

When Johnny Cash died, it was a gut-punch. I knew him. Loved his music. Loved people in his family. Loved people who were his dear friends. What was I going to write?

The only way to find clarity was to reject objectivity.

I had to allow myself to experience the moment, to feel something, and then to convey that feeling.

These kinds of things are not processes of assessment. They are nothing short of internal excavation.

Here's what I felt: I felt Johnny Cash was indomitable, but he was not.

Others wrote, "Johnny Cash, a Country Music and Rock and Roll Hall of Famer, whose sparse but electrifying sound captivated million, died blah blah blah."

I began my obituary with the five words that kept running through my head: "Somehow, Johnny Cash is dead."

When George Jones was dying, I got the call late one night, from his hospital room.

"It's going to be soon," was the word I received.

My heart dropped, and bounced around until it was badly bruise.

I stayed up all night, writing the facts of his life, and maybe drinking some of the stuff he used to like to drink. He was known to some as "The King of Broken Hearts," because of his way with a sad country ballad. I wrote the body of the obituary that night, then got word in the morning that he was gone.

I wrote the first thing I felt, at the very top of the story: "The King of Broken Hearts just broke many more."

If you write exactly what you feel, you have written an exclusive.

If you write something objective, you have most likely written a measured mediocrity.

As a writer, if you approach a subject with objectivity, you are denying what is special, what is emphatic, or what is idiotic about them.

This seems self-evident with music, but it also impacts news reporting. So many times, reasonable and unreasonable points are dealt with as equals. That's why, in recent years, the comedy reporting of humorous pundits has been received as more truthful than "objective" network reports.

The comedy folks have their bullshit detectors activated.

The network folks deactivate those detectors in favor of appearing unbiased.

Anyway, my opinion is that Cash and Jones were special. And I'm glad to have received them as such.

Also special is Tom T. Hall, who reimagined country music songwriting and who wrote staggering truths, in rhyme and meter. He is, at once, a member of the Country Music Hall of Fame and a vastly underrated talent.

Here are some words about Tom T. Hall. They are subjective, and deeply felt.

The great man sat on the side of the bed, listening to bird songs out the morning window, balancing a tennis shoe on top of his head, trying to find some humility.

He believed it to be the first virtue. Humility, not shoe-balancing. Johnny Cash told him once that he, too, believed humility to be the first virtue.

"It's the first virtue, T.," Cash assured. "And I don't have an ounce of it."

Cash did, of course, have some humility. It takes humility to admit the lack of it. But, at his core, Cash knew that both he and his rhyme-spinning, philosophizing, renegade friend, Tom T. Hall, were great men. They were exceptional, which Hall figured might be problematic.

"I have this theory that songwriters are not good songwriters," Hall said at age 79, sitting in the kitchen nook at Fox Hollow, the Tennessee estate he shared for decades with his wife, Dixie.

Miss Dixie, as everyone called her, had more bluegrass songs recorded than anyone in history. She died in the first month of 2015. After that, Tom T. sometimes thought of Emily Dickinson's words: "Parting is all we know of heaven, and all we need of hell."

But back to the theory, and to the tennis shoe that rested daily on Tom T.'s cranium.

"Songwriters aren't good songwriters," he said. "People are good songwriters. So all of my career I fought against sitting down as a 'Songwriter.' I would sit with that sneaker on my head, until I found humility and became a person.

"You sit down as a person and write a song. If you've written a song by the time you stand back up, you're a songwriter. But the person comes first.

JOHNNY'S CASH & CHARLEY'S PRIDE

You can't look at the thing from somewhere up above, or from some place of supposed knowledge. Anyway, if you look at the state of the world, mankind has a lot to be humble about."

~

Tom T. Hall came to Nashville on the first day of 1964, steering a pink Cadillac that he bought after someone told him that he'd never be able to buy a Cadillac by writing a song. He came to town because a publisher had promised him $50 a week if he'd make up songs that Dave Dudley, Jimmy Newman, and other country stars of the day could sing.

Tom T. had worked at little radio stations, where he made up hundreds of little jingles. He figured he could make up hundreds of what folks back then called "Little Darlin'" songs. "Little Darlin'" songs were the sometimes clever, sometimes hokey, rarely cerebral songs that were in favor back in the first part of 1964.

When a songwriter signed a publishing deal—and this holds true today—his job was to write songs that would please the publisher. And publishers are pleased by songs that get played on the radio. It's "Figure out what's working, and then do that." Makes perfect sense, though the end of that road is most often frustration and burnout for the creators, and for listeners who don't want to spend their day hearing twenty slightly different replications of the same tired and silly thing.

Tom T. was okay at writing Little Darlin' songs. He was fast, and smart, and he took his job seriously. He wrote every day, typing words onto paper, and then singing them into a Wollensak recorder.

His friend Kris Kristofferson accused him once of "impersonating a hack." That was said without malice. Kristofferson just meant to say that Hall approached songwriting as an office job, not as a fanciful and mysterious lifestyle choice.

Hall wrote Little Darlin' songs by making them up, the same way grown men sit in Nashville offices today, collaborating on songs about fictional farm parties. He made up songs with titles like "From Sad Street to Lonely Road," "National Everybody Hate Me Week," "Floptop Beer," and "Love Insurance." He sat down, as a songwriter, and wrote those songs.

But then, in 1968, a wonderful thing happened: Failure.

Grand Ole Opry star Stonewall Jackson was a neighbor, and one day Jackson told Hall that he was looking for songs for a prison album. At the time, Johnny Cash's *Live at Folsom Prison* was riding high, and Jackson was seeking a thematic piggyback. He asked Hall to write him some prison songs, and Hall went home and struggled mightily. He told Miss Dixie he felt phony writing about prison, since he'd never been in prison. "Make something up" wasn't working.

"Miss Dixie said, 'Write about what you know,'" he said. "I told her, 'Well, I've been in jail,' and she said, 'Write about that.'"

Hall spent a week in a Paintsville, Kentucky jailhouse, before his Cadillac-acquisition days. He wasn't supposed to spend a whole week there. He'd been pulled over for a minor offense, and was set to see the judge the morning after the arrest. But the judge's grandmother died, and it took His Honor seven days of grieving and resting before he could fine and free the restless prisoner.

That's when Tom T. Hall wrote his first Tom T. Hall song. It was called "A Week in a Country Jail." It begins, "One time I spent a week inside a little country jail, and I don't guess I'll ever live it down/ I was sitting at a red light when these two men came and got me, and said that I was speeding through their town."

It was the first song Hall never made up. He didn't have to.

"It was more relating than creating," he said. "I didn't have to make up anything. I didn't have to write it, it was just there. I just had to make it rhyme."

A year later, "A Week in a Country Jail" became Tom T. Hall's first #1 country hit. He'd gotten the record deal because his publishers didn't think they could pitch these new songs he'd been writing, the ones about his own hard truths. They weren't Little Darlin' songs, they were Tom T. Hall songs. They were at once deceptively simple and remarkably evolved, informed by life and by literature.

"I learned to write by reading," he said. "I love the simplicity of Hemingway, and I think I got my social conscience from Sinclair Lewis. Hemingway said he used the word 'town' instead of 'metropolis,' and got paid the same ten cents for both words. That stuck with me."

"Write what you know" is not anything that hadn't been tried before. But Tom T. took the approach to places that it had never been, at least in the context of country songs. The late 1960s and early 1970s found Hall charging ahead with a loosely affiliated gang of writers that included Kristofferson, John Hartford, and Mickey Newbury. These men elevated and altered the language and narrative form of country music, and they blazed a path down which Guy Clark, Townes Van Zandt, and John Prine would later meander. Witnesses have seen Jason Isbell and Patty Griffin jogging that path in recent days.

Tom T. Hall wrote the book on songwriting, or at least he wrote a book on songwriting. Johnny Cash called it "The most helpful book I know for both new and experienced songwriters." One chapter of the book is called "Rules and Tools," and that chapter includes sections headed, "Think Positive," "The Title Is the Point," and "Avoid Too Much Realism."

The trouble—and it's actually not a trouble, it's what Kristofferson would call "a table-thumping smash"—is that Tom T. Hall advice on "Think Positive," "The Title Is the Point," and "Avoid Too Much Realism" is along the lines of Bob Dylan advice on "Diction Is Respect," "Stick to the Set List," and "Avoid Changing Your Name."

Ah, Mr. Dylan. In February of 2015, at a MusiCares Person of the Year speech, he offered wobbly dismissals of Hall, saying that he recalled recording in Nashville and reading an article in which Tom T. was "bitching about some kind of new song, and he couldn't understand what these new kinds of songs that were coming in were about." Dylan also said that Kristofferson's monumental ballad, "Sunday Morning Coming Down," "blew ol' Tom T. Hall's world apart . . . It might have sent him to the mad house. God forbid he ever heard any of my songs."

By the way, Hall has heard Dylan's songs. He said he liked the one about "Blowin' in the Wind," but he also said that if Dylan had spent more time on Maggie's farm he would have come to learn that doves don't sleep in the sand. Also, to Kristofferson, he was an advocate, not a killjoy.

"I remember the first time Tom T. Hall told me he liked a song of mine," Kristofferson said. "It was 'From the Bottle to the Bottom,' and Billy Walker cut it. They put it on the jukebox at Tootsie's there, and he said, 'God, that's a great song,' and he quoted me some lines out of it. That kind of thing was enough to keep me going back then."

Dylan recorded in Nashville in the late 1960s, through the spring of 1970. During that time, Hall wasn't bitching about some kind of new song, he was writing some kind of new song. He was writing and singing "A Week in a Country Jail," and a chorus-less song called "Homecoming," in which he never says the word "homecoming." He was writing and singing a chorus-less song called "Ballad of Forty Dollars," in which he never says "ballad of forty dollars." That last one is set in a cemetery back in Hall's hometown of Olive Hill, Kentucky. It is sung from the perspective of a grave-digger. Tom T. used to work in that very cemetery.

"Think Positive." "The Title Is the Point." "Avoid Too Much Realism": Complete and utter bullshit, much like that misguided section of Dylan's speech. Asked about it, Hall simply asked back, "What the hell was that all about?" (Which is, by the way, the same question he has said he'd like etched into his gravestone.)

But then he said something more. He drew a distinction.

"There's a difference between me and Bob Dylan," he said. "Dylan's career was based on imitating legendary folk heroes, like Woody Guthrie and Robert Johnson. He made a career of imitating old folk singers, and today he's a phenomenal success who has become an old folk singer. He became what he most admired. He's a product of his subscription to another culture and another time. I invented myself."

Hall says that in enmity-free observation. It sounds colder in print than he meant when he voiced it. But the distinction is real: Dylan's genius is born of musical archaeology, fused through atypical intelligence. Hall's genius is born of internal excavation. Straight, no chaser.

Dylan is a cocktail. Hall is a shot.

As for the notion that Kristofferson would somehow have blown his world apart, Hall always considered himself and Kristofferson as part of the same world. Maybe even part of a club of two:

"Kris and I might have created what I call an illusion of literacy in Nashville," he said. "People said we were the only guys who could describe Dolly Parton without using our hands."

Tossed and turned the night before in some old motel
Subconsciously recalling some old sinful thing I'd done
My buddy drove the car and those big coal trucks shook us up
As we drove on into Hyden in the early morning sun

That's the beginning of "Trip To Hyden," another Tom T. Hall song with no chorus, and no mention of the title in the lyrics.

In songs, movies, short stories, and novels, writers know that the introduction of a plot point necessitates the resolution of a plot point. Listeners, viewers, and readers want to know what happens. Hall knows about literary convention, having spent years touring around in a consortium called "The Brotherhood," with close bookworm friends like Roots author Alex Haley and renowned poet (and daddy of Lucinda) Miller Williams.

So what was the sinful thing that caused the night's lost sleep? "Trip To Hyden" never says.

"My first line is always something I know to be completely true," Hall said. "And it is supposed to let the listener in on something. In 'Trip To Hyden,' they know immediately that the guy singing to them is a traveler, and that he's not a perfect person. Then they know he's a passenger in a car, in coal country. There's a scene that's being set there, but it's set because it's something that happened."

Start with something—an image, an emotion—that's completely true . . . that's a central lesson in American roots music lyric-writing. It doesn't have to be followed, but it should be understood. Emmylou Harris wrote, "I don't want to hear a love song/ I got on this airplane just to fly." Hayes Carll sang Scott Nolan's words: "Arkansas . . .. my head hurts." Guy Clark wrote, and sang "I'd play the 'Red River Valley,' and he'd sit in the kitchen and cry."

Most people haven't heard "Trip To Hyden." If they've heard Tom T. Hall's songs, they've heard "(Old Dogs, Children And) Watermelon Wine," or a children's song he wrote called "I Love," or the one about his childhood hero, "The Year Clayton Delaney Died," or Jeannie C. Riley's recording of his "Harper Valley P.T.A." Maybe they've heard Alan Jackson singing "Little Bitty." Those were all #1 hit singles. But Tom T. Hall was an album artist before most others in country music thought that way. He released nineteen albums in the first ten years of his recording career, and he wrote the vast majority of the songs on those albums.

So, that's two albums a year, with a rough average of twelve songs per album, and most of those songs coming from his pen (or his typewriter ribbon). Each album held only a single or two, so much of Hall's output existed outside of what anyone heard on the radio.

Hall wasn't one to record a couple of commercially viable singles and then pad his albums with filler. The vast majority of his greatest work exists below the radar, and is only available now on foreign reissues. He's a Country Music Hall of Famer because of the singles, but the genius is in the albums.

Those albums hold songs like "Million Miles to the City," where Olive Hill kids dismiss an adult's account of the nearest city: "'Why, the buildings are taller than oak trees,' but we knew better than that/ Ain't nobody could climb that high, the cities were wide and flat."

Patterson Hood of Drive-By Truckers points to "Mama Bake a Pie (Daddy Kill a Chicken)," where a wounded soldier returning from war ponders his trifling former girlfriend: "I know she'll come and see me, but I'll bet she never once looks at my legs/ No, she'll talk about the weather, and the dress she wore at the July fourth parade."

At every concert, Buddy Miller delivers a Tom T. Hall ballad. Miller says it centers him. It was never a single for Hall. It begins, "If you love somebody enough, you'll follow wherever they go/ That's how I got to Memphis." Johnny Cash, Dolly Parton, George Jones, Flatt & Scruggs, John Prine, Jim Lauderdale, and hundreds of others have recorded Hall-penned songs that Tom T. never released as singles.

As for "Trip to Hyden," the narrator and his driver head to the site of a Kentucky mining disaster, where efforts were being made to aid the victims' families. They encounter an old man who says of the mining explosion, "It was just like being inside of a shotgun." It ends with this:

Well, I guess the old man thought we were reporters
He kept reminding me of how his simple name was spelled
Some lady said, "They worth more money now then when they's a'living"
And I'll leave it there, 'cause I suppose she told it pretty well

A songwriter writes in enriched language, about miners who toiled and coughed and ached, for the comfort of those who lived above their station. A songwriter sits in judgement of society. A songwriter might be prone to smug poetry.

A person writes the words of a women who says to him, "They worth more money now then when they's a'living."

A person writes, "I'll leave it there, 'cause I suppose she told it pretty well."

It wasn't just "write what you know."

"I feel that it is important to tell you that I know far more than my songs have said," Hall wrote in his memoir.

He didn't mean that as a brag about accumulated knowledge. He knows humility is the first virtue. Hall meant that as a lesson: Don't just write what you know. Write less than you know. Know more than you write. Wonder and study and gather, then whittle to the essence.

Hall whittled to the essence of racism. His only song of overt judgement was called "The Man Who Hated Freckles." It was written at the height of the Civil Rights Movement, and it was delivered to a supposedly conservative, ill-educated country music audience. But Hall wasn't a songwriter who wrote for an audience. He was a person who wrote to other people.

"Well, he'd see a kid with freckles and he'd cuss, said 'Because of them my children have to bus/ We wouldn't have the trouble we have seen, if it wasn't for that Martin Luther Queen," he wrote and sang.

"The Man Who Hated Freckles" was a non-absurdist's song about absurdity, with "freckles" taking the place of a more sinister slur. It was a cry for help, and a howl of admonition. It ended, "The man who hated freckles may be sick, but as far as I'm concerned he was a stupid son of a . . .."

"If we didn't have people of color and culture, we would ostracize people with freckles," he says. "The nature of people is to find someone different and blame them for being different, to cast aspersion on their character and intentions.

There was a time, Tom T. Hall said, when people worried about him.

"A friend of mine said once, 'Tom T., people in Nashville think you're crazy. You don't try to fit in, you don't go to the right places, and some people are a little bit afraid of you.' Hey, if you can't get respect, take fear, which is, actually, a form of respect.

"Look, poets are unmanageable. I said, 'What's wrong with me is my greatest asset.' What creative people do is to bring original things into the world. It's a dangerous business, and you can't have both sanity and creativity. They don't run around together."

And so Hall ceded creativity in exchange for sanity. He has been written about as the greatest country songwriter since Hank Williams. Country Music Hall of Famer Bobby Bare calls him the single best storytelling songwriter we've known. President Jimmy Carter spoke of him as the singular voice of a common American conscience.

But, once he got done with his Little Darlin' era, he was not really a songwriter at all. After all, songwriters are not good songwriters. People are good songwriters.

Others work on being pithy, elliptical, and clever. Tom T. Hall wanted to be a person, not a great man. But, ultimately, the work bestowed greatness upon him. He rose from hard and isolated Kentucky poverty and found a place in the pantheon. And every time he found comfort and satisfaction in all of that, he stuck a tennis shoe on top of his head until the feeling went away.

AN ASIDE: **A BIG SADNESS**

From my perspective, Tom T. Hall's life has always looked like a grand success.

The week before his 80th birthday, he professed deep disappointment.

"When I was a kid, I was told, and I believed, that mine would be the generation to end the things that were wrong," he said. "My generation would put a stop to all this war, and to whatever this racism thing was. My generation was the future, and the future was better than what had come before.

"Well, here I am turning 80. And it wasn't true.

"It was the same lie every generation tells the one that follows.

"So that's a big sadness."

CHAPTER 7

AN INTERMISSION, FOR STUFF YOU MOSTLY DON'T HEAR

Country Music Hall of Famer Mel Tillis was backstage at the Grand Ole Opry, in the men's room.

He was relieving himself, and talking to another Opry veteran at the urinals.

"Mel, I understand congratulations are in order," said the other fellow. "A little bird tells me you're about to turn 80."

Tillis smiled, nodded in affirmation, and then looked down, forlornly.

"You'd have been gonna turn 80, too, little buddy," he said, zipping up. "If you hadn't of died."

Dolly Parton has often remarked that people in her Tennessee mountain hometown told her she'd starve if she came to Nashville.

"I'm starvin' here, so what's the difference," was her response. "I thought, 'Well, how much poorer can I be?' I was poor at home in the mountains. I figured I could be poor somewhere else."

I'd heard her speak those lines time and again. I asked her if she did in fact go hungry in Nashville.

She said not for a minute.

"To eat, I used to go over to some of the motels, and I'd go up and down the halls and find where people had left their trays out in the hallways," she said. "I'd get pieces of hamburger or whatever from their trays. I didn't feel like a bum. I felt like, 'Lord, some people waste more food than other people have.' There'd be stuff left over that people hadn't even touched."

A harmony quartet was in the recording studio.

In the recording studio, the producer and engineer are usually in their own little room.

It's called "the control room," because the soundboard and controls are there, and because producers tend to have control over the proceedings.

In a harmony quartet, each member of the quartet takes a different note in the chord. In country and gospel music, there's usually a bass singer, a baritone, a second tenor, and a high tenor. Those are the designations, but the singers sometimes switch around, just as a forward on a basketball team sometimes stands on the part of the court that one would expect the guard to stand on.

It may be unclear to the producer and engineer which member of the quartet is singing each particular note. There's a glass partition between the control room and the studio floor, and sometimes singers are behind baffles or in separated vocal booths.

The producer and engineer have something called a "talk-back" button. When they press this button, they can talk and the singers and players can hear what they are saying. Without pressing the button, they can talk freely amongst themselves, and even order take-out food while the song is being recorded.

On this day, one of the singers was having pitch problems. The producer wasn't sure which singer it was.

The producer mashed the talk-back button.

"Who's singing this note right here?" he sang, opera-style, hitting the note on which the second tenor singer kept falling flat.

"I'm singing that note right there!" sang the second tenor, ardently, and off-pitch.

The producer pressed the talk-back once again, and sang the second tenor's note, opera-style:

"You're fired."

A click track provides a mechanized rhythm accent that can be placed into each musician's headphones.

It is nothing more than a computerized metronome.

Some people hate click tracks, thinking them sterilizers that keep tempos from accelerating into choruses and relaxing into verses.

Others like them, thinking that they establish a steady tempo of the sort that a human drummer cannot equal.

> **Click tracks are neither the protagonist nor the antagonist in modern recording. They are a tool, and that tool can be used properly or misused.**

There have been wonderful songs recorded with click tracks, wonderful songs ruined by click tracks, and wonderful songs recorded without click tracks.

Click tracks are neither the protagonist nor the antagonist in modern recording. They are a tool, and that tool can be used properly or misused.

Lots of things are that way.

My friend Thomm Jutz, was producing a session on which a singer-songwriter was playing.

The singer-songwriter in question kept lousy time on guitar. He would strum before the beat, after the beat . . . anything but on the beat.

To his credit, the singer-songwriter realized that things weren't jelling.

"Things aren't jelling," he said.

"No, they aren't," Thomm said.

"Do you think we can play to a click?" the singer-songwriter said.

Thomm, by this point, was flustered. He'd had enough.

"We can play to a click," he said, motioning to the other musicians.

"You cannot.

"Perhaps if you take the song home, figure out the tempo and practice to a click, you too will be able to play to a click."

Thomm is a super-nice guy. But that session didn't end well.

Don't twist my arm and make me tell you who is the best singer
in Nashville.

Because that really hurts.

The arm stuff hurts, but it also hurts to make my inspirers arm-wrestle
each other.

Anyway, if you twisted my arm and asked about the best singer in
Nashville, the answer might be "Lee Ann Womack."

She is spectacular, more so because she doesn't have to prove to you how
spectacular she is with every line.

She can sing a straight melody and it'll make you cry.

She can augment that melody with unique phrasing, and it'll make you cry.

But she'll never take a melody and sacrifice it to curly-cues and technically
impressive-but-soul-numbing acrobatics.

She's really, really good.

Early in her career, I heard her sing in a room, unadorned, without
a microphone.

I couldn't get that out of my head. I guess I still can't.

It was like a sip of single-malt scotch after a lifetime of domestic
light beer.

Man, it was great.

It was also better than anything I'd heard from her on album.

The goal in making contemporary country records is to record country
radio hits.

The way to record contemporary country hits is to listen to what is out
there and doing well, and then try and do the exact same thing.

Lee Ann Womack isn't good at doing the exact same thing. She does better
than that. Except that in radio-land, better than that can be worse than that.
Exactly the same is good. Standing out is often problematic.

In 2005, Lee Ann made an album called *There's More Where That Came
From*.

Reviewers loved it. It was a throwback album in some ways. It didn't fall
in line with everything else that was out there. On it, Lee Ann Womack sang
like Lee Ann Womack.

Folks were excited.

They hadn't really heard that before.

Reviewers were calling it her "career album," meaning that it was the best thing she'd ever do.

I knew better than that.

I'd heard her sing in a room, unadorned, without a microphone.

I knew her power, and her talent, and her innate understanding of country music.

I also knew that *There's More Where That Came From* had a few moments of compromise. There were places where Lee Ann and her producer acquiesced to contemporary radio trends, or where song selections were short of classic.

I wound up writing a review that asserted her greatness but also said that this was not her career album, and that she could and would do even better than this.

I was in Atlanta, late at night, leaving a piano bar (don't ask), when my cell phone rang and I distractedly picked up.

"Hello?"

"Peter Cooper?"

The words came out as one: "Petercooper?"

"Yes."

"You better get your ass over here right now."

"Who is this?"

"Petercooper, it's Leeannwomack. Where the hell are you?"

"I'm in Atlanta?"

"Why?"

That one was hard to answer. I paused to ponder.

"Doesn't matter. Get your sorry ass over here right now."

"I can't. I'm in Atlanta."

"Well, get in your car and drive to Nashville. 'Cause I'm gonna give you three swift kicks to the groin."

That didn't sound particularly appealing.

"I dunno . . . ."

"I read what you wrote," she said. "You're saying I can do better? I can do better?"

Buoyed by distance from a violent volley of feet, I answered honestly.

"Yes, you can. Are you saying you can't? Are you saying this is the best you will ever do? Are you saying you've peaked?"

The next few minutes held flurries of profanity. I tried to adjust my telephone's volume, to no avail. She let me have it.

And then the next few minutes became the next twenty minutes.

"Some people would pay big money to talk to Lee Ann Womack for twenty minutes," I silently consoled myself.

But those people would be deeply regretful if the discussion went like this one did.

In the end, she vowed that she would indeed do better, if only to stick it up my sorry ass.

Which might, indeed, be better than three swift kicks to the groin.

The next time I saw Lee Ann Womack was at Madison Square Garden in October of 2005.

I was heading to a backstage bathroom.

She was holding three shining trophies, having dominated the Country Music Association Awards, winning vocal event of the year for a George Strait duet, single of the year for "I May Hate Myself in the Morning," and album of the year for *There's More Where That Came From*.

I was walking one way, alone. She was walking the other, surrounded by glad-handing handlers.

I didn't think she'd notice me.

As I passed on her right, she stuck out her arm like an angry crossing guard, palm out in a "stop" signal.

I stopped.

Then she closed her fist, then pointed her index and middle fingers at me, and then separated those fingers, slowly but ultimately severely.

"Congratulations," I said.

She just said, "Spread 'em."

Oof.

Freddie Vanderford is a superb harmonica player.

Freddie learned from the best. He was an informal student of Peg Leg Sam, who also went by the name of Peg Leg Pete. Peg was a medicine show man. He was a "draw man," which meant that he played music that drew a crowd for the "pitch man." The "pitch man" was there to sell "medicine," which was usually an alcohol-heavy elixir that country people could buy without upsetting the Southern Baptist Church or other authorities.

Peg Leg Sam called himself "the ugliest damn Negro in the world," because of some facial scarring of uncertain origin.

"He has a severe cut across the right side of his face which was incorrectly treated and left a bad scar on his cheek, disfigured one of his ears, and appears to have affected his vision, pulling down the corner of his eyes," wrote folklorist Bruce Bastin. "Another, rather less damaging scar adorns the other cheek, and a further cut is on his left breast . . . an altogether remarkable sight."

There was also the matter of the leg, from which Peg Leg Sam drew his name. That was because of an unfortunate meeting of Jackson's right leg and a train. The leg was worse for the wear, but Peg's influence directly impacted Lyle Lovett and other blues-inspired country artists. Peg was among the great entertainers of his time.

"He could tap dance his butt off with that peg leg," said Alvin Anderson, son of one of Peg's greatest friends, Pink Anderson (the band Pink Floyd drew the "pink" part of its name from Pink Anderson). "(He) was the only man I'd ever seen play harmonica with his

Searching for liberal-leaning types in Spartanburg is like combing the beachfront for hockey pucks.

nose . . . I even seen him take it around to his ear and get a note out of it. This man blew the harmonica with his ear! How he did it I will never know, but I saw this and heard this."

Freddie Vanderford saw and heard it as well. He was a white boy in Buffalo, South Carolina, during segregation times. Buffalo is outside of Union, which is outside of Gaffney, which is outside of Boiling Springs, which is outside of Spartanburg.

And searching for liberal-leaning types in Spartanburg is like combing the beachfront for hockey pucks.

So when Freddie told me that he had been a delegate at South Carolina's Democratic convention, I was on towards shocked.

"Man, I like some of the things those Republicans have to say," Freddie said. "I think a man should hold on to his money if he can, and I think hard work is important, and I don't think you should be looking for handouts.

But it seems like a bunch of the Republicans around here have some kind of problem with the black man. I don't have a problem with the black man. A black man encouraged me, taught me how to play the harmonica, and gave me something I could use and enjoy for the rest of my life. I sure got no problem with the black man."

I told Freddie that I applauded his open-mindedness.

He paused for a minute, in private thought that he then articulated.

"The crazy thing is . . . the ones around here that don't have some problem with the black man have some problem with the gay man.

"Listen, the gay man ain't saying nothing to you," Freddie said, pausing again.

"And if he does . . . take it as a compliment."

I like writing songs with Don Schlitz, in part because the songs end up being good but more so because writing songs with Don means spending time with Don. And he's a good guy: Funny and perceptive, and pleasantly elliptical.

We wrote a song one morning, and then started talking. This was at the beginning of our friendship, and he had not yet met my family. He asked about my wife—"What's she like?"—and I told him she was a very patient person.

Don asked how she got to be a patient person, and I told him that practice probably had a lot to do with it.

In the next fifteen minutes, we wrote a song about her called "Suffer a Fool."

Another time, we decided that we wanted to write a song about our favorite person in the music industry. We thought for a while, and settled on Big Steve, the door man at a Nashville listening room called Douglas Corner.

Big Steve has been in the music industry for decades, and no one has ever accused him of thievery, or of plagiarism, or of anything at all. He stands at the club entrance at the beginning of each night, and tells people that they'll need to give him some money if they want to come in and hear the music. They do, and he holds on to the money until the end of the night, when he gives the musicians all the money he has collected. What a guy. Plus, he loves music, he listens to the shows, and he usually offers up kind words. Then, he walks to the bus stop and waits for his ride back home.

Don and I wrote a song called "Big Steve," and I put it on an album, and now some people come to Nashville and head to Douglas Corner, to get their picture taken with Steve.

To me, things like that are some of the great rewards of songwriting: It's a beautiful thing when people take some kind of non-destructive action because of words I wrote on paper and sung into a microphone. I'd say it's better than a Grammy Award, but I wouldn't really know.

I'll have to ask Don. He would know. He's got Grammy trophies. He's a big-deal in the songwriting world, though you wouldn't know it to talk to him.

Don came to Nashville after what he says were a couple of unsuccessful first semesters at Duke University. He got to town in the mid-1970s, at a time when the Music City Welcome Wagon was otherwise occupied. He scuffled for a while, and finally got a job working the all-night shift at Vanderbilt University's computer lab. That's back when computers were large, whirring beasts.

Don was a beast-tamer by trade, but a songwriter at heart. He'd work all night at the computer lab, then walk over to Music Row, which is the section of town that is home to lots of recording studios, record labels, and music publishers. On the Row, Don would try to pitch his songs, in hopes

> **It's a beautiful thing when people take some kind of non-destructive action because of words I wrote on paper and sung into a microphone.**

of interesting someone. He often stopped in to see a by-then-legendary songwriter named Bob McDill, who took some interest in a song Don had written, one about a chance encounter with a wise old drifter.

Don wrote the song in August of 1976, a month after the bicentennial, when he was twenty-three years old, and he spent the next two years pitching it around, with the help of master songwriters Paul Craft and Jim Rushing, and publisher Audie Ashworth. The great Bobby Bare heard it and became convinced it was a hit. Bare couldn't convince his record label of the song's hit potential, though, and the label refused to release Bare's version as a single. Johnny Cash recorded it, but it just sat there on his *Gone Girl* album, popularly unnoticed.

Pitching songs is weary-making, as is an all-night shift in a computer lab. And Don fell into a habit of dozing off at the lab. In April of 1978, he received a letter from a supervisor, on official Vanderbilt stationery.

It was not a letter of praise or congratulations.

It was a letter documenting the supervisor's discouraged awareness that Don had been sleeping on the job, and asserting the supervisor's willingness, even eagerness, to shit-can Don from the computer gig if the sleeping stuff continued. Don determined to stay awake on the job, at least until someone on Music Row woke up and turned one of his songs into a hit.

The supervisor's letter arrived in April. A few months later, Kenny Rogers recorded the song about the wise old drifter. By December, the song topped the country chart, and it seemed everyone in America could recite the chorus about knowing when to hold 'em and knowing when to fold 'em.

The song was "The Gambler." I've heard it referenced on ESPN's SportsCenter, in insurance commercials, by failing presidential candidate John McCain, and in plenty of other contexts.

> **He'd written a song that earned him the freedom to do anything he wanted to do with the rest of his life.**

"The Gambler" wasn't just a hit. For Kenny Rogers, it was a signature and a persona, and it vaulted him to superstardom. For Don, it was a winning lottery ticket that he'd carried around for two years, unable to cash. Once he cashed it, he was free to do anything he wanted.

Lots of us think about what we'd do if we won the lottery. You might buy a home in beautiful Telluride, Colorado. I might buy an ownership share in a major league baseball team. Lots of people would quit their jobs.

Most of us would do exactly what we want to do, if we had the means to do just that.

And that's what Don did.

He'd written a song that earned him the freedom to do anything he wanted to do with the rest of his life.

So he did exactly what he wanted to do, with the rest of his life.

Here's what he wanted to do with the rest of his life: He wanted to wake up every day and write songs.

To be sure, he wanted to wake up after a good night's sleep, rather than schlep over to Music Row after working at the computer lab. The Vanderbilt job went away, and the supervisor's letter is now framed in Don's writing office.

But he'd entered the lottery by doing what he wanted to do, and he exited the lottery with the ability to do what he wanted to do, and he did what he wanted to do.

Don would be a songwriter of significant import had he only written "The Gambler."

And Don would be a songwriter of significant import had he never written "The Gambler."

Because in the years that followed "The Gambler," Don and Paul Overstreet co-wrote "On the Other Hand," which launched the career of Country Music Hall of Famer Randy Travis.

That pair also wrote "When You Say Nothing At All," a monster hit that has been covered time and again.

And Don wrote a ton of other important country songs. If you're interested in country music—and if you're not, I could probably recommend other books to be reading right now—look him up. What you'll find will impress you. It impresses me, too, but I'm just as impressed that he wrote any songs at all, when the first success he had meant that he didn't need any more successes.

He could have just stopped, except that he couldn't have just stopped. Had he stopped, he wouldn't have unloaded his heart, and the unloading was a necessary thing.

Don Schlitz didn't write because he wanted his songs recorded by Garth Brooks and Reba McEntire and Alison Krauss and Keith Whitley and George Strait and all the rest.

He wrote because he's a songwriter, not a beast-tamer.

He wrote because he had things to say about life and love and Big Steve and a bunch of other things.

Anyone with a working knowledge of country music and the people who make it knows that Don Schlitz cashed in with a layered story song called "The Gambler."

To gain a better understanding of country music and the people who make it, it's more helpful to know that he never cashed out.

Tim Carroll is a guitar player of staggering ability.

He hails from Indiana, and as a young man he played rock clubs with a group called The Gizmos.

The Gizmos once opened up for seminal Manhattan punk band The Ramones, at a club in Bloomington, Indiana. The first song The Gizmos played that night was called "Real Rock 'n' Roll Don't Come From New York."

Tim can plug a Fender Telecaster into an amp and make a thrilling, bludgeoning noise. Or he can coax sweet, clean, melodic sounds out of his instrument and make a ballad more poignant and expressive. He's one of the handful of musicians to have a song he wrote be recorded by John Prine, one of the greatest songwriters of ours or any other time.

Tim is the whole package. Most people at his skill level are like excellent golfers or tennis players who will only play with people who are close to their equal.

Tim will play with anyone, even me.

One night, Tim played guitar on the Grand Ole Opry, and then he hustled down to a dingy club off Nashville's woe-begotten Charlotte Avenue, a place called The D&D Lounge.

There, he sat in with a country covers band, because the band's regular guitarist—a guy named Bebo—couldn't be there that night.

Halfway through Tim's first solo, the lead singer pointed at Tim in appreciation, then shouted into the microphone, "Bebo WHO????"

At a set break, I asked Tim why on earth he would play the D&D Lounge, when he had just been hobnobbing with the heroes of country music.

First, he said, "Any chance to play is a chance to get better."

Then, he copped to the truth:

"I'm getting $40 and all the beer I can drink . . . The more I drink, the more I earn."

Bill Monroe could be a hard boss.

He created a great American art form in bluegrass music, but he didn't always pay his musicians a good living wage, and he was often obtuse or abrupt.

That said, he attracted the finest musicians to his Blue Grass Boys band, and those musicians knew that they would glean great things from Monroe, and that their recordings and performances with Monroe would be significant and historical.

One such musician was booked to play a tour with Bill Monroe. But on a Saturday night in the middle of that tour, the musician was backstage at a Nashville show.

"I thought you were out with Monroe," someone said to him, backstage.

"Yeah, I was," the musician said.

"But he's still out there."

"Well, I'm not with him anymore."

"Why's that?"

"He fired me."

"But you're a good fiddle man. Why'd he fire you?"

There was a pause, and then an admission . . . .

"I shit in the old man's shoe."

CHAPTER
8

THE END OF THE LINE

Hank Williams was "The Hillbilly Shakespeare."

He pioneered a backwoods poetry that changed things for the better.

"The silence of a falling star lights up a purple sky," he wrote and sang.

It wasn't the star that lit the sky. It was the silence.

Hank himself seemed a comet. He came along in the late 1940s, a sickly little wild man, like the great Jimmie Rodgers. He was plagued and self-destructive, frolicking and forlorn. In his first Grand Ole Opry performance, he encored multiple times.

He was a swiveling sex symbol, years before Elvis Presley. But he wasn't long for this world. He died in the back seat of a pale blue Cadillac, at age twenty-nine, on the first day of 1953, and since then his death has been the source of morbid fascination.

I have shared that fascination, and on the 50th anniversary of his death, I decided to drive the route Hank took to his death. I had neither a Cadillac nor a driver—Hank was driven by an 18-year-old Auburn University freshman named Charles Carr, who was ferrying the superstar in return for second semester tuition money—so mine was a lonely mini-van trip through history.

On the way, I kept thinking of Charles Carr, and of the terror the young man had to have felt. Carr's dad was a drinking buddy of Hank's who owned the Lee Street Taxi Company in Montgomery, Alabama. Charles must have thought he'd received a plum assignment when he agreed to drive Hank Williams to some shows. Instead, he'd received a spot in history, and a haunting that lasted the rest of his life.

The young man and the Hillbilly Shakespeare took off from Montgomery on December 30. Just before getting in the car, Hank took a shot of morphine. Because of his back pain, Hank was also carrying chloral hydrate, which slows the heartbeat. If you put chloral hydrate and alcohol into someone's drink, it's calling "slipping them a Mickey." Hank may not have known that: He was also carrying cans of Falstaff beer.

An Indiana police captain named Brian Turpen has researched these kinds of things. He said, "A mixture of chloral hydrate, morphine and alcohol will more than likely bring about psychosis . . . That combination is sometimes used to euthanize critically ill patients."

Carr and Williams made Birmingham, Alabama on the 30th. They left the next morning in the Cadillac, and reached Knoxville, Tennessee in the early afternoon of New Year's Eve. From there, they planned to fly to Charleston, West Virginia, but

He fell to his motel room floor, and was carried to the blue Cadillac late that night by hotel porters. Somnambulant, he rested in the backseat while Carr drove north.

their afternoon flight boomeranged back because of foggy conditions. In Knoxville again, they readied for a lengthy drive to make a New Year's Day show in Canton, Ohio.

For years, I'd seen accounts that indicated snow was the reason why their flight turned around. But when I checked newspaper weather reports from Knoxville, Bluefield, West Virginia, and Charleston, West Virginia, I found that temperatures that day were in the 40s. The snow thing was horse shit.

Back in Knoxville, Carr and Williams checked into the Andrew Johnson Hotel, a swanky place, though the old-money surroundings did nothing to lift Williams's lousy mood. Hank was back to drinking, and he received two shots of morphine and some vitamin B-12 to ease his pain. He fell to his motel room floor, and was carried to the blue Cadillac late that night by hotel porters. Somnambulant, he rested in the backseat while Carr drove north.

Speeding through Knox County, Carr was pulled over at the Grainger County line by an officer named Swan Kitts. For many years, the policeman told interviewers that he saw a passed-out Hank Williams in the back seat and asked Carr whether the singer was dead or alive.

In Kitts's account, Carr assured him that Hank was alive. In the police report, it says Carr was fined $25 for speeding. In Carr's account, he said he was fined $75, and he said that was because when a late-night justice of the peace asked how much he was carrying, he said, "seventy-five dollars."

Anyway, no one checked for a pulse.

Hank Williams was still alive when Charles Carr was pulled and fined for speeding. I'm confident of this, because I talked with the West Virginia funeral home owner who handled his body, who said Hank was neither cold nor still enough to have died so far south.

He was, however, in internal distress. Carr was in some distress as well. He was essentially alone on a doomed trip, accompanied by the shell of a country music hero who would soon be a ghost.

Folks in Bristol, Virginia will sometimes claim that Hank ate his last meal on the Virginia side of State Street, at a place called the Burger Bar. The Burger Bar is still around, and its walls are lined with Hank-affiliated stuff. But on the last day of 1952, the building that now houses the Burger Bar was the site of a dry cleaning operation. Carr did stop in Bristol, at Trayer's restaurant, near the spot where the Carter Family and Jimmie Rodgers made their first recordings at what is now called the Bristol Sessions. At Trayer's, Carr said, he bought some gas and a sandwich, and spoke briefly with a woozy Hank Williams. At that point, Williams may have taken more chloral hydrate pills, and washed them down with Falstaff beer: after Hank died, investigators found bottles on the Cadillac's floorboard.

Then it was a silent Appalachian ride across the blue-black morning, to Bluefield, West Virginia. Williams' body was under attack. Carr's mind was a thickening whirl of fearful fatigue. In Bluefield, Carr found a relief driver named Donald Surface, who worked for the Bluefield Cab Company. Carr recalled getting a sandwich and a Coca-Cola at Bluefield's Dough Boy Lunch, then talking with a cab dispatcher who found Surface.

The Donald Surface deal is mysterious. Charles Carr could never recall to anyone's satisfaction, even his own, whether Surface continued along the route all the way to the final, unplanned destination of Oak Hill, West Virginia. Some people remain suspicious about Carr's inexact recollections of the ride, figuring that an event of monumental significance would replay accurately in memory. But many trauma survivors have fuzzy memories of the ghastly things that scar them. Add to that Carr's youth and his sleep-deprived state, and it's easier to see why he never spoke with certainty.

There's another mystery figure, by the way: Hank Williams' morphine-happy personal "doctor," Toby Marshall. Witnesses have placed Marshall, who often traveled with Williams, at the Andrew Johnson hotel scene, but he was not present in Oak Hill police reports.

Williams' daughter, Jett Williams, has conducted exhaustive research into her father's death, and she believes Marshall was in Oak Hill. Jett Williams is the product of Hank's 1952 affair with Bobbie Jett. In 1952, Williams divorced his first wife, Audrey, and married the former Billie Jean Jones Eshliman. That year, he was also fired from the Grand Ole Opry cast because of his drinking, and he took a health-related leave of absence from the Louisiana Hayride radio show.

So, 1952 was a rough year to be Hank Williams. In the year's final five months, he'd moved from Nashville to Montgomery, then to a Shreveport, Louisiana apartment, and then back to Montgomery. He was hoping 1953 would bring peace and calm, and, in a way, it did so, immediately.

The Cadillac headed north, through Princeton, crossing the Bluestone River, passing farms and goats and white birch trees. Today, there's a Hank Williams Sr. Memorial Bridge in Spanishburg, West Virginia. Next to that bridge is the Valley General Store. I stopped there on my own Hank Williams Memorial Drive, and spoke with a store patron named Drema Hall. I asked her if people in Spanishburg talk much about Hank Wiliams' last ride. She said, "Very seldom. But if you want a story, I'll give you a story: There's an all-girl butcher shop, just up the road. It's just women that work there."

The main drag in Mount Hope, West Virginia used to be Highway 19, where Hank may have made the final stop of his life. Allegesa Bonifacio said she was a silly teenager back when a sleek Cadillac stopped across the street from Bon Bon's, the store where she was working behind the counter. She said a young driver came inside Bon Bon's, and that she fixed him a lemon sour because he said he had Hank Williams in his car and that Hank wasn't feeling well and needed a drink.

She made me a lemon sour just like the one she said she made Hank, passing it to me in a Styrofoam cut and saying, "Okay, don't die."

Charles Carr didn't remember stopping at Bon Bon's, but he did remember snaking on toward Oak Hill, a town where Hank had never performed, never stayed, and likely never visited in his life, though every Williams biography will tell you that he died on January 1, 1953, in Oak Hill, West Virginia.

Between Mount Hope and Oak Hill, Carr noticed that Williams' blanket had slid from his frame. The mortified 18-year-old reached back and touched a cold hand. Carr found what he called "a cut-rate service station," where a man came out, looked in the back seat, and said, "I think you've got a problem." He directed Carr to the Oak Hill General Hospital, about six miles away.

At the hospital, Carr said two interns saw Hank and pronounced him dead, whereupon he asked, "Is there anything you can do for him?"

"They said, 'No, he's dead,'" he recalled. "They took him, and they didn't use a stretcher. They put him on an examining table. I called my dad and told him what happened, and then Hank's mother called me at the hospital. One of the parting things she said was, 'Don't let anything happen to the car.'"

The number one country music singer in America—in fact, the greatest country music singer and songwriter in history—was dead. Soon, the weeping would begin. But in the moment, only two people in Hank's home state of Alabama knew what had happened. One said to call Hank's mother, and Hank's mother, Lillian Stone, said to make sure nothing happened to the car.

A law enforcement officer took the Cadillac into an empty bay at Pete Burdette's Pure Oil station, which was closed for New Year's Day. Burdette wound up with Hank's cowboy hat, and he later thought he was cursed by the hat. He wound up killing himself, committing suicide just behind his Pure Oil station.

An autopsy that afternoon found nothing in the way of foul play. Hank's heart gave out, apparently.

Joe Tyree was Hank's undertaker. He wasn't a country music fan, and this Williams body was no different to him than the other local Williams bodies he'd handled. He did feel for young Charles Carr, though, and he arranged for Carr to watch New Year's Day football games at an apartment, with Tyree's sons.

The Alabama Crimson Tide beat Syracuse that day, 61-6. Hank was a big football fan, and he would have enjoyed that beat-down. Instead, he lay dead while Tyree and others in the family funeral business prepped him for burial.

"Have you seen the pictures of him at the funeral?" Tyree said. "We put that outfit on him, and we put him in that casket."

Hank's mother arrived the next day, with papers that supposedly proved that Hank's wife, the former Billie Jean Eshliman, was not actually divorced from her previous husband when she'd married Hank. Local authorities were satisfied with Mrs. Stone's documents, and they allowed her to choose a casket and to get a stage outfit from Hank's car, to serve as burial clothes. Tyree and an assistant drove Hank to Montgomery, while

An autopsy that afternoon found nothing in the way of foul play. Hank's heart gave out, apparently.

Stone rode with Carr and his father back down South. Along the way, Hank's music played nearly constantly on radio stations. The radio play provided Tyree's first understanding of Hank's fame and artistry.

"The silence of a falling star lights up a purple sky," Hank's voice cried, over the crackling airwaves.

It wasn't the star that lit the sky, it was the silence. That was, Tyree thought, poetical.

AN ASIDE: OL' BROTHER MERLE

Merle Kilgore was fourteen years old, a Shreveport, Louisiana boy who wanted to be a music man. He asked someone in Shreveport about how to get into show business, and the advice came back, "Hang around someone famous, kid."

"That's when Hank Williams came to town," Merle told me. "I said, 'Mr. Williams, can I carry your guitar? The elevator's broken, and there are two flights of stairs.' He said, 'Grab it, Hoss.'"

Three words from Hank Williams, and Merle repeated them throughout his life. He saw those three words as the beginning of his journey. He went on to co-write the Johnny Cash classic "Ring of Fire," and to pen other major country songs for Johnny Horton, John Anderson, Claude King and many more. He was also a ubiquitous presence at the right hand of Hank Williams' only son, the man born Randall Hank Williams, nicknamed Bocephus, and most often called Hank Williams Jr. Merle was Hank Jr.'s manager and best friend.

Merle was hilarious and open-hearted, a total delight. He loved to tell the story of rap-rocker Kid Rock's manager calling to express Kid Rock's interest in meeting and working with Bocephus. Merle didn't listen to rap or to rock, and had no idea who Kid Rock was. But as he listened to the manager drone on, he thumbed through a *Billboard* magazine and found Kid Rock's song "Cowboy" was at the top of the pop chart.

"Oh, Hank *loves* Kid Rock," Merle told the manager. "He's particularly fond of the song 'Cowboy.'"

After that, Hank Jr. and Kid Rock became friends and frequent collaborators. They recorded a song together that sought to delineate the difference between musical styles.

"In country music," they sang, "You just can't use the 'F' word."

Like many showbiz people who grew up poor and managed to accumulate some wealth, Merle wore gaudy jewelry. He had a fancy neck chain with Hank Jr.'s logo on it, and each of his fingers groaned with the weight of audacious rings.

Once, I wrote a story about Kid Rock's friend Uncle Kracker, who had recorded a song called "Thunderhead Hawkins" that included lines about Merle: "Old brother Merle, he's always waiting in the wings/ Only man up in them woods wearin' all them gold rings."

"My wife called me about that story when I was fishing," Merle told me. "She said, 'The newspaper says Kracker is attracted to your bling bling.' She said, 'Merle, what is bling bling?' I had to ask around. Turns out it's hip-hop for jewelry."

Once, Hank Jr. and Merle were at a little restaurant, and the waitress greeted them in a southern chirp: "I'm Jenny, and I'll be your server this evening. How are y'all doing?"

Merle looked surprised.

"How'm I doing?" he asked, then he raised both arms and let his wrists fall, so that eight enormous rings faced the waitress. He wiggled his fingers and said, "Are you shitting me?"

Merle fought through a heart surgery, a couple of back surgeries, and lung cancer. He spent a lot of late-life time in hospitals. I came to see him in one of those hospitals, and asked him how he was holding up.

"Just great," he said. "I have beautiful nurses. Bee-yoo-tiful, brother. I'm thinking of sticking around after I'm well. Maybe get a pecker extension. You know, kill two birds.

"Brother, I had to get an extra room just for the flowers," he said. "And it makes a difference when people care enough about you to come and see you. If you're an asshole, nobody comes by. That must be real depressing."

Merle died on February 6, 2005. He was in Mexico, undergoing some kind of experimental treatment, hopefully with beautiful nurses all around. It was the night of Super Bowl XXXIX, And the score was tied at 7 when my phone rang with the word about Merle. We were having a Super Bowl party at the house, and I had to excuse myself, compose myself, and eulogize my friend on a tight deadline. In forty-five minutes, I had to write something appropriate and send it in.

One of Merle's songs had the hook line, "When you get on the whiskey, let somebody else drive." That was a particularly well-whiskeyed Super Bowl, as I recall. It's good that I didn't have to drive anywhere, and also good that newspaper obituaries don't require blood or breath tests.

In the newspaper piece, I wrote of Merle as "one of Nashville's great characters. I got "Grab it, hoss," up high, and managed to get in "Hank loves Kid Rock" as well. "Are you shitting me?" became "Are you kidding me?"

Merle is buried at Hendersonville Memory Gardens, near his great friends Johnny and June Carter Cash.

John R. Cash's tombstone reads "Let the words of my mouth, and the meditation of my heart, be acceptable in thy sight, O Lord, my strength, and my redeemer."

June's reads "Bless the Lord, O my soul, and all that is within me, Bless His holy name."

Merle's features an artistic depiction of the dearly departed's hands and wrists, with rings and bracelets and such.

It reads, "Are you kidding me . . . I've made the biggest deal of all."

CHAPTER 9

A SHORT, STRANGE TRIP WITH PORTER WAGONER

Robert Hunter was the lyricist for the Grateful Dead.

When people say things like "What a long, strange trip it's been" and "A friend of the devil is a friend of mine," they're quoting Hunter.

Jim Lauderdale is a tremendous, Grammy-winning singer-songwriter. I knew him when he was a tremendous, achingly unknown singer-songwriter. He's the same guy now as then. He's a deep thinker with a penchant for slapstick oddity. I've seen him under burning stage lights, saying to the crowd, "You're a warm audience. I'm sweating up here like Newt Gingrich at an Indigo Girls concert." Another time, after mentioning that a song of his had been recorded by country star Patty Loveless and the iconic George Jones, he said, "Aw, I should know better than to name-drop. Name-dropping is terribly rude. I was just having a discussion about that last weekend, during a party held at the home of Judge Lance Ito."

If you swung and missed on those references, dear reader, Google away.

Lauderdale and Hunter wound up as friends and occasional collaborators, which is how I wound up at a restaurant table with both of them one evening in the early new century. Hunter lives in California, but he was in Nashville for a few days. I asked if there was anything he wanted to do while in Nashville, and he said he'd always wanted to go to the Grand Ole Opry. I told him I'd be glad to take him to the Opry, and that we could go backstage and meet anyone he'd like to meet.

"I'm not much of a meeter-greeter," he said. "But I would love to meet Porter Wagoner."

Porter Wagoner was bigger-than-life. Life was smaller than Porter Wagoner. Known as "The Thin Man From West Plains, Missouri," Wagoner wore the flashiest rhinestone suits in country music. He'd leave the suits on a hanger at the back of his dressing room. Once, he motioned to the suits and told me, "Pick one up, man." I didn't quite understand, and he said, again, "Pick one up." I thought for a moment that he might be giving me a suit--we were similarly sized--but actually he just wanted me, literally, to pick one of the suits up.

I walked over to the suits, grabbed a hanger, and lifted. It was like lifting a weighted barbell. The rhinestones made the suit unexpectedly heavy. I looked like a small child trying to hoist a suitcase. Porter got a kick out of that.

Back to Robert Hunter. I asked him why, out of all of the Opry's cast of performers, it was Porter Wagoner that he wanted to meet.

He said that in the late 1960s, when he and Jerry Garcia were writing the songs that appeared on the Grateful Dead's classic *Workingman's Dead* and *American Beauty* albums, they would stop whatever they were doing on Sunday evenings and tune into Porter Wagoner's syndicated television show, which aired in the Bay Area on a television station based in Marin, California. Hunter

> "I'm not much of a meeter-greeter," he said. "But I would love to meet Porter Wagoner."

said he loved Wagoner's flash and his easy way with a country song, and that he and Garcia particularly loved Wagoner's "girl singer," a young East Tennessee thrush named Dolly Parton. Wagoner thrusted Parton into the spotlight when she was little-known, and the *Porter Wagoner Show* became her vehicle to notoriety. Parton's and Wagoner's partnership ultimately came to a messy, legality-drenched end, though they ultimately reconciled. Parton's song "I Will Always Love You," a hit for her and for Whitney Houston, was written with Porter Wagoner in mind.

The walls of Wagoner's Opry dressing room groaned with the weight of dozens of framed photos of Wagoner with country music stars and sports figures. On the same visit where I picked up one of Porter's suits, I pointed at a photo of Porter and Dolly and asked, jokingly, "Oh, you sang with Dolly Parton?"

He said, not at all jokingly, "She sang with me, Hoss."

Porter's love for Dolly was deep and real, but that didn't mean he approved of everything she did. In the 1970s, a *Playboy* magazine writer described Dolly disrobing and streaking in a gravel parking lot, just for the hell of it. An interviewer later asked Porter if he would consider such an action himself. He said that he wouldn't. When the interviewer asked why not, Porter said, "The gravel hurts my dick too bad."

Porter's gravel-scraping pecker was, however, not why Robert Hunter wanted to meet Porter Wagoner. Hunter was just impressed by the man and his music, and wanted to take a moment to tell Porter of his admiration.

At the Opry, some dressing room doors were always open. Visitors were constantly in and out of Little Jimmy Dickens' dressing room, gabbing and cutting up.

"Where's your wife tonight?" I once asked Dickens.

"She's at home, sitting on the ice chest, keeping the beer cold," the little man replied, winking.

George Hamilton IV, a gentle and welcoming man who performed in Russia during the Cold War and served as country music's greatest international ambassador, always kept an open door, as did Jimmy C. Newman, the "Cajun Country" star who loved to host jam sessions.

Porter's door, though, was always closed. You had to knock, and you had to knock loudly, because Porter was constantly listening to demo recordings at high volume. If you knocked loudly enough for Porter to hear the knock, he'd raise his voice above the music and say, a little aggressively, "What?"

In case Porter wasn't in the mood to be met and greeted, I left Hunter in an adjacent hallway and knocked, loudly, on Porter's door, and I met his "What?" with a squeaky, "It's Peter Cooper."

He turned the music halfway down and opened the door a little. Porter liked me, because I wrote stories about him that delved into the depth and breadth of his talents and revealed the substance of the man, rather than just going on about his flashy suits or his Dolly connections. He wrote me a note once saying that he'd liked a story I wrote about him so much that he'd gotten it laminated.

When Porter opened the door, I told him that I had a new friend who would very much like to meet him, and I told him that the friend was the lyricist for the Grateful Dead. Porter said, "Bring him in here, man, but I've got my Taco Bell coming in a minute."

I went and got Hunter, and brought him in to Porter's dressing room. A shy man by nature, Hunter looked a little overwhelmed to see all the photos on the wall and the rhinestone suits hanging up. Porter stuck out his over-sized right hand and greeted Hunter with the same easy confidence with which

> I told him that I had a new friend who would very much like to meet him, and I told him that the friend was the lyricist for the Grateful Dead. Porter said, "Bring him in here, man, but I've got my Taco Bell coming in a minute."

he greeted everyone from fans to fellow Opry members to, in 1974, Beatle Paul McCartney.

Hunter haltingly shook Porter's hand, and then began rattling off the story of how he and Jerry Garcia loved his television show, and how Porter's music had impacted the Workingman's Dead and American Beauty albums.

Hunter talked fast, and more than a little nervously, and in a moment Porter looked over Hunter's shoulder.

"My Taco Bell's here," Porter said, and, sure enough, a flunky had arrived, weighted down with take-out bags filled with tacos, quesadillas, and MexiMelts.

The presence of the Taco Bell bags meant it was dinner time, which meant visiting hour was over. This was readily apparent, and Hunter and I said quick thanks and headed for the door.

"Hey, man," Porter said, as Hunter and I backed out. "I never did hear nothing by that Grateful Dead that I didn't like."

AN ASIDE: OPRY BANTER

After our brief brush with Porter Wagoner, Robert Hunter and I went out to our seats and watched the Opry show unfold. Hunter enjoyed the music, particularly the songs of a brash and whip-smart singer-songwriter named Elizabeth Cook, but he took even more delight at the stage banter.

That night, Jumpin' Bill Carlisle--who earned his nickname as a young leaper but by this time moved around with the aid of a walker--was joined by sideman George Riddle.

"Hey, Bill, didn't I see you up in Goodlettsville last week, with a pretty young blonde on your arm?" Riddle said.

Carlisle said, "Yeah! Doctor's orders! He said, 'Find a hot mama and be cheerful!'"

"No, Bill, I took you to that appointment. He said, 'You've got a heart murmur, be careful!'"

Little Jimmy Dickens told the same jokes he'd been telling for years. Dressed in his own flashy suit (Dickens was the first performer to wear rhinestones on the Opry), he said he looked like Mighty Mouse in his pajamas. Then he asked, "Would you like to hear my latest hit single?" When the audience clapped in affirmation, he said, "Then I'll sing it for you. It's from 1965, and it's called 'May the Bird of Paradise Fly Up Your Nose.'"

And it really *was* from 1965, and it really *was* called "May the Bird of Paradise Fly Up Your Nose."

Then Dickens said he was from a large family, because his mother was hard of hearing: "At night, daddy would turn to her and say, 'Do you want to go to sleep or what?' She'd say, 'What?'"

As for Porter, he told a story about going to a Nashville restaurant and overhearing the man in an adjacent booth order cow's tongue. The waitress took that order and then tended to Porter, asking what he'd like to eat.

"I sure ain't gonna order a cow's tongue," he said. "I'm not gonna eat something that comes out of an animal's mouth . . . I'll just have some eggs."

CHAPTER
10

MERLE HAGGARD AND THE DOOR TO HOPE

Kris Kristofferson called Merle Haggard "The greatest artist in American music history."

The two men shared similar motivations, and a deep friendship. They each believed that creativity is a divine calling, a spiritual necessity. I don't know whether Haggard was the greatest artist in American music history, though I believe he's in the discussion. You can make a case for Louis Armstrong, Bob Dylan, Aretha Franklin, Hank Williams, Johnny Cash, Jimmie Rodgers, Paul Simon, Ray Charles, Johnny Cash, Stephen Foster, and others, including Kristofferson. I guess you might ponder Georgia O'Keeffe and Jackson Pollack, as well. Maybe Muhammed Ali, too, for that matter. I'd rather tell you about Haggard than sit here and make my heroes' legacies arm-wrestle each other for superiority.

Haggard said the act of creativity got harder as the time passed. He said the only way to make it easy on yourself was to work on writing better and better versions of things you'd already written. And he thought such an endeavor was pointless.

"It's really hard, as an old human being, to press as much weight as you pressed when you were a kid," he told me at age 73, six years before his death in 2016. He pressed the weight until the very end, making his last recording two months before he died. He wrote the last song he recorded,

"Kern River Blues," while he was in the hospital. His body was shutting down, but his mind was still restless.

"I've always known that I was a gifted person," he said. "I've always felt like I would be punished, severely, if I didn't continue to make use of that gift."

He occasionally cursed his gift, as it was as much a chore-assignment as a cause for celebration. But he took it seriously, and he lugged it across the world and he used it to ease a lot of loads, and he presented it to all of us on 77 studio albums and tens of thousands of performances. He used it to create a catalogue of remarkable significance.

In a song called "Oil Tanker Train," Haggard sang of a train that "would rumble and rattle the old boxcar we lived in." His father, James Haggard, converted a train car into a family home, in a town called Oildale, near Bakersfield, California. James played a little fiddle, though music took a backseat to hard days of work for the Santa Fe Railroad. Then those hard days ceded to harder days, as James suffered brain hemorrhages. He died when Merle was nine years old, far too young to process sorrow. He was too young to process anger, too, and he channeled that anger into a young life of crime and recklessness. Notorious to local authorities by age 14, he was also under the spell of music from his country music inspirations Bob Wills, Jimmie Rodgers, and Lefty Frizzell. Haggard spent years attempting to mimic Frizzell's slurred style of singing, and he has always been open, even emphatic, about Frizzell's impact on his art. In 1953, Frizzell met Haggard at a concert and inviting the young man onstage at Bakersfield's Modesto Garden.

"That was the first time, and I was hooked," Haggard later told historian Daniel Cooper.

In that same time period, Haggard was working to learn song-craft. In so doing, he looked beyond his country heroes and took notice of the burgeoning rock and roll scene.

"The first good song I wrote was probably "If You Want To Be My Woman," he said. "Glen Campbell opened his show with that for years, and I wrote it when I was 17. It was a good example of the rock and roll thing that was happening then; Chuck Berry and Carl Perkins were the kings of the kind of rock and roll I liked. I was trying to be a guitar player, too, and they were both guitar players and both writers.

"Songs that I later wrote, like 'Workin' Man Blues,' were patterned after listening to 'Blue Suede Shoes.' And so many of my songs were takeoffs of Chuck Berry. He was the first guy I ever heard that did the original rock and roll thing with a guitar, and I think he was the originator of a lot of that. I think Chuck is one of the most underrated heroes in the business. He's impacted most everyone I know and appreciate, and Chuck had a great influence on the business as a whole."

Haggard's Berry-picking lessons were put on-hold in late 1957, when he and a friend were arrested after attempting to "break in" to a restaurant that was still serving customers. The subsequent arrest, added to his already checkered record, cost Haggard years. He didn't get out of prison until late 1960, and he left committed to trying to right his ship.

In "Mama Tried," he wrote, "I turned 21 in prison, doing life without parole." He did turn 21 in prison, but he determined in time (and through the self-analysis that comes with solitary confinement) that he would not be a lifer in crime. Bakersfield was bustling by 1960, with Buck Owens, Dallas Frazier, Tommy Collins and others spurring plenty of excitement. Upon Haggard's release, musicians Fuzzy Owen and Lewis Talley took an interest in his songs and singing, and Owen and Talley released Haggard's early sides on their Tally Records. Haggard's first successful single, "Sing a Sad Song," was penned by Wynn Stewart. That one peaked at No. 19 on the national country charts, and its sound caught the ear of Leonard Raymond Sipes, the singer-songwriter-entertainer who worked under the name "Tommy Collins."

> **He did turn 21 in prison, but he determined in time (and through the self-analysis that comes with solitary confinement) that he would not be a lifer in crime.**

"Tommy Collins was a songwriting mentor," said Haggard, who wrote about Collins in the biographical song, "Leonard" (Tommy's real name was Leonard Sipes). "Tommy was way down the songwriting road already when I came onboard, and he showed me a lot of pointers: Methods of conjuring up or projecting the right thing after the thought has been conjured. I think it was Tommy who told me, 'When your song is called 'XYZ' or whatever, every line has got to make sense against your title.' He showed me little methods of proving to yourself whether the line belongs, and ways of finding out whether you were able to get more out of a line if you tried."

Collins wound up penning some hits for Haggard, George Strait and others.

"Well, Leonard gave me lots of inspiration," he wrote in 'Leonard.' "He helped teach me how to write a country song/And he even brought around a bag of groceries/Back before 'Muskogee' came along."

"Muskogee" would be "Okie from Muskogee," one of Haggard's most profitable, most discussed and most alternately beloved and reviled songs. He and drummer Ray Edward Burris penned the song after the tour bus passed through Muskogee, Oklahoma. The rumor is that someone was smoking some non-tobacco on the bus, and that the idea was proffered that folks in Muskogee didn't likely smoke marijuana.

Released in late 1969 while conservatives railed against long-haired, counterculture Vietnam War protesters and the protesters railed against a mainstream culture that would accept such a mess of a war, the song was taken by most listeners as an indictment of those who would question authority. It was a four-week Number One country record, a Country Music Association single of

Haggard changed his own opinion of the song, half a hundred times.

the year in 1070 and a thorn in the side for people who disagreed with its message. Merle wound up being one of those people, and he certainly came to question authority at every turn.

At a 1972 show that was released decades later as *Live At The Philharmonic*, Kris Kristofferson and his band performed a version of the song "With apologies to our good friend Merle Haggard, who is neither a redneck or a racist, he just happens to be known for probably the only bad song he ever wrote." Kristofferson has since then changed his opinion of the song. Haggard changed his own opinion of the song, half a hundred times.

"It's a different song now," he said, in 2010. "I still believed in America then. I don't know that I believe now."

In between "Sing a Sad Song" and "Okie," there was a near-constant stream of creative activity for Haggard. Fuzzy Owen worked as Haggard's manager, and he and Lewis Talley released a Top 10 Haggard single called "(My Friends Are Gonna Be) Strangers," and that Liz Anderson-penned song hit country music's Top 10 in the same 1965 week that Buck Owens' "I've Got A Tiger By The Tail"—recorded on the west coast and released on L.A.-based Capitol—was in the top spot. Left-coast country was hitting national airwaves with snarl and twang that were lacking from many Nashville recordings, and Capitol had the funds and the interest to sign Haggard away from Tally. As his star rose, he wrote at a frenetic pace, sometimes scribbling lyrics by hand but often asking his then-wife, Bonnie Owens, to take his rhyming dictation.

"Sometimes the songs got to coming too fast for me to write, and sometimes they still do," he said. "So if I had a lady with me that I trusted, I'd have her write. Bonnie grabbed a lot of stuff that I might have missed. I just want 'em to write down what I say, not to critique it. Just get it down the way that looks impressive to me, before I lose it. A real good pencil lady is real good to have around."

In 1966, Haggard recorded his first No. 1 country hit, Liz and Casey Anderson's "I'm A Lonesome Fugitive." That song's recording found Haggard arriving at a sound that combined a plaintive acoustic guitar with James Burton's lead electric guitar, and the single topped the charts in March of 1967.

"Really, there is no way to describe the ensuing three years of Merle Haggard's career, no way to elucidate the artistic growth he underwent beginning with those August 1966 sessions," wrote Daniel Cooper in the liner notes to Haggard's boxed set, *Down Every Road*. "For country music, there is nothing comparable, no other time when a country singer has delivered as broad—or varied—and as consistently deep and moving a body of work in so short a time as Merle Haggard did from 'The Fugitive' through the close of the 1960s."

In that period, Haggard released an incredible eight albums, including a live record, and his Strangers band put out an instrumental album on Capitol. In the studio, Haggard sang "Branded Man," a song that revealed the fear and shame that followed his prison release, death-row ballad "Sing Me Back Home," plainly worded masterpiece "I Started Loving You Again," blistering rave-up "Workin' Man Blues," the sadder-than-sad "Silver Wings," and numerous other classics.

"Okie" brought him, unshielded, to public light, but it did not dim his run of epic songwriting. And, though, "Okie" and "The Fightin' Side of Me" were ideological opposites of friend Johnny Cash's open-minded "What Is Truth," the men remained close.

"Johnny Cash and I, we believed in the freedom of speech," Haggard said. Haggard also believed in freedom of expression, and he was unfazed when some conservatives who had flocked to "Okie" were shocked by "Irma Jackson," Haggard's pro-tolerance take on interracial romance. That one shouldn't have surprised anyone: He's recorded Tommy Collins' similarly minded "Go Home" years earlier. Haggard was speaking his mind, not speaking from a platform.

"Merle is arguably the best songwriter that our genre has ever seen," said Grammy-nominated songwriter Odie Blackmon. "At the level of songwriting he's achieved, and the honesty and the depth, that man wears his heart on his sleeve. He's a moody, emotional person, and everyone around him understands that. It's a little like his burden, his curse."

The heart-on-sleeve approach extended to the stage, where Haggard's mood and outlook made their way into each night's song selection.

"I took a set list onstage for the last time in 1969," Haggard said. "And what we wound up with was so far away from what we set out to do, I thought it was stupid to put everybody through the stress of that: Why don't we just walk out there with our songs and our talent, and see what happens?"

That's what he did: He walked out there with his songs and his talent, and he saw what happened. But he did more than that. It wasn't just his talent, or his creativity. It was an indefatigable belief that, conceived and delivered properly, music was of practical use.

"People don't need to be badgered anymore, I don't think," he said. "We need to have music that contributes to the well-being of the spirit. Music that cradles people's lives and makes things a little easier. That's what I try to do, and what I want to do. You don't want to close the door on hope."

AN ASIDE: TOMMY COLLINS' FUNNIES

"Hello, Opal? This is Frank. Did the man give you the divorce papers?" Thus begins one of country music's under-beloved classics, a spoken-word number by Tommy Collins called "Opal, You Asked Me." Tommy was a mentor and friend to Merle Haggard, and he was a kingpin in the 1950s Bakersfield, California scene that spawned Haggard and Buck Owens. After that, he went into the ministry, and then he got disgusted at the ministry and went back into country music. He wound up in Nashville, where he often tacked funny songs on to the end of his recording sessions.

In the Opal song, a man named Frank tries to end his marriage with a phone call, offering his soon-to-be-ex-spouse "the house, the car, the money in the bank, the muffler shop" and anything else she wants, in exchange for a quiet ending to a bad situation. But wife Opal insists on an explication.

"Okay, okay, okay Opal . . . remember, you asked me," Frank says, before unleashing a litany of complaints. The first involved Opal's insistence on wearing an old faded formal dress to a neighbor's open house.

"The top of that dress kept falling down, and I kept pulling it up," Tommy said. "You know, the years kind of take their toll on us, Opal. It wasn't as much indecent as it was sickening . . . You asked me, now . . .

"Another thing . . . did you ever notice how when you walked through the house, you just kind of stomped? Oh, I used to hate to walk anywhere with you. And when you would drink out of a glass or a cup or whatever, you just kind of sucked it out, and made that funny sound. Oh, that used to disgust me."

There were other Tommy Collins funnies, as well. There was one where a fellow named Clifton Hartness calls home to explain where he's been for the last six months and goes on to say that he's now a show-biz professional under the name of "Cigarette Milner."

"Got a ring to it, hadn't it? With a name like that, I ought to pack 'em in. Get it? Pack 'em in? Why I'll have 'em rolling in the aisles . . . rolling. Let 'em watch my smoke.

"Now, baby, for that big surprise. I'm gonna cut a record. It'll cost me $500, so I think you better stay on down at the creamery until I get this thing going. Then you can tell 'ol Whatenbarger to hang it . . . I know he's giving you a bad time. When I get back there, I might just let him hold one, too. He's beggin' for it . . . well, kiddo, send me some money."

CHAPTER 11

DON LIGHT AND THE IMPOSSIBILITY OF UNSCRAMBLING EGGS

The music business is not hard. It moves too slow to be hard.

That's what Don Light said, anyway. And most of us in Nashville made it a point to believe whatever Don Light said. After saying the music business moves too slow to be hard, he'd say, "I believe in establishing goals and objectives: Knowing where you think you're going, and knowing how you think you can get there. Then, it's about keeping your goals and objectives in front of you. That's the reason they put the carrot right out in front of the mule. Otherwise, the mule might forget."

We all called him "Don Light."

Not "Don," and never "Mr. Light."

I don't know why that was, but it was a community practice clearly established before I came to Music City, in the year 2000.

By then, Don Light should probably have been dead for thirty years. In July of 1969, he underwent a then-experimental surgery to combat ulcerative colitis: He had his colon removed.

"See, I don't even have a rectum," Don Light said. "I tell people my butthole is in a jar of alcohol on the mantle, but it's really not. It's in the bedroom."

Don Light could barely be heard. He talked softly, not out of lack of conviction but because of another health condition.

He was stooped and bent, not from age or submission but because of yet another health condition.

His work frequently went uncredited, which was okay with him. He distrusted the means by which credit is bestowed.

"Columbus didn't know where he was going, didn't know where he was when he got there, and didn't know where he'd been when he got back," Don Light said. "But he got credit for discovering a country he didn't discover."

> **His work frequently went uncredited, which was okay with him. He distrusted the means by which credit is bestowed.**

Allow me to give Don Light proper credit, so you'll understand why we believed him when he talked.

Don Light was a Marine, and then he was a disc jockey, and then he was a drummer on the Grand Ole Opry and on studio sessions. At the same time he was drumming, he ran the Nashville office of *Billboard* magazine. And then, in 1965, he opened the first professional outfit for booking gospel music, Don Light Talent, and he co-founded the Gospel Music Association.

After creating the Jesus music business, he discovered, promoted, and enabled the ascent of irreverent folk singer/songwriter Jimmy Buffett. Don Light even convinced one of his gospel clients, the Oak Ridge Boys, to sing harmony for Buffett on the sinner's tale, "My Head Hurts, My Feet Stink, and I Don't Love Jesus."

He also raced stock cars, and he managed Grand Ole Opry star Steve Wariner, doomed singing genius Keith Whitley, award-winning new century bluegrass duo Dailey & Vincent, and former Louisiana Governor (and "You Are My Sunshine" co-writer) Jimmie Davis, among others. When he asked Davis about his final term as governor, Davis said, "I didn't do much, but I didn't promise 'em anything."

Don Light talks . . .

The Marine Corps? It's something I'm glad I got to do, and glad I don't have to do anymore. When you first arrive, I remember one of the drill instructors has you do all the pushups you can do. After what you think is the last one, he makes you do one more. "You telling me you can't do one more pushup, for your mother?"

Well, yeah. He ends up getting ones for a couple of other people, and one for himself. He gets another five out of you before you fall, and you didn't think you had any left in you. So, that shows you something about motivation.

But I didn't agree with everything those people were about. I've watched World War II footage of those beach landings, and that was not good military strategy, in my opinion. Those guys dug holes and are shooting out of them, and you're running across a beach?

I had a totally undistinguished career in the Marines. I didn't get court marshaled or anything, but they didn't weigh me down with a bunch of medals, either. I fell through the cracks. I was too young for the Korean War, and too old for the Vietnam War, so I don't know anything about combat. I knew they didn't always appreciate my humor, and that I wasn't going to stick around long enough to tell time their way.

The Marines help teach you patience, and patience is a virtue. My old friend Les Beasley was in the Marines, too. When we first got in the Marines, they gave us these little white pills, so we wouldn't think about girls. Not long ago, Les told me that his little white pills had just started working. See, patience.

"I've never had any original ideas," Don Light said. "What I've been able to do is see something working in one area and realize it could be applied to another area. If you can find a need and fill it, you've probably got a job."

He watched what happened with the Country Music Association, a trade organization formed in 1958 to combat the rock 'n' roll onslaught and bolster Nashville-based country music. The CMA worked, quite successfully, to convince radio stations of the worth and popularity of country music. Don Light figured a similar organization could be a boost to gospel music, so he plotted the Gospel Music Association. The plotting worked, and he's now a member of that association's Hall of Fame.

He also saw the country music industry's creeping professionalism, and he thought he could bring some legitimacy to gospel music by booking gospel artists via then-unheard-of methods: contracts and constructs. Starting with the Oak Ridge Boys and the Happy Goodman Family, Don Light would negotiate a date, a time, and a length of performance, and agree with a promoter on what pay would be received for a performance of a particular length on a particular date. Then he would issue a contract, and all parties would officially agree on the terms.

This was in stark contrast to the handshakes, hopes, and prayers on which the rest of the gospel business ran. That business was lucrative, but less than legitimate. It wasn't sinister, but it was under-the-table. Don Light pissed some gospel promoters off with his contracts, because those contracts put an end to the Oaks, the Goodmans, and, later, acts like the Chuck Wagon Gang doing "all-night sings." Don Light held fast to the agreed upon fact that the night ends at the stroke of midnight. If he'd booked an act to play on August 18, the contract asserted, correctly, that the post midnight hours that followed August 18 were, in fact, August 19.

August 19 was nowhere in the contract.

August 19 was a separate negotiation.

Gospel promoters bemoaned that they should have included the early morning hours in the original contract.

Don Light told them, gently but firmly, "You can't unscramble eggs."

Don Light Talent was thriving in 1968, when Herman Harper was a bass singer for the Oak Ridge Boys. Harper wanted off the road, and Don Light wanted some help, and they reached an agreement: Harper resigned from the Oaks and became head of Don Light Talent's gospel division. Without Harper, Don Light Talent would have gone under. Don Light had ulcers in his colon. He was losing weight, and otherwise weakening. He was throwing up water.

"People thought I was dying, probably because I was dying," Don Light said. "I was taking Prednisone, about twelve a day, and I'd never want to do that again. It gave you a false sense of well-being. You think you're doing good, but you're bleeding to death. I'd go in to work every day, but what I was actually accomplishing you could stick up a gnat's ass."

On July 20, 1969, Don Light watched from a hospital television as Neil Armstrong walked on the moon. The next day, he went in for surgery, not knowing whether he would recover or die while under sedation. But you can't unscramble eggs.

Days later, when Don Light awoke, the first words he said were, "Did we get the moon guys back?"

He knew they didn't have jumper cables up there, and that they were out on a limb.

The moon guys came back, and so did Don Light.

"It's a drastic surgery, but a big improvement over the way I was before the surgery," he said. "I can change my bag in less time than it takes for a woman to put on her makeup. When they told me about what this would be, I fought it a lot. But in hindsight, it's a lot easier to maintain than your butt. And I can't ever get hemorrhoids. I've never had to look very far to find somebody that's worse off."

Don Light was big on what he called "separation from the pack." He worried less about who could do things better than he did about who could do things differently. He himself did things differently. He was the first *Billboard* magazine writer to play drums on the Grand Ole Opry, and the first talent agent in gospel music.

He was, most probably, the first gospel executive to walk around every evening after 5:00 p.m. with a can of beechwood-aged Budweiser in his suit jacket pocket. He took care to remove the beer can from his pocket before going onstage at the Opry.

"If you drop your drumstick and need to bend over and pick it up, you might have a problem," he said.

When he recovered from his colectomy, he began looking outside of gospel music for artists to represent. He had an affinity for bluegrass music and for storytelling songwriters, and he started booking bluegrass and folk singers into colleges and listening rooms. He stayed true to his notion of seeing

> **He was, most probably, the first gospel executive to walk around every evening after 5:00 p.m. with a can of beechwood-aged Budweiser in his suit jacket pocket.**

something that works in one area and applying it to another. Traditional bluegrass worked on the festival circuit, and he thought it would work on college campuses.

He took Lester Flatt—of Flatt & Scruggs fame—for a showcase at the national association of college talent buyers convention in Cincinnati. Flatt played a twenty minute set, and Don Light booked seventy seven college dates based on those twenty minutes.

In the early 1970s, Lester Flatt was bitter towards his old partner Earl Scruggs. He was especially negative towards Earl's wife, the broad-minded and tough-nosed Louise Scruggs. Louise was a huge Bob Dylan fan, and in the 1960s she encouraged Flatt & Scruggs to record Dylan's songs. Flatt despised Dylan's songs, and he sang compositions like "Rainy Day Women #12 & 35," with its repeated assertion that "everybody must get stoned," as if he had a gun pointed at his temple.

After Flatt & Scruggs' big bluegrass breakup, Lester saw television footage of Earl playing at an anti-Vietnam rally and figured Earl had become a communist. The men didn't speak for years, though Scruggs' distance was less antagonistic than Flatt's. But, after an eventful heart attack and a renewed religious commitment, Flatt began to soften.

"He was driving home from church with Marty Stuart, and Lester said, 'When you've been through something like I have, you start to see things different,'" Don Light said. "And he went on from there. He said, 'I don't even feel the way I used to about Earl. In fact, I wouldn't mind talking to him, and wouldn't mind seeing him, if he wanted to see me.'

"Marty said, 'What about Louise?' and Flatt said, 'Why, hell, I ain't been that damn sick.'"

One day, Don Light's phone rang. On the other end of the line was Bill Williams, who was running Nashville's *Billboard* office and who was a rhyming weatherman on WSMV television.

Right, a rhyming weatherman. Poetic forecasts, and there aren't many rhymes for "sunny."

Williams was calling on behalf of a young guy who was writing for *Billboard*'s sister publication, *Amusement Business*, but who wanted to be a professional singer-songwriter. Williams thought maybe Don Light could help.

That evening, the writer Jimmy Buffett came to Don Light's office, at 816 19th Avenue in Nashville, and he played a reel-to-reel tape with original songs like "The Great Filling Station Holdup" and "Pencil Thin Mustache."

"When Buffett came through the door that very first night, he was there to see me because he wanted to play the Bistro club in Atlanta, Georgia, and he'd heard that I was booking singer-songwriters into places like that," Don Light said. "If you're in the doctor's office, you're not just stopping in. Something has caused you to be there, and in this case Jimmy was in my office because he wanted to play the Bistro. He asked if I could do that for

> **"I thought I was right about Jimmy Buffett. It just took me a long time to get anyone else to think that."**
> **—Don Light**

him, and I did. And then he wanted to play the Quiet Night in Chicago, and the Cellar Door in Washington, DC. And we did that.

"He was a delightful guy, and after awhile I told him, 'I think I can get you a record deal, and if I do then I'd like to be your manager.' Looking back, I hadn't gotten anybody else a record deal. I didn't really know I could do that. I thought I was right about Jimmy Buffett. It just took me a long time to get anyone else to think that."

After two years of playing songs for record company executives who liked the songs but didn't think they would get played on country radio stations, Don Light and Jimmy Buffett found two receptive ears attached to the head of ABC Records' Don Gant. Buffett signed a contract, and then Gant found that the other honchos at ABC didn't see much commercial potential.

"They wanted the next Waylon Jennings, and didn't think Jimmy was it," Don Light said. "They were right, he wasn't the next Waylon. He was the first Jimmy Buffett. Gant offered us an escape before the first record was even released. He said, 'ABC isn't going to do much promotion, so if you want to get out of the deal and try for another label, I'll let you out.' Well, this was the only record deal we had, so I said, 'No, we'll stay right here.'"

Meanwhile, Buffett was playing the same club and college circuit Don Light had opened up to Lester Flatt. He went to a regional collegiate talent bookers conference in Texas, and booked nineteen of the twenty one Lone Star colleges represented there.

"If he'd left off the song about getting drunk and screwing, we'd have gotten Baylor and Texas Christian," Don Light said.

Buffett stayed in Nashville for a time, but then he decided to make Key West, Florida his home, and he started working on a beach bum persona that would serve him well. He wrote about the island life, and Don Light knew to leave business messages for him at Key West's Chart Room bar.

"He put a lot of Key West people in his songs, like a guy named Ace," Don Light said. "Ace walked around the island with a cigarette in his mouth, never lit. Ace was pretty smart, and he figured cigarettes lasted longer if you didn't light them."

Don Light was pretty smart, and he figured success in the music business was based seventy percent on pure determination. He was 100 percent sure that Jimmy Buffett was the most determined artist he ever worked with. Buffett had the ability to make people think what he wanted them to think. They thought he was a shuffling, scuffling, nary-a-care type, when in fact he was methodical and thought-out and damn serious, a business man bent not just on success but on establishing an empire.

Through 2016, Buffett notched a total of five Top Ten hits, and one solo chart-topper, "Margaritaville." Yet his fortune extends far beyond peers who have scored dozens of major hits. Don Light didn't foresee all of that, but he knew Buffett augmented his determination with charm that verged on the magical.

"His stage persona and awareness from day one was as good as it ever got," Don Light said. "He got better at playing and singing and writing songs, but from the beginning, in any setting, he could make people love him."

Those settings moved from small clubs to bigger clubs, and then on from there. Don Light booked Buffett for the 1974 Willie Nelson Fourth of July Picnic at Texas World Speedway in College Station, because he thought his clever story songs would go over well with Nelson's crowd. By then, Buffett had released two albums on ABC, and he had little in the way of radio success (though he'd just put out "Come Monday," which became his first radio hit).

"I felt like we were doing well, and I knew everywhere I booked him he was getting to go back for more money," Don Light said. "But at Willie's show, I looked out at the crowd and the audience was just as deep as I could see, singing every word to every song. They didn't hear those songs on the radio. They heard those because they owned the album, or one of their friends did, and they listened to it. Other people were starting to think the same things about Jimmy Buffett that I was thinking."

Two years after that 1974 Willie Nelson picnic, Don Light and Jimmy Buffett re-upped with ABC Records. The label gave Don Light two checks: The one for $100,000 was to record a new album, and the one for $132,000 was for tour support. Three years before, Buffett had been denied a bank loan because, the banker explained, he needed to stabilize his work efforts. Don Light handed Buffett the two checks from ABC and encouraged him to take them back to the banker and ask, "Is this stable enough for your ass?" Buffett smilingly declined.

By then, Buffett had written "Margaritaville," which Don Light thought, correctly, would be his breakthrough. He did not have any way of knowing that the song would spur a casual dining restaurant chain, and lines of chicken wings and frozen seafood and beach furniture and blenders, or that it would become the key to Buffett earning hundreds of millions of dollars.

"First time I heard it, it was at the Roxy in Los Angeles, before the show," Don Light said. "He came down the hall in shorts, no shoes, a t-shirt, a guitar, and lyrics in a yellow notebook, and he said, 'Listen to this.' I did. Not a bad, throwaway phrase in it. Singable. Well-written. I knew it was his hit."

Norbert Putnam produced Buffett's *Changes in Latitudes, Changes in Attitudes* album, which held "Margaritaville." The album came out in January of 1977, the same month Don Light got an unexpected phone call. Buffett had just moved his home and bus and bank account to California. Now, he wanted to move his management to California. Don Light didn't want to move to California, and Buffett knew that. Don Light had several years left on his management contract, and Buffett knew that as well.

"It was never not civil," Don Light said. "I was disappointed, and I didn't think it was the right move, but Jimmy's right more than he's wrong. We all try to be. So we proceeded along with a settlement."

Don Light didn't get ripped off. He claimed no malice, and he and Buffett remained friends. When Don Light died in 2014, I wrote his obituary, and I called Buffett for his reaction. He said, "Don Light was an honest guy that took an interest in me. He had this unique eye for talent, unlike anyone else

. . . He was the only guy that 'got' me at that time in Nashville. I was lucky to have him in my life."

There was a settlement, in which Don Light kept twenty-five percent interest in the publishing revenues from "Margaritaville," "Cheeseburger in Paradise," and a bunch of others. That interest would have meant millions, had he not later sold it for $125,000.

"When I think about horrible mistakes, I've used up all mine and two or three other people's," he said, softly as ever. "But there's no substitute for experience, and only one way to get it. Experience is what you get when you don't get what you want. One hundred percent of the blame rests squarely on me, if I'm going to be fair about it, and I try to be."

Early 1970s.

Bluegrass festival.

Berryville, Virginia.

Don Light was there, managing Mac Wiseman, who would later enter both the bluegrass and country music halls of fame. Mac was in a field near a camper, singing and playing with Doyle Lawson and John Starling and a 17-year-old kid named Keith Whitley.

Don Light didn't know his name was Keith Whitley, but as soon as he heard him sing, he asked his name, and his name was Keith Whitley. He was from Kentucky, and took full advantage of that commonwealth's riches of roots music and bourbon. Don Light heard him sing and told him, "If you ever get serious about being a star and move to Nashville, I think I can get you a record deal. You don't have to live in Nashville to have a career, but things can happen accidentally here that wouldn't happen on purpose somewhere else."

Years later, in 1983, Whitley came walking through Don Light's back door. He hadn't called, just came on in and said, "Well, I'm here."

Keith Whitley was a magnificent, tradition-drenched singer who filtered his evident Merle Haggard idolatry through a Kentucky-cured sensibility. Don Light managed Steve Wariner, who was on RCA Records, and he took a Whitley demo tape to the label's chief, Joe Galante.

"We're going to pass on Keith Whitley," is what Galante told Don Light, who responded, "You don't have one of these, and you need one."

He meant that other labels had traditional country singers, and RCA did not. He meant that there was only one Keith Whitley, and RCA didn't have him and they'd do well to have him. Six months went by before Galante agreed with him and signed Whitley to an RCA Records deal.

Whitley's first RCA release, *A Hard Act to Follow*, was not. It wasn't exceptional, and it didn't sound much different than what others were doing at the time. Don Light believed in separation from the pack, but this stood cozily among the pack.

While he was making *A Hard Act to Follow*, producer Norro Wilson called Don Light, saying that Whitley was at the studio, drunk and passed out.

"I don't remember ever smelling alcohol on Keith's breath," Don Light said. "But I learned from his first wife, Kathi, that sometimes he'd go missing for a few days."

Whitley agreed to seek treatment, but didn't have the money for it. Don Light met with Joe Galante and asked if RCA would pay. Within a half hour, Galante produced a check. Days later, Whitley was at Cumberland Heights alcohol and drug rehabilitation center.

"I took him there, and visited him a couple of times," Don Light said. "He had a brand new record, and I had an alcoholic artist on my hands. I came to know later a lot about this, because I studied. But at that point, when he got out, I thought, 'Well, we fixed that.' For six months after that, he was straight as a string."

And then he wasn't. There were two more rehab stints, and in between those there was some brilliant music and a full embrace of Whitley's affable personality. He was, Don Light always said, a delight. But with the third rehab stay, Don Light resigned as Whitley's manager: He wasn't helping, and didn't know how to help.

> **"He had a brand new record, and I had an alcoholic artist on my hands."**
> **–Don Light**

"Keith was very funny, and very enjoyable," he said. "There was nothing wrong, except the problem, which greatly interfered with what we were trying to do. He told me he was going to quit drinking, and that he didn't want to die. Two years and one more trip to rehab later, he was dead, and he was dead because of the problem. It was a sad thing for country music, and for this town. I'd regret dropping him more if there'd been a way that

I could have fixed it by staying involved. I don't have to win, but I have to think that I can."

If you didn't want to see Don Light cry, you'd do well not to ask him about Keith Whitley, who died in May of 1989, at the age of 34.

Four months before Whitley died, RCA released his single "I'm No Stranger to the Rain." It became the third of his five career chart-topping hits. Just after he died, the company released a song he'd recorded that April, one called "I Wonder Do You Think of Me." That song went to Number One, as well, though Whitley never knew that triumph.

Don Light was sick for forty years.

There was the colostomy, and there was a spinal disease, called Ankylosing Spondelitis, that left him four inches shorter than he'd once been and turned his posture into a question mark. There was another disease that made it a struggle to speak.

He could deal with all that, but when his brain got sick he had no interest in continuing. His memory suffered, and he developed an exit plan to use prior to the point at which he would become a burden to others.

He was 77 when he put that plan into action, and then he was gone.

Don Light said the music business moves too slow to be hard, but when he died, it got real hard, real fast.

I spoke at his memorial, but I didn't have any original ideas. I just repeated things Don Light had told me . . . .

Sometimes we did it because we didn't know we couldn't do it.

In the music business, three people can keep a secret if two of them are dead.

I'm okay with mistakes and accidents. I'm not okay with pre-meditated screw-ups. You have to be able to depend on somebody.

Nashville didn't invent jealousy, but we perfected it pretty good.

Tenor singers and left-handed guitar players are all crazy. I know of no exceptions.

If that guy had ever been accused of singing, it wouldn't have come to court.

Beware of somebody who tells you, "Don't worry about a thing."

That guy may have heard about diplomacy, but he didn't catch it.

He was one of those people who would complain about not having anything to complain about.

You can look back on some things I've done and say, "That's a hillbilly way of doing things." Well, we're hillbillies, so why shouldn't it be?

He's from that part of Alabama that knows how to hold a grudge and stay mad.

I've been right more than wrong. I don't take a lot of credit for that, but I don't take any blame. I'm grateful.

AN ASIDE, FROM DON LIGHT

"Every day when I'm in Daytona Beach, I climb the Ponce de Leon Lighthouse, which is the tallest lighthouse in Florida. It's the second tallest on the east coast. 175 feet. With my back and hips and respiratory problems, I'm never the first one up. It takes me a long time. I have to stop at every other landing and rest. But I like it up there. And when I finally get to the top, I've got the same view as everybody else."

—Don Light

CHAPTER 12

TAYLOR SWIFT AND THE HYBRID ART OF UNDERSTANDING

"The cookies are a hybrid version," the 19-year-old told me. "I put bread flour in with the regular flour. Makes them rise."

Taylor Swift didn't offer that information up clinically or hopefully. She was explaining her process, and trying to be pleasant and helpful. And she figured I might be hungry. The cookies were good. If you aren't happy with your cookies, try putting bread flour in with the regular flour. It can work out just fine.

We were talking in advance of her first headlining show in Nashville. She was a burgeoning success, not a global superstar. I was an industry veteran, and not a member of Swift's intended audience. She was a young person, singing to young people about young people things. She didn't write lines like "She wears short skirts, I wear T-shirts/ She's cheer captain and I'm in the bleachers" with people like me in mind ... though, come to think of it, I do wear T-shirts, and when I'm at a Cubs game I often sit in the bleachers.

She was still figuring stuff out. And I was quickly figuring out that she was the most pleasantly, intelligently, self-possessed person I'd ever met. Already, she'd done some things that no one else in country music history had done. She had written about her own real life, in her own language, by herself, and found that her own teenage experiences resounded with mass audiences.

"It's ingrained in me to have these dreams and crazy wishes, and pray every night that my career might, on some off-chance, skyrocket," she said. "But I never expect it to happen."

It happened, in ways that were unprecedented and monumental. And Taylor Swift became a resounding commercial force by doing something no one else had done, which was, simply, being Taylor Swift.

To sit down face-to-face with a 19-year-old Swift was to comprehend that she was someone of uncommon intellect, palpable presence, and perfectly risen cookies.

"At 14, 15, and 16, I was hanging out at the Bluebird Cafe in Nashville, or meeting with songwriters to hear their opinions on the world," she said.

> **Taylor Swift became a resounding commercial force by doing something no one else had done, which was, simply, being Taylor Swift.**

"I wanted to know what people thought of the prospects of a teenaged girl making it in country music, and the forecast was grim. I had a lot of people prepare me for the failure that never ended up happening. Just because you're 16 does not mean you have to think like a 16-year-old."

In truth, she did think like a 16-year-old. But she also thought like a 26-year-old, and a 36-year-old. I'm not sure that there's anything particularly wise about a 46-year-old perspective, but if there is then she thought like that, too.

She knew that no one had ever done what she was wanting to do. She knew that no teen music superstar since Brenda Lee in the 1960s had blossomed into her twenties with her musical vision, her perspective, her audience, and her personal life in good order.

"Going crazy is not on the agenda for me," she said, and she clearly had no space on her agenda for anything that was not on her agenda.

"When I get fearful, it's that I'm fearful of people getting tired of me, or fearful of my life ending up a cliche of a person who has people around them all the time but in what matters most they're alone," she said. "I want to have a life that looks warm and feels cozy, where I'm surrounded by the people I love. I'm scared of losing the kind of love that I have around me now, with my family. I'm always worried of things going wrong, but now I'm less worried than before."

Death, taxes, and backlash are inevitable for those fortunate enough to be successful.

In 2009, Taylor Swift was anointed as a pop-country queen. And so, in 2010, there was backlash. That February, she was pitchy and uncomfortable during a Grammy Awards performance.

I might have been pitchy and uncomfortable myself during a Grammy Awards performance, had I ever been asked to perform at the Grammy Awards. As it stands, I have been nominated for one Grammy Award, as producer of a Tom T. Hall tribute album. People have asked me about the most exciting part of the Grammy Awards process. I tell them that it was the moment just prior to the announcement that I had lost. After the Grammy Awards are done, lots of folks will tell you that they are Grammy-nominated musicians. If they tell you that, in actuality they are Grammy-losing musicians.

Taylor Swift is a Grammy-winning musician. But she offered up a less-than-commanding performance in 2010. A *Washington Post* writer called her "incredibly wretched." A widely-read industry blogger, Bob Lefsetz, pontificated that her "dreadful" performance would kill her career.

Spoiler alert: It didn't.

The whole episode seemed pre-ordained. The world was waiting to pounce. Suddenly, the young woman who had inspired thousands of girls to play guitar and put their own feelings to rhyme and meter was "talentless." In short order, she was, and I quote, a "lily white," "pin-thin," "vindictive," "disgusting," "slut-shaming misogynist" who made "training-bra music."

I wrote, "I've read, over and over again, people volunteering that they 'hate' Taylor Swift. Now, the world has plenty of hate-able things, from war to famine to whoever's playing our favorite football team. And we're going with the barely post-teen who sings about fairy tales and princesses and stuff? Really?"

Really.

I also wrote, "I'm not saying that Taylor Swift sang well at the Grammys ... I'm saying we really don't have to be so mean about it."

Swift was silent in the aftermath of all that. As is her habit, she flung herself into her work, not emerging until she had written an album's worth of songs drawn from her own life's experiences.

"Someday, I'll be big enough so you can't hit me," she sang. "And all you're ever gonna be is mean/ Why you gotta be so mean?"

When she started writing songs, Taylor Swift heard melodies in her head. She didn't know enough about the acoustic guitar to know what chords held those melodies, so she got out a book of guitar chords and played each chord according to diagram until she found the chord that matched the melody.

Chords are terrains. Notes are flora, fauna, people, and structures. Taylor Swift has spent her life finding the terrains that fit her experiences and her creations.

Though she is from Pennsylvania and spends time in New York City, Martha's Vineyard and other environs, the terrain that best fits her experiences and most informs her creations is Nashville.

"It has shaped me into who I am," she said of Music City. "We don't have an ocean, or mountains: People come here because of the feeling they get. It pulls you in, and turns you into who you're going to be."

What Swift was going to be was not what the country music industry wanted her to be. She accepted no prescriptions, and the result has been a career that is fascinating to millions and frustrating to some in country music. Unlike Shania Twain, Dolly Parton, and others, when Swift explored full-scale pop music she did so without shading it as "country" in any way. In 2014, she emerged with a pop album called 1989, one that she didn't pretend was anything but a pop album. In so doing, the biggest star in country music became the biggest music star in the world.

> **She accepted no prescriptions, and the result has been a career that is fascinating to millions and frustrating to some in country music.**

"The only choice I had was to paint a wall green and tell people it's blue," she said. "I decided to be honest about it."

Swift views herself from, to borrow from songwriter Greg Brown, "one cool remove away," instantly aware of repercussions and insinuations, yet wholly present in every conversation. She is the actor, the writer, and the director, always. She's the critic, too.

"Right now, knock on wood, things are good," she told me. "Ugh, I hate it when I rhyme and don't mean to."

In our first conversation, Taylor talked about how she was the only girl at her high school who played guitar and wrote songs. She went on to donate four million dollars to the Country Music Hall of Fame and Museum, to establish an education center that encourages young people to voice their feelings through music. It was through her voicing of feelings that she was heard, and appreciated, and hated, and beloved.

"I'm really lucky, and I feel very thankful for that," said the 19-year-old. "I have never felt misunderstood."

Taylor Swift no longer claims to be perfectly understood.

She became tabloid fodder, though there was never much there to fodd. She didn't taste alcohol until she was twenty-one, she has no issues with drugs, and she hasn't made any of the kinds of mistakes that tend to be made by people who come into enormous fame at a time when other people their age are in high school.

One tabloid "get" on Swift came when she was photographed drinking a beer at a New York Knicks game. I found it particularly unfair of people to criticize Taylor for this, as the Knicks were terrible that year and it was practically impossible to sit through a game without a drink or two.

With paparazzi and tabloid writers documenting Swift's every pratfall, here's the worst thing they've come up with: Sometimes, she goes on dates.

When Swift made her first pop album, there was plenty of anger, to the point that some people asserted that the Country Music Hall of Fame and Museum should be "ashamed" to have the singer's name on the Taylor Swift Education Center.

She contributed to the center because she was the only girl she knew at her high school who played guitar, and the only one she knew who wrote songs. She didn't want future creatives to feel themselves alone or atypical.

"So many of the girls that come here to take lessons, they're playing because of Taylor," said Pamela Cole, co-owner of a Nashville music store where dozens of young girls learn to play guitar. "She's responsible for this boom."

That's not to say that we should feel sorry for Taylor Swift. She'll be fine. She has enough money in the bank that she was actually criticized for making a $50,000 donation to New York City's public schools. Apparently, the gesture wasn't generous enough.

But it is to say that, while Swift will be fine, I'm not sure that we will.

We take the unprecedented success story of an inspirational woman, and we use it as a dartboard.

A lot of us do, anyway, and it makes us seem tacky.

Why do we angrily flail away, bullying the privileged?

We we gotta be so mean?

Townes Van Zandt used to say that there are two kinds of music: "blues" and "zippity do da."

I'll buy that. And sometimes I like zippity do da.

Sometimes I like a hybrid, too: "The Zippity Do Da Blues."

AN ASIDE: SHEL SILVERSTEIN, HYENA GENIUS

Shel Silverstein's artistry was of the renaissance variety.

He wrote children's books, like *Where the Sidewalk Ends*, *The Giving Tree*, and *Don't Bump the Glump!*

He drew dirty cartoons for *Playboy* magazine.

He wrote plays, like *The Lady or the Tiger* and *The Devil and Billy Markham*.

Most important to our country music matters at hand, he wrote songs.

He wrote "A Boy Named Sue," the rollicking Johnny Cash single that in which an absentee father explaining to his long-lost, furious son why he'd given him a girl's name.

He wrote "One's on the Way" and "Hey Loretta," both hits for the great Loretta Lynn.

He wrote numerous songs recorded by his best friend, Country Music Hall of Famer Bobby Bare. Shel didn't live in Nashville, but he often came into town to show Bare his songs. Bare delighted to see him, because Bare loved creative types and Shel was the embodiment of creativity.

Bare recorded an entire album of Shel songs, called *Bobby Bare Sings Lullabys, Legends and Lies*. It's a classic, with songs including "The Winner," in which a barroom fighter's teeth "rolled away like Chicklets down the street in San Antone." Another highlight is She's tale of voodoo queen Marie Laveau. On that one, which topped the country charts in 1974, Shel made an ultra-rare contribution: He was a featured vocalist.

See, Shel was possessed with one of the worst singing voices ever heard. Musical appreciation is inherently subjective, and it's normally senseless to write about vocalists or instrumentalists as "good" or "bad." But in Shel's case, it's a practical necessity. His voice was a razor-gargled hyena screech. But Bare needed just such a screech to embody the voodoo holler of Marie Laveau. In the song, Marie screams her curses, and then Bare sings, "Another man done gone."

Shel starred on that recording, as the howling witch. But he didn't have to sing in anything but his unnaturally natural voice. His was a frightening, disturbing instrument, as discomforting as his stories and lyrics were pleasing.

Bare was a song hound, and sometimes he would rent a hotel room and have songwriters come sing him their works in the room. One day, he rented a room and a succession of musicians came by with works of varying quality. Shel came along in the still-early evening, and he grabbed a guitar and began to sing.

"He hadn't been singing for more than ten seconds when some woman in the next room started banging on the wall and hollering, 'Shut the fuck up!'" Bare said. "I mean, we'd been going for hours and hours with no complaints. Then Shel starts playing and the woman just couldn't stand it. I said, 'Shel, I love you, but you're a *terrible* singer.'"

JIMMY MARTIN, HOTSHOT WITH A TEARDROP IN HIS EYE

Jimmy Martin was immediately captivating.

He was a star of bluegrass music, a genre that is most often well-mannered and serious minded.

Jimmy was serious-minded, but not well-mannered. He was brash, and sometimes rude. He was, above all, positive. Not "positive" meaning "prone to looking on the bright side." "Positive" meaning "convicted." Pick a subject, he was sure about it. And he would convey his beliefs with a preacher's countenance, or a drunkard's tears, or a loudmouth's loud mouth.

Lord, he was talented. Martin was the most invigorating frontman in bluegrass, strutting around the stage like a corn-fed, Pentecostal-bred Mick Jagger.

He worried about heaven and hell, though they weren't the most crucial of his concerns.

Once, he told someone he suspected of lying that they should be wary of stretching truths: "You can go to hell for lying," he said.

The accused truth-stretcher noted Jimmy's quickly disappearing cup of booze:

"You can go to hell for drinking, too," he said.

Jimmy snapped back, "Yeah, but I *like* it."

He liked applause, too. Before recording songs in the studio, he gathered some musicians together and played them a cassette tape.

"It was nothing but applause," said one of those musicians, Jeff Hanna, of the Nitty Gritty Dirt Band. "It was three minutes of people clapping. Jimmy sat there with a big grin on his face and finally said, "You know what that was? That was the applause from the last time I played the Grand Ole Opry. I went over pretty good there, didn't I?"

Jimmy didn't play the Opry much, because the Opry bosses wouldn't let him. It wasn't that he lacked in talent, it was his volatile moods that spoiled the deal. A child of East Tennessee poverty who was four when his father died and whose stepfather often physically abused him, Martin was sensitive to exclusions of any sort. The Opry's refusal to make him a member was wrenching to him, every day of his life.

"Ever since I was a little boy, I've felt left out of things," he said in 2002, tearing up.

Jimmy's proud gravestone reads "Now Sings in Heaven," which was a cocoon of a lie that he hoped would butterfly into truth.

In bluegrass circles, Bill Monroe was seldom called "Bill." He was most often "Mr. Monroe" and sometimes "Big Mon." Jimmy Martin, a fiery and audacious presence in a music normally made by people wearing sober suits and inscrutable expressions, was never "Mr. Martin." He was "Jimmy," and Jimmy was the King of Bluegrass. And if you didn't believe it, you could ask him.

> **He was "Jimmy," and Jimmy was the King of Bluegrass. And if you didn't believe it, you could ask him.**

Jimmy often visited his own grave. He purchased it when he discovered he could secure a plot straight across from Roy Acuff's resting place. Acuff was the first solo singing star of the Grand Ole Opry, and he is known as "The King of Country Music."

"The King of Country Music and the King of Bluegrass, right there together," Jimmy would say, standing on the well-tended grass of the Spring Hill Cemetery.

"What do you think?" he asked, not really caring what I thought.

But I thought it was cool.

Sometimes people are asked what they'd like written on their headstone.

Todd Snider and I wrote a song that goes, "I want a six-foot gravestone, two feet thick/ With the words engraved, 'I'd like to tell you all I was sick'/ So you will know that I was right when you go walking on past/ You tried to tell me I was well, but look who's laughing last."

But nobody knows for sure what's actually going to be on there.

Nobody except Jimmy Martin.

He bought the stone, and paid for the carving.

A SELF-DESCRIBED "POOR BOY FROM SNEEDVILLE, TENNESSEE" IN REFERENCES TO HIS EARLY YEARS, JAMES H. MARTIN WAS DUBBED "THE KING OF BLUEGRASS MUSIC" DURING THE 1970S. A MAJOR FORCE IN DEFINING AND ESTABLISHING THE MUSIC'S SO-CALLED "HIGH-LONESOME SOUND." HE BEGAN AS LEAD SINGER/ GUITARIST WITH THE BLUE GRASS BOYS IN OCTOBER, 1949.

AMONG OTHER LABELS, JIMMY MARTIN RECORDED 138 TITLES FOR A MAJOR RECORD COMPANY, MANY OF WHICH, INCLUDING "OCEAN OF DIAMONDS," "SAPHRONIE," "WIDOW MAKER" AND "SUNNY SIDE OF THE MOUNTAIN" DID WELL IN THE COUNTRY MUSIC CHARTS OF THE 1950S-1970S. VIRTUALLY ALL OF THE SONGS HE POPULARIZED CAME TO BE RECORDED AS STANDARDS.

A COLORFUL AND CONSUMMATE ENTERTAINER AND MUSICIAN, JIMMY MARTIN PRODUCED PROFOUND AND ENDURING INFLUENCES ON THE IDIOM DURING ITS CRITICAL, FORMATIVE YEARS AND THROUGHOUT THE REMAINDER OF BLUEGRASS MUSIC'S FIRST HALF CENTURY.

Under the "Now Sings In Heaven" information is an etching of a photograph. To the left, the stone read SHAKE HANDS WITH MOTHER AND DADDY AGAIN. To the right was the song title WILL THE CIRCLE BE UNBROKEN.

Jimmy Martin got fired for singing on the job, back in Sneedville, Tennessee. He was on a paint crew, and singing wasn't supposed to be a painting work. But singing was a part of Jimmy Martin, and Jimmy Martin was in the business of letting everybody else know all the parts of Jimmy Martin. If it was in him, it would come out. Loudly.

In 1949, after being fired, he went to Nashville and found himself a job as the guitarist and strong-singing frontman for Bill Monroe, the Father of Bluegrass Music. Martin returned to Sneedville, but only briefly enough to inform his foreman that if the boss man ever missed Jimmy's singing he could tune into the Grand Ole Opry every Saturday night.

Jimmy's entry into Monroe's Blue Grass Boys heralded a new era of bluegrass music. Jimmy's high-pitched voice forced Mr. Monroe to sing even higher harmonies, and thus developed what is now known as "the high, lonesome sound" of bluegrass.

"You know, a lot of people will say that Jimmy Martin put the high, lonesome sound into bluegrass music," Jimmy told me. "I believe you ought to put that in your article, don't you? Say?"

If Jimmy asked, "Say?" he meant for you to say. He never knew a rhetorical question. He always demanded a response, and the response would only go unchallenged if it were positive.

As did most all of Mr. Monroe's great supporting musicians, Jimmy left the Blue Grass Boys and formed his own bluegrass outfit, the Sunny Mountain Boys, in 1957, the same year that Hank Aaron and the Milwaukee Braves won the World Series title over the New York Yankees. He employed genius-level musicians like mandolin player Paul Williams and banjo great J.D. Crowe in his Sunny Mountain Boys band. Together, they recorded a

In the early 1960s days when Jimmy would have been a natural for membership in the Grand Ole Opry, Monroe fought hard to keep him out.

bevy of genre-shaking songs. This was exciting music, captivating in its intensity and its musicality. And delivered live, it was even better, with Jimmy's frenetic fervor every bit the equal of contemporaries like Elvis Presley and Chuck Berry.

"There was nobody like that," said Sunny Mountain Boy Bill Emerson. "He'd just smoke those people, and they'd be waiting in line for him when he got offstage."

In the early 1960s days when Jimmy would have been a natural for membership in the Grand Ole Opry, Monroe fought hard to keep him out. Mr. Monroe prided himself in having created bluegrass music, and he felt that others who played in that style were competing against him using his own sound. He felt that way about Lester Flatt and Earl Scruggs, who were only able to join the Opry because of pressures from their sponsor, Martha White Flour. And he felt that way about Jimmy Martin.

"Bill Monroe said he was going to do everything in his power against me," Jimmy said. "Bill said he'd resign if they let me on. He just didn't want me on that Grand Ole Opry."

Jimmy didn't have a powerful sponsor to force the Opry management's hand. He just had his music, which he thought should stand on its own.

"Jimmy Martin is one of the two greatest rhythm guitarists in Nashville history, with Lester Flatt," said another phenomenal guitarist, Kenny Vaughan. "But there's nothing I could tell you about him that he won't tell you himself."

Seldom does music stand all on its own.

In 1971, a group of long-haired folk-rock musicians came down to Nashville from Colorado and set upon Woodland Sound Studios in East Nashville. With the help of Earl Scruggs and his persuasive wife, Louise, they invited numerous heroes of country and bluegrass music to be part of the Woodland recording sessions, and those sessions became a generation-jumping delight of a triple-LP called Will the Circle Be Unbroken. Today, it is considered one of the classic albums of country music, with contributions from Scruggs, Acuff, Doc Watson, Mother Maybelle Carter, Merle Travis, and many more.

Bill Monroe didn't want to take part in the album, perhaps because the Dirt Band boys had hair longer than was normal in the burr-cut Nashville of 1972.

Jimmy Martin was more than happy to contribute, but not before he made some points.

"Vassar, who helped Bill Monroe write 'Uncle Pen?'" he asked, while the tape rolled, of Vassar Clements, the father of hillbilly jazz.

"You did," Vassar said.

"Who helped write 'Memories of Mother and Dad?'"

"You did."

"Let's see, what was the other one? Who helped write 'When the Golden Leaves Begin to Fall?'"

"You did."

"Thank you."

Those songs were all Monroe standards, and Jimmy went to his grave—and, remember, he went to his grave many times before he died—asserting that he helped create them, uncredited.

Earl Scruggs and Lester Flatt were in Monroe's band in 1945, when bluegrass music was de facto invented on the stage of the Ryman Auditorium. Flat and Scruggs left the band fewer than two years later, and went out to form their own monumentally successful band. After that, Monroe brought in the great Mac Wiseman to sing sonorous lead vocals. When Mac left, Jimmy entered the picture.

"When I joined, it changed it completely, didn't it?" he asked. "Say? Changed his rhythm and the timing of his music, didn't it? Say? Well, all you have to do is just put the damn records on the record player. It don't sound a thing like Flatt and Scruggs to me."

Jimmy's agreement to participate on the Nitty Gritty Dirt Band's project didn't come without strings. He insisted the Dirt boys come to his house and practice before they committed anything to tape.

"He said, 'You're going to be the Sunny Mountain Boys for a few songs,'" said the Dirt Band's Jeff Hanna. "That basically meant, 'We're going to do this right.' He beat the crap out of us, but it paid off."

When the Dirt Band's Will the Circle Be Unbroken album came out, it led off with Martin singing "The Grand Ole Opry Song," a tribute to the show that wouldn't have him.

"There'll be guitars and fiddles, Earl Scruggs and his banjo, too/ Bill Monroe singing out them old Kentucky blues/ Ernest Tubb's number, "Two Wrongs Won't Make a Right/ At the Grand Ole Opry, every Saturday night."

The verses are name-checks of country greats. All of them are dead now, every one. Jimmy, too, though his name is nowhere in the Opry song.

Jimmy Martin burned to be a part of the Grand Ole Opry.

It was the burning that was the problem. The Grand Ole Opry was founded as the radio outreach of the National Life and Accident Insurance company, which owned WSM radio. This was a company that was in the business not only of insurance but of assurance. It was there to provide security and peace of mind, not agitation. And Jimmy Martin was an agitator. So was Hank Williams, who was fired from the Opry because he consistently showed up for work drunk and angry.

Jimmy felt that his own anger, drunkenness and unpredictability were judged too harshly.

"It seems like they hate to give me any loose of the rope," he told me.

"Jimmy comes on strong," Bill Emerson said. "I never thought they'd let him on there, because of the way he is. "Jimmy comes on strong, and he's got a mouth on him. Underneath all that, there's a big heart, but he burned a lot of bridges in Nashville."

In late 1996, Jimmy entertained a writer named Tom Piazza, who wrote a story on Jimmy for *The Oxford American* magazine. Piazza is a superb writer, and he was drawn to Jimmy's

Jimmy walked in, unannounced and uninvited, and proceeded to curse at next-generation bluegrass ace Ricky Skaggs and to try to pick a fight with Whisperin' Bill Anderson, one of country music's gentlest giants.

catalogue of material and to his force of personality. When he came to interview Jimmy, he found a man of brilliance and unsteadiness. He went along in Jimmy's Cadillac on a ride to the Opry, where Jimmy walked in, unannounced and uninvited, and proceeded to curse at next-generation bluegrass ace Ricky Skaggs and to try to pick a fight with Whisperin' Bill Anderson, one of country music's gentlest giants. Piazza's story was well-received, and ultimately made into a book. Jimmy Martin never set foot backstage at the Opry again, much less onstage.

"People ask him why he ain't on the Opry show," sang Tom T. Hall, in a song called "Jimmy Martin's Life Story," written after a conversation with Dixie Hall and with Jimmy. "'Ain't good enough,' is what he'll laugh and say/ But the songs that he sung and the work that he done is in the books, they can't take that away."

Jimmy Martin died in 2005.

Complications from bladder cancer.

He was interred at Spring Hill Cemetery, and then he was buried under that stone he liked to visit.

He's still there, to my knowledge.

His music is still here, too, as vibrant and thrilling as any Opry star's.

"I'm just an old country boy with a third-grade education, and I'm liable to say anything," is what he told me.

Blessings and curses are often one and the same.

"There was a write-up in *Bluegrass Unlimited* magazine that said, 'The name Jimmy Martin has become a big, big, big conversation piece amongst all bluegrass pickers and singers," he crowed. "That's true, isn't it? I believe you ought to put that in your article. That's good and bad, but if it's all good, it ain't worth a shit, is it? Say?"

AN ASIDE: BUS RUINED BLUEGRASS

"You wanna know what ruined bluegrass?"

Jimmy Martin hollered the question, and expected the answer.

I didn't know the answer, but I wanted to know the answer, and I told him that. I didn't tell him that I didn't know that bluegrass had been ruined. Too afraid.

"Bus!"

He didn't say "The bus."

He said "Bus."

He looked at me as if I should nod in understanding.

"You know what I mean by that? Say!"

"No, sir, I don't."

"Back when Jimmy Martin brought the high, lonesome sound to Bill Monroe and his Blue Grass Boys, we were traveling over mountains and rivers and whatnot in an old station wagon, all five of us, with a big old bass fiddle either strapped to the roof or laying across the middle," he said, his index finger jabbing the air. "We'd be coming back to Nashville to play the Grand Ole Opry, from Georgia or South Carolina or North Carolina or West Virginia or Alabama or Ohio, usually coming over them Appalachian mountains, trying to get to Nashville in time for the Saturday night Opry. And you know what we was doing the whole time? Say!"

"No, sir."

"We was singing! And you know what singing is? Say!"

"No, sir. I mean, I guess singing is singing."

"No, singing is practicing! Practicing! That's what we was doing while we was riding all over the place, speeding through them hills!"

I think I said something super-smart, like, "Cool, sir."

"Nowadays, my Sunny Mountain Boys, after a show they walk on bus (again, no "the bus") and they put their instruments up and you know what they do?"

"Go to sleep?"

"That's right! And you know what sleeping is? Say!"

"Not practicing?"

"Sure as shit, sleeping ain't practicing! Bus ruined bluegrass!"

CHAPTER
14

LORETTA LYNN, THE ANTI-POET

For decades, anyone who knew anything about country music knew that Loretta Lynn was born and raised in Butcher Holler, Kentucky."

Loretta wrote a famous song called "Coal Miner's Daughter" that told people, in plain-speak rhyme that thrilled millions and troubled grammarians, "I was borned a coal miner's daughter/ In a cabin on a hill in Butcher Holler."

Then came a big Hollywood movie about Loretta, starring Sissy Spacek. The film is called *Coal Miner's Daughter*, and its scenes of a Butcher Holler childhood are known to people who have never paid great attention to country music and country artists.

In the *Encyclopedia of Country Music*, a quick glance at the Loretta Lynn entry will tell you she was born in the coal mining town of Butcher Holler.

But the thing is, there was no such thing as Butcher Holler, Kentucky when Loretta was born. She made the town's name up in 1970, when she wrote the "Coal Miner's Daughter" song.

Celebrities and people of accomplishment are often credited with putting such-and-so a town on the map, but they don't actually do that. The town was already on the map, and you could look it up.

But look for maps that said Butcher Holler before 1970, and you'll look in fruitless vain.

"The whole thing is really Webb Holler," said Lynn, who was born into the Webb family and married a man named Oliver Mooney "Doolittle" Lynn, who Loretta usually called "Doo." "The Webbs owned the holler, and the Webbs started marrying into the Butchers. I thought the syllable come out better saying 'Butcher' than saying 'Webb,' so I made it Butcher Holler. They say 'Butcher' since I wrote that song."

They not only say it, they believe it, and they make maps and plaques and encyclopedia entries about it. I believed it, too, until 2003, when I went on a trip to Butcher Holler in order to do some research for a newspaper story I was writing about Loretta. I followed the signs to Butcher Holler, and then went on my own fruitless search for town records. Then I went looking into old newspaper stories about Loretta in the 1960s, when she began recording, moved to Nashville, signed with Decca Records, became a member of the Grand Ole Opry, and made significant steps towards proving herself as, in the words of rock star Jack White, "the most significant female singer-songwriter of the twentieth century." In some stories she was from Webb Hollow, in others she was from Van Lear, and a 1966 Tennessean story listed her as being from Miller's Creek Hollow.

The "Coal Miner's Daughter" song isn't about the name of a place. It is about poverty, struggle, and ascendance. And it was powerful enough to become a Country Music Hall of Famer and Kennedy Center Honoree's signature song, and powerful enough to spawn a major motion picture, and powerful enough to instantly change the name of a place that already existed. Most towns need at least a council vote to do that sort of thing.

Hers was the sort of childhood that won't ever again be lived.

"Was it dark when you was up there?" she asked me, and I told her that it was. She said, "I remember that cold and dark, and no food. When we'd get down to nothing and go to bed hungry, sometimes in the middle of the night I'd smell chicken cooking, 'cause Lee Dollarhide (a moonshining cousin) had stole a chicken. Mommy'd get us all up in the dark, let us eat, and then put us all back to bed."

Hers was the sort of childhood that won't ever again be lived. The theft of a chicken was cause for midnight thanksgiving. Snow made it through cracks in the thin hemlock boards that served as walls. Loretta's father brought in water from the well each evening, and in the winter time that water would freeze by daylight.

Loretta came back to the sad little home, after she had become a major music star. She saw a stringless Kay guitar on a bed in a frigid room, and recognized it instantly as the one that belonged to her mother and father . . . the guitar that turned her heart towards music. And then she walked out on the porch and wondered how in the hell she'd ever gotten out of that dear, dark place.

Until his death, Loretta's younger brother, Herman Webb, collected $5 from pilgrims who came to tour their childhood home, to glimpse the well, the Kay guitar, the sausage grinder and the moonshine boiler, to walk through the old doorway into another, thin-walled time.

"I can shut my eyes and see my family, settin' there," Webb said. "You know, I had one lady that complained that she didn't get her money's worth. I gave her the money back and told her, 'I don't know what you was expecting. All this is, is just an old house and the way we lived.'"

Loretta left when she was fifteen, already married, and eight-and-a-half months pregnant. Her mother and father cried about the leaving, and she'd later regret choosing adulthood so soon. But the thing was done, and she boarded a train with Doo's sister, bound for Washington state, where she and Doo could work in the strawberry fields.

For her three-day journey, she had some chicken gizzards and a candy bar, and no pillow for her head.

"Mommy had wrote the conductor a letter and told him to take care of me," she said. "That conductor gave me a pillow, even though you wasn't supposed to get a pillow unless you gave twenty-five cents. And for three days, the conductor would bring us something out of the dining room."

Doo loved Loretta's singing, and thought she sounded like the Queen of Country Music, Kitty Wells. For her eighteenth birthday, he managed to scrape enough money together to buy a guitar, and that guitar became a lifeline.

"The first songs I wrote that got recorded were 'Honky Tonk Girl' and 'Whispering Sea,' and I wrote them in the same day, sitting outside by the toilet, on a $17 guitar that couldn't stay in tune," she said. "I had to put my heart and soul into them. I'd close my eyes and go through it in my mind. You know, you've got to close your eyes when you're a writer. You need to get to yourself."

Loretta and Doo painted a cat head on a coffee pot, and set it next to where she'd sing in little honky-tonks in those early days. They called the coffee pot "the kitty," and song requests were only met after someone fed the kitty a nickel or a dime.

"I saved up enough money to get me an old felt hat, a $14 pair of Acme boots, and a little black skirt with fringe on it. Looked good to me. Annie Oakley wasn't nothin.'"

With that guitar, the boots, the skirt, and the kitty, a young mother of four found hope that life might involve something beyond hard labor and a body that would soon stoop from work in the fields. Onstage, she had spark and gumption, and she used that to convey a perspective that was at once entirely her own and instantly relatable to people who had shared her country upbringing.

She impressed west coast impresario Buck Owens, and she found her way to a record deal with Zero Records. Her first single came out in 1960, and her memoir and her Hollywood movie depict her cross-country efforts to promote the single. She and Doo drove across America, looking for radio towers. When they'd see a tower, they'd stop by the station office and hand out a copy of the record, hoping for airplay.

> **With that guitar, the boots, the skirt, and the kitty, a young mother of four found hope that life might involve something beyond hard labor and a body that would soon stoop from work in the fields.**

The song, "Honky Tonk Girl," was sung in a vibrato-heavy voice that offered a fine but uncomfortably close imitation of Kitty Wells. But the narrative perspective was entirely different than Wells, who sang of honky-tonks and divorce as unholy things. ("Will your lawyer talk to God for you?" Wells asked, in one song.) By contrast, Loretta's song was from a plain, heartbroken first-person, as she ordered a bartender to fill her glass to the top: "I've lost everything in this world, and now I'm a honky-tonk girl," she sang.

Loretta, Doo, and family wound their way to Nashville, where the honky-tonk girl made her debut on the Grand Ole Opry in October of 1960. Soon, she was managed by the stage-savvy, business-wise duo of Doyle and Teddy Wilburn, and in 1961 she signed to Decca Records and began working with esteemed producer Owen Bradley, who told people that Loretta was the only "lady writer" in Nashville that could touch Hank Williams.

The "lady writer" thing was different. Until Loretta Lynn, female country music singers tended to sing the words and melodies of male songwriters. There was no major country music female (in the day, they were called "girl singers") star who sang from her own singular perspective. Loretta Lynn invented that role, just as she invented Butcher Holler.

Her first #1 hit was autobiographical enough to bother her husband. It was called "Don't Come Home A'Drinkin' (With Lovin' on Your Mind)": "Many nights I've laid awake and cried here all night long/ Then you come in, kissin' on me, it happens every time/ Don't come home a' drinkin', with lovin' on your mind."

Doo's love for Loretta was of the faithful variety, but feelings and actions sometimes diverge. When he was running around with another woman, Loretta wrote and sang, "If you don't wanna go to fist city, you better detour around my town/ 'Cause I'll grab you by the hair of the head, and lift you off the ground."

"The woman I wrote that about, her name's Ann Dunn," Loretta once said from stage, as the audience roared approval. "She's wearin' a wig, wherever she's at, 'cause I took her hair out. I crippled her up pretty good."

Loretta didn't consider herself a part of the women's liberation movement, but her songs demanded something approaching equality at home.

"Doolittle didn't like some of those songs, but that doesn't matter," she said. "They were true."

The "true" part was most important to her. And in singing what was true to her, she gave voice to the pent-up feelings of so many others, who loved her for it.

"It was a pure, straight from the holler, unadorned and un-acrobatic woman's voice, said Mary Chapin Carpenter, a fan who would become a singing, songwriting footstep-follower. "She wrote her life and sang her truth."

As was the case with her friend Johnny Cash, Loretta Lynn's creativity floundered in the 1980s. By then, her legacy seemed secure, but her songwriting was suffering and she struggled to make recordings that could compete with younger artists in the contemporary market. Her strident, mountain-reared voice was at odds with the synthesizers and electric guitar tones that marked that era, and the 1990s were an even tougher fit.

Doolittle had diabetes, and Loretta spent six years in the early '90s caring for him at their ranch in Hurricane Mills, Tennessee.

"I hung everything up and took care of him, and nothing else mattered," she said.

There marriage had been marked by great love and deep contention. Doolittle was an easy man to carry on with, but not an easy man to live with. He was fun-loving, and he found a lot of fun in women and whiskey bottles. Still, his decline and death was crushing to her. After he died, Loretta wrote a song for him, but, as usual, it was an internal excavation of her own feelings. In it, she sang, "Now he's gone to a distant shore, and I can't hear the music anymore."

When she was awarded a Kennedy Center Honor in 2003, Loretta looked to the world like a woman who had created a significant legacy but who was more than two decades past productivity. She was relevant as an influence, not as a modern-day force.

But by that time, she had already begun a remarkable resurgence, it's just that no one knew it yet. She had some help from Jack White, a rocker who had moved to Nashville after spurring a garage rock revival as the leader of wildly successful duo The White Stripes. The two struck up a friendship that would seem unlikely to anyone who doesn't understand the way great and willful people are drawn to each other. And White, who by then had embarked on a solo career, agreed to produce a Loretta Lynn album that would at once recall her past glories and incorporate new and edgy ideas. She told him to pick the studio and the musicians, and that she'd show up to sing.

White had plenty in the way of reputation and funding, so he had his choice of studios in Nashville, and Nashville is home to more than a dozen of the world's most important and advanced studios. So Loretta was on the shocked side of surprised to find herself in the passenger seat of White's car when he stopped at the shabby corner of 14th and Boscobel streets in what was then a dodgy part of town.

"Jack, where are you taking me?" she asked.

White explained that a friend of his, Eric McConnell, had a studio inside the paint-chipped walls of the home behind the metal gate at that corner.

With trust and reluctance, she walked through the gate, up the steps, and into her own life's revival.

"I wanted to hear Loretta in the way everyone wants to hear her: no modern country production, no commercial-tasteful overtones, just Loretta in a real environment, like how it used to be and how it always should be," said White, then twenty-eight years old. "I've recorded tons of bands, and she's the best voice I've ever heard in person. She can sing the daisies out of the ground."

> **"I've just cut a new album," she told a crowd in Wheeling, West Virginia. "The boy that produced the album is Jack White. He's a White Stripes. He's rock 'n' roll."**

Loretta was more excited about the album than her fans were, at least as she broached the idea.

"I've just cut a new album," she told a crowd in Wheeling, West Virginia. "The boy that produced the album is Jack White. He's a White Stripes. He's rock 'n' roll."

Crickets.

Van Lear Rose, the album White produced, was released in late April of 2004, when Loretta was seventy-two years old.

Most of us figured the album would be a pleasing diversion from Loretta's long, slow decline.

Instead, it wound up as one of the grand highlights of her life and career.

Rob Sheffield of Rolling Stone wrote, in a four-star review, "Anybody who worships Loretta Lynn dreams about being able to thank her for all the music, but Jack White has pulled off the ultimate fan fantasy: He's helped her make the album we all dreamed she would make."

The lead-off single was "Portland, Oregon," a song about hooking up over sloe-gin fizz. It was a winking, even leering, duet with White, and it blended rock aggression with Loretta's plainspoken storytelling, and that daisy-raising voice.

The album wound up peaking at #2 on the country chart, giving Loretta her best chart performance since April of 1977, when Jack White was a one-year-old. It also won two Grammy Awards, Loretta's first Grammys since the Nixon administration.

The afternoon before the 2005 Grammy Awards in Los Angeles, I visited with Loretta on her tour bus, parked in a television network lot. She showed me the sparkling dresses hanging in the bus's shower, and she showed me the state room where she kept a hot plate. She hated to fly, and she was often restless at night. She said many a night she would get up in the middle of the night, about the time her mother would wake the kids if Lee Dollarhide had "stoled a chicken," and cook eggs on the hotplate. She said she usually had to use the state room phone to call and admonish the bus driver, who too often drove at rates of speed and bumpiness that could cause less than perfect egg outcomes. She said she was glad for the attention Van Lear Rose was getting, but that she was anxious to leave Los Angeles and take the bus to Florida, where she had gigs the next week.

> "I was just sayin' it like I was livin' it. People'd go around that, but I went right through the middle. If you don't tell it like it is, it's not a very good story, is it? Tell the dadgum story like it is."
> —Loretta Lynn

The night of the Grammy Awards, Loretta was there to collect her trophies. She was pleased, but not overwhelmed. She mostly wanted to make sure that White, who she called "Little Jack" that night, even though he towered over her, would take his award-grabbing turn in the spotlight. Loretta was always more concerned with truth than with rewards.

"Cultural contributions? What's that?" she asked, upon getting the Kennedy Center Honor in 2003. "I was just sayin' it like I was livin' it."

People'd go around that, but I went right through the middle. If you don't tell it like it is, it's not a very good story, is it? Tell the dadgum story like it is."

We can take many lessons from the life and work of Loretta Lynn.

"Her voice alone would have been enough," said her fellow Country Music Hall of Famer, Emmylou Harris. "But she wrote great songs, songs that told the truth from a woman's point of view—a strong woman who was a wife and a mother."

Talking about Loretta, Jack White said, "No other female in the last century was doing what she was doing: writing her own songs at a time when no woman was really doing that in Nashville, and to top it off just burning down walls between men and women."

But the main thing I draw from her is, "Tell the dadgum story like it is."

I played bass on a Loretta Lynn recording.

That's an amazing thing to say, and an even more amazing thing to say truthfully, especially because my bass guitar skills are nothing to write home about (though I'm sure I wrote home when I got to play with Loretta).

I played bass with Loretta for the same reason I played bass on Jay Leno's *Tonight Show* and on *Late Night with David Letterman*: I'm friends with a tremendous singer-songwriter named Todd Snider, and he enjoys my company enough to excuse my bass-playing. The Loretta thing came about because Todd had written a song with Loretta called "Don't Tempt Me," and because he was recording an album that included that song, and probably because he thought quite correctly that I would like to spend a few decades telling people that I played bass for Loretta Lynn.

So, thanks, Todd.

As much of a gift as it was to play on that song, the bigger gift may have come when Todd told me about writing the song.

Now, dear reader, I shall share that gift with you.

Loretta and Todd worked on "Don't Tempt" me for a couple of hours. It was a barroom song, in which a man (Todd) flatters himself by assuming a woman (Loretta) is interested in him. She floors him with a verbal punch near the end: "Big boy, don't you flatter yourself, that mirror must be showing you something else/ You've been sitting here since two o'clock, and anyone can see you're stoned as a rock."

"Stoned as a rock" was Loretta's line, I believe.

Anyway, Todd thought they'd finished the song, and he was well-pleased. He'd just written a song with the great Loretta Lynn. He thanked her, profusely. And she said, "No, we're not done."

But, he said, it was a good song.

Yes, she said, it was.

But, she said, the way Todd heard it, "We've got to take the poetree out."

"Come again?"

"We got to take the poetree out."

Todd looked at Loretta like a hog staring at an iPod.

But then he got it.

"Oh, the poetry."

"Yeah, the poetree. See that line there? That sounds like poetree. I wouldn't speak it like that. We've got to go in there and get all the poetry out of this thing."

Most songwriters work to put the poetry in.

Loretta spent a life trying to get it out of there.

Most songwriters work really hard to make something good up.

Loretta Lynn told the dadgum story.

AN ASIDE: **LORETTA AND ERNEST**

I was in Loretta Lynn's kitchen.

My presence there had been approved by Loretta's publicist. I hadn't previously met Loretta.

I was a little anxious.

She was not.

"What was your name, again?" she asked.

"Peter Cooper."

"You from England?"

"Um, no. I'm from South Carolina."

"When I went to England with Ernest Tubb, I kept meeting all these men named Peter. Seemed like everybody that come up to me was named Peter. I told Ernest, 'Ever since I got to England, I ain't never seen so many Peters in all my life.'

"He laughed and laughed. What do you think that was all about?"

CHAPTER 15

LLOYD GREEN, AND SIGNIFICANT STEEL

The steel guitar is decidedly difficult to play.

People who strum an acoustic guitar smile and nod their heads while they are playing.

People who play bass tend to act kind of disaffected and stare off into space, like they are sitting on a subway or standing in line at the Department of Motor Vehicles.

People who play lead guitar make funny faces, like they're looking in a mirror and trying to crack themselves up.

But steel guitarists stare at their instruments, with expressions of vaguely irritated wonder. They look like they're taking college board exams. The lead singer cavorts at the front of the stage, while the steel player sits and takes the ACT.

Regular guitars have steel frets, and if you put fingers in between the correct frets, the notes will be in tune.

Steel guitars have no frets. Each millimeter above the neck produces a different tone. And a steel guitarist applies pressure to the strings with a steel bar, held in the left hand. It's much more difficult to control the steel bar than it is to control individual fingers.

Ah, but that's just the start. Then there are the foot pedals and knee levers that are affixed to a pulley system that bends notes quarter tones and half tones, up and down.

I can strum an acoustic guitar in a reasonable facsimile of correctness after downing a six pack of beer, while hollering at someone to get me a seventh beer.

But playing a steel guitar requires intense and total concentration. It's way harder than flying a helicopter, and only slightly less dangerous.

That's why when you see a country band, you may see a bunch of strutting, emphatic, young people onstage, while one gray-haired fellow sits and labors. The laborer is the steel guitar player. And the reason why the young and emphatic people's image consultants allowed the gray-haired guy onstage is that young and emphatic people aren't able to play the steel guitar. This is an instrument that requires the sober certainty of experience.

In the 1950s, 1960s, and 1970s, the steel guitar was among country music's defining instruments. It is a distinctive instrument, both in appearance and in sound, and its expressiveness is positively human. It is capable of symphonic volume swoops, and its range is like that of a grand piano. But its masters are few: Everyone reading this book knows someone who plays guitar, but very few know someone who plays the steel. It's just too freakin' hard. I bought one, once, and played it for enough months to realize that I would either close myself off to the world, its women, and its wonders for a decade or more and learn to make suitable sounds, or I would just go back to playing other instruments passably.

> **Playing a steel guitar requires intense and total concentration. It's way harder than flying a helicopter, and only slightly less dangerous.**

I ditched the steel. I did not become, as rock 'n' roller Webb Wilder calls steel players, a "hillbilly scientist."

All that said, the steel is my favorite instrument. The electric guitar is a strip mall. The steel guitar is a prairie. One is over-explored, while the other is largely unchartered.

Steel guitar devotees tend to pick favorites.

Some pick Ralph Mooney, who played propulsive steel guitar for Waylon Jennings and Merle Haggard, and who co-write the classic country song "Crazy Arms."

Some—a lot, actually—pick Buddy Emmons, who brought a jazzy ethic to country steel and who was an absolute gas.

My man, though, is Lloyd Green.

Lloyd—and in musicians' lexicon, the first name is all that is needed—is to steel guitar what Sandy Koufax was to the pitcher's mound.

He is grace and mastery, personalized.

He is the most elegant steel guitarist of all time.

And he is eminently adaptable. Lloyd played the rapid-fire, "chicken-pickin'" steel on Warner Mack's "The Bridge Washed Out," and the high, keening, trebly parts on the whacked-out Johnny Paycheck songs of the 1960s, like "(Pardon Me) I've Got Someone to Kill."

He helped invent country-rock with the Byrds on the Sweetheart of the Rodeo album, and he brought playful gentility to the 1970s music of Country Music Hall of Famer Don Williams. In the 1980s, he ushered in the neo-traditionalist era by playing heart-breaking solos on the ballads of Ricky Skaggs, and then he conceived of genius-level progressive parts on the groundbreaking Americana recordings of Nanci Griffith.

Lloyd is a Mensa. And an Egyptologist. And a hillbilly scientist.

"There are certain players that are magicians rather than musicians," said steel ace Steve Fishell, nodding to Lloyd as the former.

Junior Brown, whose solo albums brought the steel guitar to greater public awareness in the 1990s, said, "The way a linguist knows how to use words, Lloyd can use notes."

Lloyd Green figured he was done in the late 1980s.

By then, he had played on more than 100 top-charting country songs, and had established himself as one of the greatest instrumentalists in Nashville history. But he was reeling from something called Maniere's Disease, a disorder of the inner ear that caused him to hear a half-tone difference between ears. Each note he played on the steel sounded to him like two competing notes, which rubbed up against the cacophony he heard when others were playing. The stress of all that was excruciating, and his blood pressure soared. All of this came to a head when he was playing a 1988 session for Lorrie Morgan's debut album, and he was unable to complete a solo to his satisfaction.

"At midnight, I was still working on the solo, and the only two people left were me and the recording engineer," he said. "I wouldn't give up, but finally the engineer said, 'Lloyd, you're a great steel player, but we ain't gonna get it tonight.' At that moment, I was so exhausted and I just accepted defeat. It was a strange feeling to be called on to do a job and not be able to do it. I left that session thinking, 'My career is over.'"

Had Lloyd's career been over in 1989, it would have been among the most stellar and impactful careers in Nashville music history.

He arrived in Nashville on Christmas day of 1956, and in 1957—the same year fellow Mobile, Alabama resident Hank Aaron won the National League's Most Valuable Player award and helped the Milwaukee Braves to a World Series title—he began working the Grand Ole Opry and touring with highly combustable country artist Faron Young.

> **Had Lloyd's career been over in 1989, it would have been among the most stellar and impactful careers in Nashville music history.**

Back then—and this is still the case—"road work" on tour with singing stars did not necessarily lead to "session work," in which musicians are paid top dollar to play on studio recordings. On the road, the wages are iffy, the accommodations can be lousy (especially in the 1950s and '60s), and the glory is largely hypothetical. In the studio, the money is good, the musical contributions are documented and certified, and travel is unnecessary. Session work is good work, so much so that in 1974 Lloyd turned down Paul McCartney's offer to join his band, Wings: There was no sense in hitting the road, even with a Beatle, because there was no guarantee that someone else wouldn't take Lloyd's place in the studio.

Road work with Faron Young was neither productive nor lucrative, and Lloyd ended up taking a job as the assistant manager of a Little Rock, Arkansas shoe store.

"It was a miserable experience," he said. "(wife) Dot and I decided to leave Arkansas, and so we sold what furniture we had, put our belongings in a U-Haul, and came back to Nashville."

That decision was very, very good for Nashville. In 1964, Lloyd took a job at SESAC, a music-licensing organization. He also began playing on demo (short for demonstration) recordings, on which musicians create lo-fi versions of songs, so that the songs can be more easily perfected in "master" recordings. A demo recording is like a dress rehearsal, or a football scrimmage.

In demo recordings, Lloyd was working on a unique sound.

"I'd been experimenting with a different style, where I would use a sharp-edged sound but mute the strings with the bottom of my hand," he said. "They call it chicken pickin' now. Well, when Warner Mack heard me playing that way, he said, 'I've got a song that's perfect for that style.' He came over one night and we worked up 'The Bridge Washed Out,' just him and me."

Warner Mack's producer was Owen Bradley, an architect of the "Nashville Sound" who normally used session steel player Pete Drake. Mack asked to use Lloyd rather than Pete Drake, and Owen Bradley answered in the reluctant affirmative.

"When I got to the session, it was a strange relationship with Owen," Lloyd said. "He tried his best to humiliate me . . . But when we got to 'The Bridge Washed Out,' Bob Moore (the greatest bass player in Nashville history) put his bass down and said, 'That's a hit sound you've got there. That's going to get you some bucks.'"

"The Bridge Washed Out" became Warner Mack's first (and only) top-charting hit, and it was the first Number One country hit to feature significant steel guitar from Lloyd Green. Other steel players emulated Lloyd's style, and chicken pickin' was all the rage. Yet Lloyd refused to replicate himself, and he wound up playing differently on each session. For Johnny Paycheck, his tone was biting and trebly. For Lynn Anderson, he played strong and full. On Tammy Wynette's "D-I-V-O-R-C-E," he used his pedals to produce a crying effect that was in keeping with the song's sad story. On Charley Pride's In Person album, he was richly dominant.

In 1968, California rock band the Byrds came to Nashville to record, hoping to make an album that would ingratiate them with country music fans and that would point their longtime fans to the beauty and worth of country music. On March 16, 1968, Lloyd joined the Byrds on the stage of the Grand Ole Opry, as the only "straight" Nashville player joining band of rockers. That night, the Byrds were booed by the normally docile Opry audience.

"Lloyd had to know it was going to be that way, and he had a lot of guts to get up there with us," said Chris Hillman, leader of the Byrds. "He was a gentleman, but a courageous gentleman, and such a great player."

Lloyd says he actually didn't expect the booing, and that he was embarrassed enough to want to crawl off the stage. He wasn't embarrassed to be part of a band that was being booed, he was embarrassed at what he calls the crowd's "rude" and "redneck" behavior.

The album that grew out of the Byrds' Nashville recording sessions is called *Sweetheart of the Rodeo*. Upon its release, it was viewed, at best, as a sidestep, and, at worst and most often, as a failure. Now, it is viewed as a groundbreaking recording, one that is honored in the Grammy Hall of Fame as being of "lasting qualitative or historical significance" because it blurred the lines between country and rock.

Hillman told journalist David Fricke, "We were the pioneers—with arrows in our backs."

The years removed the arrows, and now Hillman, Gram Parsons, and the rest of the circa-1968 Byrds are viewed as musical heroes. Lloyd is a hero as well, and he's one of the reasons why Nashville is a truly ecumenical "Music City" rather than a "Country Music City." In 1966, Bob Dylan came to Nashville to record an album called *Blonde on Blonde* with Nashville session musicians, and that album signaled to other musicians that Middle Tennessee was one of the world's best places to make music, because of the musicians who lived and worked there. Dylan's embrace led the Byrds, Joan Baez, Gordon Lightfoot, and many others to come to Nashville, but it was the musicians' ability to shift between country, rock, and R&B that made all of this possible.

Business people divide music into categories. Musicians don't divide music. Musicians are into addition, not division, and the great ones are multipliers.

Paul McCartney, late of the Beatles, came to Nashville in 1974.

McCartney was of the reputation, wealth, and proficiency that he could go anywhere to make music, and he could record with anyone he chose.

He chose to come to Nashville, and to record with Lloyd Green.

With Lloyd, McCartney recorded a song called "Sally G," and another called "Junior's Farm."

Lloyd was impressive enough that McCartney asked him to join his band on the "Wings Over America" tour. Had Lloyd agreed to the tour, each concert would have featured a fifteen-minute country music segment. It would have clued hundreds of thousands of listeners into the wonders of the pedal

Lloyd turned down the Beatle. It is, he says, the biggest regret of his career.

steel guitar. It also would have cost Lloyd a lot of money: He was playing multiple sessions each day in Nashville, and sleeping in his own bed. And a disappearance from the Music City recording scene would have come with no assurance that studio work work would be waiting for him when he returned.

Lloyd turned down the Beatle.

It is, he says, the biggest regret of his career.

His regret doesn't stem from financial concerns. Rather, he thinks he could have bolstered the perception, direction, and popular appeal of the steel guitar had he gone on the road with McCartney.

The steel guitar is country music's greatest, most mysterious, most evocative instrument. But very few folks know how to play it, which means very few folks get to hear it. I played a show in a little town near Athens, Ohio one time, with a fine steel player named Jerry Brightman. Jerry was in one of Buck Owens' classic bands. He was a pro. And the people in this little town had never heard anything like him. Most of them had never been up-close to a steel guitar. After the first set, they were walking up next to the stage, looking at the instrument, and taking selfie photographs of themselves with the steel.

Another time, I was recording a song called "Cheatham Street Warehouse" with Todd Snider. I was playing bass and singing harmony, and we'd called Lloyd Green to play steel guitar. The recording was done in the same home studio where Loretta Lynn had recorded her Grammy-winning Van Lear Rose album, and Lloyd was set up in the kitchen. Todd had been around steel guitars some, but he'd never been around a steel player the caliber of Lloyd Green. Since Todd had already sung his vocal and we were "overdubbing" (that means adding instruments to the song, after the song's basic elements have already been recorded) Lloyd's part, Todd was free to be anywhere he wanted to be in the studio. He went to the kitchen and lay down on the floor next to the steel, so he could look up as Lloyd operated the knee levers and foot pedals. He was quite literally at the master's feet. Lloyd didn't mind. He thought it was cute.

Like I said, Lloyd thought his career was done, back in 1989.

A steel guitarist trying to play through Meniere's Disease is akin to a baseball pitcher playing through a broken elbow. The player, who must command his instrument with a level of precision that other instruments do not require, can't hear the proper note. Even if he plays it right, it sounds all wrong.

"It was a nightmarish experience," he said. "One day, everything started sounding terrible. The steel guitar sounded like a tin can. I picked up the phone one day, then switched ears and realized I was hearing a half-tone difference between ears. The stress exacerbated the problems, and my blood pressure was going through the roof."

And so he walked away.

For a year, he didn't play the steel. He studied history, and he ran long distances, and he did anything else he could to keep his mind off of country music. He tried not to ponder the extent to which the steel was losing favor with country music producers. In the 1990s, the instrument began being used not as a featured instrument but as sonic padding. In his prime, he'd developed

In a Madison, Tennessee basement, just north of Nashville, Lloyd Green began again.

a different sound and approach for each artist with whom he worked. In the '90s, steel players on hit country records—with notable exceptions including Vince Gill's "Look At Us"—played simple parts that said very little, like a reluctant husband at his wife's office Christmas party.

That's what was happening on the radio. But in a Madison, Tennessee basement, just north of Nashville, Lloyd Green began again.

Through the 1990s, the master was a student. He had to re-learn and re-imagine, battling atrophy and some measure of private indignity as he chipped away at Maniere's. To the music world, he was the shining hero who had transformed thousands of recordings. But in his windowless basement, he flailed away. In 1991, his practice sessions were like a past-prime boxing ex-champion's grim training in the months after being KO'd by an upstart. But by the century's closing years, he was a wizard once again. Plenty of instrumentalists had fallen from the precipice and lost their mastery. Lloyd was bent on being the one to regain everything he had lost.

As it turns out, he did just that.

"I wouldn't have come back if I wasn't capable of doing it," Lloyd told me in 2003, one year into his purposeful return. But he worried, with good reason, that he was a skilled soldier fighting a war that was already over.

"I'm not sure some producers think it's a viable concept to use steel as a legitimate instrument instead of just as a color," he said. On some sessions, he was asked to essentially dumb down his playing: His steel was there to remind people that they were listening to something that was supposed to be "country" music, not to play anything of significance.

But in the spring of 2003, he got a call from Keith Stegall, who produced tradition-minded country music superstar Alan Jackson.

Jackson normally worked with another steel guitar great, Paul Franklin. But he was recording a ballad called "Remember When," and it cried for a Lloyd Green solo.

Lloyd entered the studio, a 65-year-old man among much younger musicians who were tasked with making a commercially viable recording for the contemporary market. One minute and fifty four seconds into the song, Jackson's simply expressive words and melody give way to one of the most gorgeous instrumental parts in country music history: Lloyd Green was back, and he knew it.

"This will be Alan's next single, to be released in the fall, and is the solo opportunity I've been waiting for since I restarted sessions," Lloyd said. "Good melody, good lyrics, major artist, almost certainly a Number One record . . . and a long solo that doesn't sound like anybody else except me. I never gave less than my best on any session, large or small. Yet this one does take on a larger magnification of importance, much akin to that long-ago session of anther era with Warner Mack, "The Bridge Washed Out," when a lot of my future as a musician seemed to ride on the capricious whims of a song, a singer, and a producer.

"I was all of twenty-seven years young, full of ideas and enthusiasm, and ready to add to the musical vocabulary of the steel guitar. Damn, this has a quality of deja vu."

"Remember When" is probably the last of the 117 Number One country singles Lloyd Green has played on.

That's not because his skills dissipated: into his late seventies, he played with the speed, finesse, and musicality evident in recordings from a half century before. The decided lack of Lloyd in commercial country recordings of the first two decades of the new century is due to changes in the sounds favored by radio programmers. Once one of country music's signature instruments, and a defining element in the records of Country Music Hall of Famers Hank Williams, Charley Pride, Merle Haggard, Buck Owens, Connie Smith, Don Williams, Patsy Cline, and the majority of country artists from the 1940s through the 1990s, the steel became at worst a non-entity and at best a color (gray is a color, right?) in radio-ready country music.

> **The decided lack of Lloyd in commercial country recordings of the first two decades of the new century is due to changes in the sounds favored by radio programmers.**

"The steel guitars no longer cry, and fiddles barely play," sang George Strait and Alan Jackson in a stylistic protest song called "Murder on Music Row." "But drums and rock 'n' roll guitars are mixed up in your face."

That song came out in the year 2000. Ten years after that, "rock 'n' roll guitars" were being deemphasized as well, and "drums" were often computerized facsimiles of actual drum sets. Radio programmers began requesting versions of songs in which guitar solos were either cut short or edited out entirely.

"The listeners' attention spans are shorter and shorter, and if they start getting bored . . . it's too easy for them to go somewhere else," radio consultant Joel Raab told Tom Roland of *Billboard* magazine, in 2015. "So it's really about forward momentum on the radio station. Is that guitar part moving everything forward? If it is, great. If it's not, then maybe it needs to be edited."

That's one perspective. But a radio programmer's notion of "moving everything forward" can be vastly different from a music producer or musician's idea of the same.

"On country radio, there's a tendency to edit out the guitar solos to save time," is what Brad Paisley, one of modern country music's most skilled guitarists, told Roland.

Radio stations also speed songs up, sometimes as much as 4%, to save time. If you feel some barely perceptible difference between a song you hear on the radio and the same song heard via other means, that's likely the difference.

Music most often makes an impact via surprise and delight. The former can lead to the latter. But terrestrial radio station playlists aren't designed to surprise or to delight. Programmers seek familiarity and uniformity. For the listener, the best radio experience is to hear something new that we instantly love. For the radio programmer, the best thing that can happen is for the listener not to change the station.

Surprise can not only lead to delight, it can lead to displeasure. If you hear new music that makes you want to seek out the music-maker's recorded works or live shows, and I hear that same new music and it causes me to change the channel to a sports talk station, this is a poor outcome for the programmer who played that new music. If you and I hear a song on the radio that we've heard for months, or that sounds like the other songs on the radio that we've heard for months, and the result of this is that we listen passively but don't change the station, this is a fantastic outcome for the radio programmer, who can tell the local automobile dealership that advertising on his or her (and it's usually a "he") station makes perfect sense. The folks who run the automobile dealership certainly don't care whether you are surprised or delighted by music. They want you to listen to the Chevy truck ad and decide that you would be delighted to drive a brand new Silverado.

If, dear reader, you are anticipating a rant about tin-eared radio programmers, or a remembrance of the long-gone days when stations would program the Beatles and Johnny Cash, back-to-back, or an angry screed detailing my disgust at the lack of steel guitar in general and Lloyd Green in particular on the radio . . . well, then I may surprise but will not delight you by telling you this:

It's not radio's fault.

It's your fault.

Well, maybe not your fault, personally.

It's our fault, as a nation of people who tend to lack musical curiosity.

If you aren't satisfied with what you're hearing on the radio, simply quit listening to the radio and go listen to something else. You have the entirety of recorded popular music at your fingertips. There are no gatekeepers between you and the music you want to hear. Radio isn't obligated to serve you, and you are not obligated to sit there and wait for your service.

If you aren't satisfied with what you're hearing on the radio, simply quit listening to the radio and go listen to something else.

People who complain about the lack of quality music on the radio are people who would sit at Commander's Palace in New Orleans, eating pecan encrusted drum fish and complaining about the lack of fresh seafood at the Applebee's out by the interstate.

As the Traveling Wilburys sang, "Anything you want, you got it." And, as a bonus to you and a severe minus to content creators, you can usually get it for free.

If you like steel guitar, you don't have to wait in vain to hear some significant steel on the radio. You can go online and access an abundance of steel guitar. Lloyd Green, Buddy Emmons, Ralph Mooney, Don Helms, Sneaky Pete Kleinow, Al Perkins, Ben Keith, and all the rest of them are up there in the cyber-beyond, waiting for you to have a listen.

Whatever kind of music you like, the beauty of our digital age is that you don't have to be passive about it. Yet people still gripe about their dissatisfaction with radio gate-keepers.

Friends, there is no gate left to keep.

We act as if radio programmers fail at some hypothetical responsibility to music.

We act as if the "best" (there's another hypothetical) music "deserves" wider attention, and more airplay.

Bullshit.

Well, mostly bullshit.

Lots of music does "deserve" wider attention, it just doesn't deserve more airplay on terrestrial radio stations.

Radio stations aren't equipped to spoon-feed you the music that pleases you most.

You are equipped to spoon-feed yourself the music that pleases you most.

Your connection to the music world is a champion rock climber. Why wait in line for the escalator?

For three Nashville years, a ferocious singer named Chris Stapleton sang lead for a soulful, Grammy-nominated bluegrass band called The SteelDrivers. That band played once a month at the Station Inn, a wonderful Music City club, and everyone who saw and heard The SteelDrivers marveled at the power and emotion in Stapleton's voice. The guy was, clearly, a monstrous talent. He was immediately compelling, surprising, and delightful, and many of us who heard him wondered (stupidly) why a voice like that wasn't on the radio.

Stapleton left The SteelDrivers in 2010, and he wound up signing a record deal with a major country label, Mercury Nashville. He recorded an album called *Traveller*, which came out in 2015 to great critical acclaim, and to decent sales (it made its debut at number two on the *Billboard* country album chart).

Country radio programmers' give-a-shit meter was fundamentally unmoved by the critical kudos or the album sales. *Traveller*'s debut single made it to number seventeen on the country charts, meaning it failed to gain any kind of positive consensus among radio people. Stapleton continued on as a little-known performer who sang his ass off every night onstage. People in the Nashville music industry understood how good the guy was, though, and when it came time to vote for the Country Music Association's CMA Awards, they voted in his favor. Without a single in the Top 40 of the country charts, he triumphed as top new artist and best male vocalist, and *Traveller* was named Album of the Year.

Those wins were as close to shocking as industry awards can get. Stapleton won out over well-established artists who had sold millions of records. He won because the voters found it difficult, even out of self-interest or company loyalties, to assert that anyone in contemporary country sang better than Chris Stapleton.

That's not the important part.

The important part of that CMA Awards night came when Stapleton took the stage. He was up there for eight minutes, sharing a performance with pop star Justin Timberlake. Stapleton was, as always, commanding and endearing and undeniable. But this time, he was commanding and endearing and undeniable in front of sixteen million television viewers and, later, a whole bunch of people who watched and listened via the Internet.

> **He won because the voters found it difficult, even out of self-interest or company loyalties, to assert that anyone in contemporary country sang better than Chris Stapleton.**

Instantly, Chris Stapleton became the biggest phenomenon in country music. *Traveller* shot to the top of the charts: country and pop. It had been absent from the all-genre Billboard 200 chart since September, but it was atop that chart the week after the CMA Awards.

The album sold more in the week following the CMA Awards than it sold in total from its May release until November. Soon, sales topped the million mark, and then it was on to the next awards show, and Stapleton dominated at that one, winning six trophies.

Stapleton was, by far, commercial country music's biggest story of 2015 and of 2016, though you'd have never known that by listening to the radio.

Immediately after the CMA Awards, Mercury Nashville released a Stapleton single called "Nobody to Blame." I figured that radio programmers would have to play it, and that it head quickly to the top of the airplay charts, like the album had gone to the top of the sales charts.

Nope.

Radio people didn't have to play it.

It didn't fit their format.

Some of them played "Nobody to Blame," and it wound up scraping its way up to number ten on airplay charts. "Nobody to Blame" was named song of the year at the Academy of Country Awards, but it was never even a song of the week on country radio.

Maybe the lack of radio play had to do with a decision Stapleton and co-producer Dave Cobb made in *Traveller*'s planning stages: They decided to call a virtuoso musician named Robby Turner into the studio, to play an assload of significant steel guitar.

It's not the case that Lloyd Green's comeback resulted in numerous high-profile recording session gigs with contemporary country artists. But he has made stupendous contributions to multiple recordings that fall into the amorphous, country-affiliated sub-genre called "Americana."

There is an actual Merriam-Webster dictionary definition for "Americana," but it is best defined as "music someone might define as 'country' that is not played on country radio." Early in the 2000s, some music-loving friends of mine formed the Americana Music Association, and they formally embraced the music of artists like Cowboy Jack Clement, Nanci Griffith, Emmylou Harris, John Prine, the Byrds, and Buddy Miller, all of whom Lloyd has worked with. They also claimed as "Americana" the contributions of Country Music Hall of Fame members Johnny Cash, Loretta Lynn, and Willie Nelson, all of whom Lloyd has played with.

As an Americana recording artist myself, with dozens of fans all over some of the world, I asked Lloyd's help in making music. I featured him on more than a handful of albums, and I have been roundly praised for my supposedly generous gesture of asking Lloyd Green to play significant steel.

Asking Lloyd Green to play on an album is akin to asking Michael Jordan to play on your pickup basketball team in 1991. It is a gesture of inherent selfishness, yet of irrefutable logic.

That said, Lloyd has had fun with it. I give him recordings of my guitar and vocals, and he sits in his basement and works out mind-bending steel guitar parts. Then he comes into the studio and plays those parts. And then I bring in other players to color around Lloyd's steel.

Works like a charm. I can legitimately say that if people want to hear some of the greatest pedal steel guitar of all time, they can listen to my albums. I even called one of them *The Lloyd Green Album,* just to clue people in to what they were hearing.

Many times, Lloyd has said something to me that no guitar player or keyboard player could say: "I've come up with something for your song. Something that's never been played before."

I treasure a photograph taken by my friend Stacie Huckaba. It is from a night at the Station Inn, when Lloyd was playing in my band. He had just played a remarkable solo, one that brought people to their feet and caused Station Inn booker Lin Barber to ring the cowbell up by the bar. Lloyd played the solo with characteristic seriousness and attention, appearing hard at work to everyone there. But when he completed the solo, he smiled broadly and acknowledged the crowd's riotous applause. When the song was over, the show was over, and people stood and cheered. Lloyd stood up and walked to where I was, and shook hands like we were agreeing on some solid deal. In truth, we had long ago agreed. The handshake, and Stacie's photo, were only happy reminders.

AN ASIDE: LLOYD GREEN AND MIKE AULDRIDGE

Lloyd Green was rehearsing with me. Or, more properly, I was rehearsing with him.

We were sharing a rehearsal room with my pal Eric Brace, and with Eric's band.

Eric's band included my original dobro hero, Mike Auldridge, from the Seldom Scene. Mike was a gentleman, a groundbreaking musicians, and perhaps the biggest Lloyd Green fan on the planet. Mike wrote a song called "Lloyd's of Nashville," just to solidify his appreciation for all things Lloyd Green. Mike studied every note Lloyd ever played, and Lloyd was a Mike Auldridge fan as well: He considered Mike to be the first elegant dobro player in music history, and he had great admiration for Mike as a player and as a person.

At the rehearsal, I called for a song called "Wine." I'd written the song with my friend Baker Maultsby, and Lloyd had invented an incredible steel guitar part for "Wine." Lloyd's part involved a super-human bending of the metal steel guitar bar, one that would pull most every other steel guitarist far out of tune.

When Mike heard me announce that we would be rehearsing "Wine," he walked up to where Lloyd was playing, and he asked if Lloyd would mind if he stood behind Lloyd and watched Lloyd play the song.

"It'll be like a lesson for me," Mike said, and Lloyd said anything Mike wanted to do was fine with him.

We played the song, and Mike got an up-close understanding of what and how Lloyd played his part. He watched Lloyd's hands fly like birds across the steel guitar neck, and I watched him watching Lloyd. Mike Auldridge, one of the most beloved instrumentalists of my time, looked like a 12-year-old kid watching a sports hero. People use the term "slack-jawed admiration" a lot, but this was the first time I saw a musician's jaw drop in the presence of another musician.

At the song's end, Lloyd turned towards Mike, with a slightly cocky, slightly cautious half-smile.

Mike, the creased-jeans gentleman and musical innovator, just said, "Fuck you, Lloyd," and walked off in profane agitation and evident admiration.

REQUIEM FOR A SHORT BITCH

Ann Soyars initially thought she'd had a light stroke. As it turned out, she had tumors on her brain, liver, kidney, and lungs.

She was dying, at age 67.

And her dying was cause for great grief among a great number of musical Nashvillians, many of whom grabbed their guitars and headed to a sixth floor hospital room at Saint Thomas Midtown in Nashville, so that she spend the little time she had left around the thing she most loved, which was music.

Not just music, special music. The sixth floor at Saint Thomas became the greatest concert venue in Nashville for a few weeks in 2014. Then, when the doctors admitted there was nothing in the hospital that could turn Ann around, she went home, and her picker friends followed.

John Prine, the closest thing Nashville has to a poet laureate, came and sang "Souvenirs": "I hate graveyards and old pawn shops, for they always bring me tears/ I can't forgive the way they rob me of my childhood souvenirs."

Chris Stapleton, soon to become a country star, came with his sweet-singing wife, Morgane, and played a Townes Van Zandt song called "Rex's Blues": "It's legs to walk and thoughts to fly, eyes to laugh and lips to cry/ A restless tongue to classify, all born to grow and grown to die."

Contemplative songs were welcome, but Ann didn't allow expressions of sorrow or, God forbid, pity. The Van Zandt lyric that the Stapletons sang commands, "Tell my friends to mourn me none," though Ann was less poetical in her admonitions. I walked tentatively into the hospital room, only to be greeted by Ann's weathered but familiar bark: "No sad motherfuckers allowed up in here."

Country music superstar Dierks Bentley came to sing, as did bluegrass legend Del McCoury, gospel quartet The Fairfield Four, Country Music Hall of Famer Bobby Bare, and so many more. You'd have thought Ann Soyars was some kind of dignitary, or a revered performer, or a record executive, but she was none of these things.

"I feel like the luckiest person in the world, and I've had some really bad luck," she said, a year before she died. "I worked in Kentucky for BellSouth for thirty-two years, took a buyout, and was going to live happily ever after. Then the market went to hell in a hand basket, and I lost everything."

Everything but her fondness for music and musicians. Broke and nearly broken, she wound her way to Nashville and found a soft place to fall in the form of the Station Inn, a dumpy treasure that is one of the world's greatest places to listen to bluegrass and acoustic music.

The Station Inn is situated in Nashville's Gulch, an area of skyscrapers, luxury condos, impossibly expensive restaurants, and singers who work as parking valets while waiting for their big break. Amidst all of that bustle and gleam is the Station Inn, a window-less, ground-level rectangle that looks from the outside to ready for a wrecking ball. Inside the door, though, the Station Inn is a rare and righteous room that features tremendous music, seven nights a week. Every major figure in bluegrass music has played the Station Inn, and superstar guests frequent the

> **Amidst all of that bustle and gleam is the Station Inn, a window-less, ground-level rectangle that looks from the outside to ready for a wrecking ball.**

place, often popping up onstage. Anytime someone asks about the "soul of Nashville music," I point them to 402 12th Ave. S., and tell them to get their early: There are no advance tickets, and everybody pays at the door.

The "everybody pays at the door" thing is the cause of numerous nightly discussions, which is where Ann proved herself invaluable. She ended up befriending Station Inn owner J.T. Gray, who asked her to help out around the Inn, in exchange for meager pay and great happiness. Among Ann's many duties was "working the door," which meant collecting the entry fee from each patron at the beginning of the night, and giving that money to the musicians at the end of the night. An honest door-person is a universally beloved figure in the music industry.

At the door, Ann became "Short Bitch," the no-nonsense counterpart to her buddy Lin Barber, who was known as "Tall Bitch."

"She was always a joy," John Prine said. "She and Lin would work these running comedy bits on you, like Abbott and Costello doing 'Who's on First.' She was so outgoing and showed her love for you as soon as you walked in the door. She was a short little woman, but her capacity for putting out love was way, way bigger than she was."

Ann was a lover, but she was not a negotiator. The door charge was the door charge, unless the person seeking entrance was a musician who Ann knew to be down on their luck. When an attractive couple walked up to Ann and Ann told them that the cover was $20, the man asked, "Do I look like I have twenty dollars?" Ann eyed him, then eyed his well-dressed date, and said, "I don't know, but she looks like you have twenty dollars."

As a tandem, Ann and Lin called themselves "the huggingest bitches in town," and those hugs often involved ass-grabs that would have gotten others in hot water. If they backed a legend of American song into a corner and posed for a photo, the legend of American song was likely going to get goosed, just before someone snapped the picture. Without fail, everybody loved it.

Another thing musicians loved about Ann was her complete devotion to the music that was coming off the stage. The Station Inn serves beer, and sometimes people who drink beer together get talkative. Chatter is distracting, and distraction is the enemy of art. If people were talking at the Station Inn while music was playing, Ann became the world's least physically impressive bouncer.

She'd walk over to chatterers and say, "Those people onstage are the greatest of the great, and you are either going to shut the fuck up and take in the best music you've ever heard or I am going to take you out of here."

Most of the time, they shut the fuck up and took in the best music they'd ever heard.

Some of the time, she took them out of there.

Ann wasn't there for confrontation, though.

She was there to love. Unless you were there to talk through what she loved, and then she was there to tell you to shut the fuck up.

In addition to working the door, booking talent, shushing rowdies, and hugging everyone in the room, Ann worked as a talent scout. This work was unofficial and unpaid, but she took it seriously. She understood music, and she spotted potential where others did not. When a funny-named Vanderbilt drop-out began making sporadic and cautious appearances behind the Station Inn microphone, Ann knew immediately that he would one day be a star.

She befriended the kid, and learned to spell his unusual name. Then she started going to all of his shows, selling his independently produced CD for him, and telling buyers, "You'd better hang onto this. He's going to be big someday." Then she made two t-shirts, each of which read "#1 Fan of Dierks Bentley, Future CMA Winner." She kept one of the shirts, and gave the other to Bentley's mother.

In 2005, Bentley won the Country Music Association's Horizon Award, as the most impressive country music newcomer of that year. On November 5, 2014, he was nominated for five CMA Awards and had a performance slot on the show. Upon learning of his nominations, he asked Ann to be his date for the show.

She promised she would, but cancer had attacked too hard and too fast. Dying was bad enough, but to Ann the crueler blow was missing Dierks' big night.

Though he couldn't take her to the show, Bentley made several trips to Ann's dying bedside. When she was out of the hospital and back at the house, he came and got her out of bed, then took her for one last car ride, in his black 1967 Camaro.

When he got her back to bed, he climbed in to hold her, and Ann temporarily allowed one sad motherfucker up in there.

Ann's other big talent scout find was Chris Stapleton, who she believed was an undeniable talent, even in the years that record executives spent actively denying that talent. She worked the door at Stapleton's first sold-out show, when he was singing lead for the SteelDrivers. Chris and his wife, Morgane, often came to sing for Ann as her health deteriorated. They'd sing songs they knew Ann cared about. One was Van Zandt's "Rex's Blues." Another was "Traveller," which would become the title track to Stapleton's first country album, which came out in May of 2015, six months after Ann died.

Stapleton wrote "Traveller" after his father died, in 2013. The song is about the cycle of life.

"I can't tell you, honey, I don't know/ Where I'm going, but I've got to go/ 'Cause every turn reveals some other road."

Music gets recorded a long time before the public hears it. It takes a long time to get the art finalized, get the promotions team ready to roll, book concerts and television shows around the official release, and all of that. Sometimes music gets recorded and it never gets released at all, it just sits on some hard drive in silent obsolescence. Ann was anxious to here the music Stapleton had recorded, and Stapleton was under orders to keep that music to himself. Instead, he and Morgane gave a CD copy of *Traveller* to Ann. It became the soundtrack to her dying. Her CD player was tucked in bed beside her, and Chris's rich and soulful leads and Morgane's silken harmonies filled the somber room. When she died, nine days after she was supposed to have accompanied Dierks Bentley to the CMA Awards, Ann's friends fulfilled her request to have her CD copy of *Traveller* cremated with her.

One year after Ann died, Chris Stapleton became a country music star. The music from *Traveller* touched millions, and the woman who loved it first wasn't around to hug and cuss and pinch asses and celebrate about it. I could say that Stapleton's ascent came a year too late, but if Ann were here she'd tell me to shut the fuck up about all that.

I don't think she'd mind me mentioning that she was a delight, or that she bolstered spirits and pricked puffy attitudes, or that she was mean about meanness, or that she was hilariously rude to the rude. Or that Dierks Bentley said she was the best friend to music that he's known in Nashville. Or that Chris and Morgane Stapleton made a point to tell the world about her when they were finally in a position to bend the world's ear. Or that she created a vibrant and beautiful music community simply by opening her heart and mind and arms and mouth.

"She asked me after she got sick, 'Why does everybody love me like this?'" said Melonie Cannon, another supremely gifted singer whom Ann loved and supported and championed, and who nursed Ann on her way to wherever the hell she is now. "I said, 'Ann, because you have loved us like this.' She has been the cheerleader and the therapist. She fed us if we were hungry, and let us in the club when we were broke. This town is full of wanderers and gypsies and vagrants. She had a way of connecting us all together, and believing in us when we didn't believe in ourselves. That's why we became her family."

AN ASIDE: THE MAYOR OF EAST NASHVILLE

Skip Litz was a soundman, which is different from a sound man.

I won't assert that he was a sound man. He was happily unsound. But he was good at sitting behind the soundboard at a show, and adjusting the levels and frequencies so that the music sounded its best when it came out of the speakers.

He was also a road manager, which means he was responsible for checking musicians in and out of hotels, and for getting the music-makers to the proper place at the proper time.

He was also the unofficial mayor of East Nashville, and since there was no official mayor of East Nashville—because East Nashville is not a city—that made Skip the actual mayor of East Nashville. By the way, East Nashville isn't an actual city. It's just the stuff on the east side of the Cumberland River. Because it was one of the last parts of town where "creative types" (code for "non-wealthy") could buy property, it got a reputation as a freewheeling neighborhood. In that neighborhood, Skip got a reputation as someone simultaneously welcoming and foreboding. He was the mayor: if you knew him and he liked you, things were going to get easier in your life. If he knew you and he didn't like you, things were going to be tough. If he didn't know you, you didn't play music and thus you didn't figure into the equation.

Being the mayor did not place Skip above the law. One night, he was riding his motorcycle at a rapid rate of speed, and he caught the attention of the East

Nashville police. When he saw the flashing blue lights, he slowed his Harley down to four miles per hour, but he didn't stop. The cop called more cops, and soon there were multiple police cars "chasing" one Skip Litz, who drove slowly past every bar in East Nashville, waiving to the proletariate.

The cops beat Skip up once they finally apprehended him. But Skip thought it was worth it: He had been at the forefront of the greatest low-speed police chase in the history of East Nashville.

Skip had a website. If you went to his website, you could read about him.

Name: Skip Litz.
Location: Earth.
Favorite things to do: Live music, drink whiskey, enjoy life.

Skip had a hard life.
Combat duty in Vietnam.
Biker gang stuff.
Run-ins with the law.
Bad heart.
Bad liver.
Hernia operation.
Man, we all loved him.

On his website, there was a link headed "Ladies Only," and when visitors clicked on it they received the message, "This is just for the ladies. Just in case no one told you today, you are beautiful."

He was road managing Todd Snider one time, which meant he had to sneak Todd's tiny dog, Lulu, into hotels. In Atlanta, Skip checked Todd into a hotel that didn't accept dogs. Then Skip carried Lulu in his arms, right through the lobby, and a guy behind the hotel desk saw this happening and said, "Is that a dog?"

Skip looked the guy square in the eye and said, "No." Then he and Lulu got on the elevator, and no one said another word about it.

Another time, Skip was supposed to take gig proceeds and feed everybody who needed feeding.

This was a Todd Snider gig, and Todd was paid in $100 bills.

Skip went to the local Taco Bell, guided the van to the drive-through, and when the Taco Bell lady said, "Welcome to Taco Bell, how may I help you?" Skip asked, "Can you change a hundred dollar bill?"

She could not.

Skip was nonplussed. He said, "Then give me $100 worth of tacos."

CHAPTER 17

"HELLO, I'M JOHNNY CASH"

Johnny Cash was reminiscent of no one.

No one as a singer.

No one as a songwriter.

No one as a person.

He was a singular force, communally received.

And, while most country music standouts inspire imitators, Cash did not. After Jimmie Rodgers died in 1933, generations mimicked his Mississippi drawl and his blue yodel. Lefty Frizzell's sliding, slurring singing style inspired Merle Haggard to sing in a similar manner, and ever since Haggard's first hits in the mid-1960s, "traditional" country singers have been imitating Haggard (and, thus, imitating Lefty Frizzell).

If you sing like Haggard, you are a traditionalist. But if you sing like Cash, you are just doing a Johnny Cash impression. You might as well do Richard Nixon saying "I am not a crook," or do Marlon Brando doing the Godfather. You might entertain, but your entertaining will be based in replication, not in creation. And so, other than Johnny's brother, Tommy Cash, no hit-making country singer has emerged who sounds even remotely like Johnny Cash. There's really no point.

I can claim no great personal relationship with Cash, other than the deep relationship that I have with his music. That music sprung from inside of him, so in a way I'm closer to Johnny Cash than I am to many of my friends. Maybe you are close to Cash in that way, too. I knew him well enough to know that he was as layered and deep and mysterious and hilarious as we all suspected he might be. And I can tell you that he was the most charismatic presence I've ever witnessed.

Roger Miller, the most quotable of Nashville geniuses, said Cash had "Animal magnetism . . . . In fact, he was undressing the other day and a dog bit him."

If you and I were standing in a room facing north, and Johnny Cash walked silently through an open door at the south end of the room, we would know instantly that the room had changed. We would feel a presence. And when we turned around, we'd be freaked out to see Johnny Cash standing there, because he has been dead since 2003.

Hearing that Johnny Cash had died was like hearing the Grand Canyon had died. It didn't make sense. Dolly Parton said "Johnny Cash has only passed into the greater light. He will never, ever die."

But I went to the visitation, and to the open-casket funeral. He was dead, alright.

I know what Dolly meant, though. She meant that his dying did nothing to end his impact and import. She meant that people will still be talking about Johnny Cash many years from now. He just can't talk back.

Merle Kilgore, Cash's longtime friend and the co-writer of his 1963 hit, "Ring of Fire," heard about Cash's death and said, "Man, an earthquake hit us this morning." A truck driver named Bobby Williams said, "He was the greatest man ever picked a guitar."

There were millions who grieved, and they grieved with a sorrow that was personal. Though he was in some ways unknowable, everybody knew Johnny Cash.

A friend of mine named Andy McLenon said, "I guess I'll try to numbly get through the day as I start trying to adjust to the total alien concept of a world without Johnny Cash in it."

Cash was elemental, is what I'm trying to say. He was more granite and fire than flesh and blood.

He wrote a song once where he pondered, "I wonder if I ever really did leave, how many would there be to grieve?" The day he died, the answer was evident: There were millions who grieved, and they grieved with a sorrow that was personal. Though he was in some ways unknowable, everybody knew Johnny Cash.

Now, what he meant to everybody was different.

To Kris Kristofferson, he was "a true American hero," but also "a walking contradiction, partly truth and partly fiction."

To Snoop Dogg, he was "A real American gangsta."

To me, he was a bunch of things. He was a believer, in people and in kindness and in God, though his daughter Rosanne accurately wrote, "He believes what he says he believes, but that don't make him a saint."

That's what he wasn't: a saint. But he was a bunch of other things.

For sure, he was an attention-payer. I remember interviewing him on Wednesday, October 18, 2000, the morning after Democrat Al Gore's final presidential debate with George W. Bush.

"Did you see the debate last night?" he asked. "I thought Gore stomped him. Everybody's got an opinion, but I thought Gore was so much better."

Being so much better didn't wind up helping Gore, who wound up winning more votes than Bush but losing the electoral vote and, thus, the election.

After Cash died, I told the story of the Johnny Cash endorsement to Al Gore. He kind of pumped his first when I told him. It made him feel better about the whole losing-the-election thing.

It didn't make him feel good about it . . . just made him feel better.

Cash was born in Kingsland, Arkansas, in the middle of the Great Depression. His name wasn't "John," it was "J.R." His father wanted to name him John, and his mother wanted to name him Ray. "J.R." was the compromise.

When he was three years old, his family moved to Dyess, Arkansas, northeast of Memphis, Tennessee. The move was one of desperation: The Cash family agreed to farm a plot of lousy land, in a Roosevelt administration rehabilitation project.

"Actually, it was a socialistic setup with a co-op store and a co-op cotton gin," Cash wrote in an autobiography, *Man In Black*. "The intention being that the farmers would share any profits form the gin and the store."

Cash was forever changed when he was twelve years old, and his brother Jack was fourteen. Jack took a job cutting timber, for $3 a day, to help his family. John, the more whimsically minded of the brothers, went fishing. While trying to cut a board, Jack lost his balance and fell into a head saw, which is the saw that makes the initial cuts in large pieces of wood. Days later, after hours of horrific pain, he died. Johnny Cash felt guilt, remorse, and sadness over the incident for the rest of his life.

Jack died on a Saturday morning in May. The following Monday, the Cash family was back chopping cotton. Mother Carrie Cash fell to her knees in the field.

"Lest you get too romantic an impression of the good, natural, hard-working, character-building country life back then, back there, remember that picture of Carrie Cash down in the mud between the cotton rows, on any mother's worst day," Cash wrote, in a second memoir.

There in the sticky Arkansas mud, which the locals called "gumbo soil," Carrie Cash's head dropped to her chest. Father Ray tried to take her arm, but she rebuffed him, saying, "I'll get up when God pushes me up."

Later, God pushed her up, and she went on about her work, bent at the waist, saw briars cutting her legs, cockle burrs sticking to her common clothes, the images of her son—an infant, a smiling boy, a bloody mess, a corpse—in her head. Her lot was to grieve and to work, but not in that order. J.R. saw this, and understood more about life and living than he'd ever wanted to understand.

Eight days after Jack died, J.R. Cash walked the aisle at the Church of God, shook the preacher's hand, and said he'd accepted Jesus Christ as his Lord and savior.

Johnny Cash's daughter, the singer-songwriter Rosanne Cash, told author Michael Streissguth that her father was profoundly wounded by Jack's death, and by his own father's blame and bitterness: "If someone survives that kind of damage, either great evil or great art can come out of it. And my dad had the seed of great art in him."

Dyess cotton fields offered nothing in the way of transcendence, unlike the radio.

J.R. listened voraciously to the radio, and particularly to the Grand Ole Opry, which beamed from Nashville each Saturday night. He loved gospel music, and songs about hard times, like Vernon Dalhart's "The Prisoner's Song." He loved Jimmie Rodgers, and the Carter Family. When Jack was alive, the brothers sang together in the cotton fields, lifted by words and melodies that offered grander possibilities than anything they saw with their own Dyess eyes. In a 1970 songbook, Johnny Cash wrote a dedication to Jack: "Though the songs that we sang are gone from the cotton fields, I can hear the sound of your voice as they are sung far and wide."

One of the acts J.R. heard on the Opry was The Louvin Brothers, a harmony duo from Sand Mountain, Alabama that embodied the pentecostal fervor, the worldly wonder, and the mortal terror that reverberated through J.R.'s brain. In 1947, the Louvins often played Smilin' Eddie Hill's High Noon Roundup on Memphis radio station WMPS, and the Cashes would listen as Ira Louvin's smooth and ethereal high tenor melded with Charlie Louvin's dusky, earth-bound voice. In the summer of 1947—the same summer that Jackie Robinson integrated major league baseball, a dark black man wearing the pressed white uniform of the Brooklyn Dodgers—the Louvins came to Dyess, for a concert at the schoolhouse.

J.R. got to the concert two hours before it was slated to begin, hoping to meet a singing star. The Louvins arrived in a black Cadillac. J.R. watched them unloading equipment, and then Charlie Louvin walked right up to the fifteen-year-old Cash and asked him where the restroom was. It was the first time Cash had met a famous person, a voice from the radio. He pointed Charlie to the restroom, and noticed that the singer had soda crackers in his pocket. Cash asked if the crackers were good for your throat. Louvin

> **He called that evening the greatest of his childhood, and he never forgot Charlie Louvin's unspoken lesson: Small kindnesses can impact a life.**

said, "No, but they're good for your belly if you're hungry."

Asked before the show if he had a request, J.R. asked that the Louvins dedicate a song to his mother, who was listening at home. The song they chose to dedicate "to J.R.'s mother" was a gospel song about dying, called "I'll Have a New Body (I'll Have a New Life)":

"Won't it be so bright and fair, when we meet our loved ones there/ I'll have a new body, praise the Lord, I'll have a new life."

Cash walked two-and-a-half-miles home in the pitch-black dark that night, but not before Charlie Louvin waved goodbye to him from the back seat of the Cadillac. He called that evening the greatest of his childhood, and he never forgot Charlie Louvin's unspoken lesson: Small kindnesses can impact a life. In later years, when his own fame far eclipsed that of Louvin or of any other country singer, he took care to take care, praising unknowns, lifting the fallen, or speaking truthfully when his truth would bring some measure of joy.

At times, these tendencies got him in trouble. At a prison concert, Cash was moved by a song written by inmate Glen Sherley. He not only recorded the song, he aided Sherley's release from prison, he gave Sherley a job, and he brought him the road. Sherley wasn't meant for straight life, though, and Cash had to dismiss him after the ex-con made violent threats to others in the House of Cash operation. Sherley killed himself in 1978, after shooting another man in a drug dispute. Sherley was buried in Salinas, California, and the funeral was paid for by Johnny Cash.

Cash graduated high school in 1950, whereupon he moved from Dyess to Michigan, making car hoods on an assembly line. He figured that gig would at least be better than cotton farming, though his figuring wasn't necessarily correct. In short order, he joined the U.S. Air Force, though the military wouldn't accept "J.R." as a legitimate first name. J.R. Cash became John R. Cash, and all of that eventually led to "Johnny." Around friends and family, he never much went by "Johnny": In 1981, he sent a hand-written letter to Tom T. Hall, in which he wrote, "You are my all time favorite writer." He signed that one, "John."

In the Air Force, Cash learned some guitar chords, and he saw a movie called *Inside Folsom Prison* that helped him conceive of his half-borrowed hit song, "Folsom Prison Blues." He was shipped to Germany during the Korean War, where he worked as a radio operator, learned to intercept and decipher Russian morse code, and, depending on who you believe, may have been the first American to learn of the death of Soviet Union Premier Joseph Stalin.

"Radio operator, in a tiny foreign room," sang his daughter Rosanne Cash, in a 2007 song that was part of her Grammy nominated *Black Cadillac* album. "We can hear you now and later, calling out and coming through."

Discharged in 1954, John R. Cash moved to Memphis and married the former Vivien Liberto. He worked as an appliance salesman, and he enrolled at the Keegan School of Broadcasting. In those

> **It was Phillips who told Cash that Sun Records had no use for a gospel artist. He asked Cash to write secular material, and Cash came back to him with "Hey Porter!" and "Folsom Prison Blues."**

days, musicians often launched their careers as disc jockeys, and Cash had hopes of becoming a gospel singer. He put together a little group of rudimentary-level players—a guitarist named Luther Perkins and a bass player (once he and Cash worked to figure out how to tune an upright bass) named Marshall Grant—and went to see producer Sam Phillips at Sun Records. It was Phillips, an uncommon visionary, who recorded Elvis Presley in July of 1954 and launched the rock 'n' roll revolution. And it was Phillips who told Cash that Sun Records had no use for a gospel artist. He asked Cash to write secular material, and Cash came back to him with "Hey Porter!" and "Folsom Prison Blues," the latter of which borrowed mightily from Gordon Jenkins' 1953 song "Crescent City Blues." (Which takes its melody from a 1930s Little Brother Montgomery instrumental, also called "Crescent City Blues.")

Phillips liked the songs but wasn't sure they were hits. He asked Cash to write what he called "an uptempo weeper love song," and Cash responded with "Cry! Cry! Cry!", which was paired with "Hey Porter!" as Cash's first Sun single. In addition to setting a Guinness World Record for exclamation points, "Cry! Cry! Cry!" became Cash's first Top 20 country hit.

Writers Colin Escott and Martin Hawkins claimed that Cash's first single offered an originality that had been absent in country music since Hank Williams' death on the first day of 1953. But Escott and Hawkins also wrote that "Musicians scoffed" at this new and original music. To say Cash's band was lacking in technical virtuosity is to say that slugs are lacking in fast twitch muscle fiber: These were people who were just learning to play their instruments. Perkins' playing frustrated Cash, but Phillips saw the beauty in what the producer termed "perfect imperfection." Perkins filled Cash's songs with little electric guitar runs that any other guitar player could easily play, but that no other guitarist had conceived. The primitive and inelegant sound became an instant signature, and when Phillips perceived that Perkins had been practicing his way towards deftness, he would take Luther's guitar and keep it at the studio, to keep refinement from the realm of possibility.

Perkins played the simplest of riffs, Grant played the simplest of bass, and Cash threaded folded paper through his guitar strings, to produce a tone that, when captured on microphone, sounded vaguely like a snare drum. The outfit was dubbed Johnny Cash and the Tennessee Two, and together Cash and the Tennessee two created a clicking sound that came to be called "boom-chicka-boom."

Cash later wrote that the men didn't work to get that "boom-chicka-boom": It's all we could play. But it served us well, and it was ours."

Springtime of 1956, and Johnny Cash and the Tennessee Two were at 706 Union Avenue, recording a song called "I Walk the Line." The song's lyrics offered pledges of faith from Cash to his young bride, and the melody was a marvel of Sam Phillips' preferred kind of artistry: Perfect imperfection.

That melody was inspired by Cash's time in the Air Force, when he was listening to a reel-to-reel tape player and heard what he called a "haunting drone full of weird chord changes, something that sounded like spooky church music."

The tape turned out to be a recording of Cash's Air Force band, which he called the Landsberg Barbarians. But it had been placed incorrectly on the tape player, resulting in the odd sounds. Cash kind of liked the odd sounds, and composed music that replicated them.

Cash, Perkins, and Grant recorded a fast and a slow version of "I Walk the Line" on that Memphis day. Cash preferred the slow one. Sam Phillips preferred the fast one. Since Sam owned the label, the fast one was released. Soon, "I Walk the Line" became Cash's first chart-topping country hit, and it also crossed over into the pop charts.

That July, two years to the day after Elvis Presley recorded Bill Monroe's "Blue Moon of Kentucky" at Sun Records, Johnny Cash played the Grand

Ole Opry for the first time. He wore a white jacket with black trim that his mother, Carrie, had made for him, twelve years after she buried J.R.'s brother Jack.

Cash was introduced by Opry star Carl Smith as "the brightest rising star of country music," and he introduced himself backstage to Carl's wife, June Carter. She was the daughter of Maybelle Carter, who was the first guitar hero of country music and the originator of the influential guitar style known as "The Carter Scratch."

When Cash met June, he told her, "Someday, I'm going to marry you." She grinned and said, "Do you think so?" He said, "Yeah, someday I'm going to marry you, June."

A week later, Nashville Banner reporter Ben A. Green reported what happened when Cash first took the Opry stage.

"He had a quiver in his voice, but it wasn't stage fright," Green wrote. "The haunting words of 'I Walk the Line' began to swell through the building, and a veritable tornado of applause rolled back. The boy had struck home . . . . One

> **When Cash met June, he told her, "Someday, I'm going to marry you." She grinned and said, "Do you think so?"**

onlooker told us, 'He'll be every bit as good as Elvis Presley. Probably better, and he'll last a whole lot longer. He has sincerity, tone, and he carries to the rafters.'"

When it was over, Cash told Green, "I am grateful, happy, and humble. It's the ambition of every hillbilly singer to reach the Opry in his lifetime."

"I taught the weeping willow how to cry/ And I showed the clouds how to cover up a clear blue sky," Cash sang in "Big River," a song released in 1958 and heard on the radio by a young man named Robert Zimmerman, who by then was beginning to call himself "Bob Dillon." That name would morph to "Bob Dylan," and Bob Dylan would become a transformative figure in American song. In 1969, Cash wrote liner notes for Dylan's Grammy-winning *Nashville Skyline* album. But in 1958, Dylan was Zimmerman, and Zimmerman was enraptured. He later told writer Nicholas Davidoff that Cash's "Big River" lyrics struck him as "words that turned into bones."

The first day of 1959, Cash was an established star, and he chose to celebrate the new year with a concert at San Quentin State Prison, in Marin, California. By then, he was also celebrating with amphetamines, habit-forming drugs that dogged him the rest of his life. The drugs often made him hoarse, turning his cave-deep baritone into a rasp, a squawk, or nothing at all. On New Year's Day, it was a rasp, and yet it commanded the assembled prisoners, one of whom was future Country Music Hall of Famer Merle Haggard.

"Prison is a good place to find out the truth, because them convicts won't lie," Haggard said. "They ain't got no reason to give you any clout that you don't deserve. And we saw the truth that day."

After Haggard was out of prison, he met Cash, who told him he should come clean with the public about his past. Haggard worried that if his burgeoning audience knew he was an ex-convict, they would abandon him. Cash told him that people are prone to forgiveness, and that openness and honesty trumped perfection. Haggard took the advice, and it proved true, in his case at least.

Johnny Cash wound up on Columbia Records. He left Sun in 1958, frustrated by Sam Phillips' reluctance to let him do a gospel album and, no doubt, excited by the prospect of recording for a major record label. He and Sam bickered about the arrangement, but they got over it. Cash was an honorary pallbearer at Sam's funeral in 2003. And Sam's insistence on perfect imperfection helped Cash find his way as an artist.

> **He left Sun in 1958, frustrated by Sam Phillips' reluctance to let him do a gospel album and, no doubt, excited by the prospect of recording for a major record label.**

"When it dawned on me that I didn't sound like anybody else naturally, I let it come naturally," Cash told Bill Flanagan in 1998. "Of course, that was the secret of my success. It ain't no secret: Be yourself."

In the late 1950s, Cash triumphed with an album called *The Fabulous Johnny Cash* and a chart-topping single (for six weeks) called "Don't Take Your Guns to Town," and he was on his way to popular ubiquity.

"The 1960s were probably my most productive time, creatively speaking," he wrote in his second memoir, Cash. "Often I wasn't in my best voice, because the amphetamines dried my throat and reduced me, at times, to cracks and whispers, but that wasn't the story all the time, and my energy and output were high."

His destruction was also rampant. He messed up hotel rooms, cancelled shows, started fires, kicked out the footlights at the Grand Ole Opry, served jail time, and frightened his wife and four daughters. He was a holy terror. And his marriage to Vivien Liberto was in grave danger. In 1962, June Carter, then married to Rip Nix, joined the Johnny Cash road show. She was Florence Nightengale, and Cash was something of a trainwreck. In 1963, she wrote a song with Merle Kilgore that Cash made a classic: "Ring of Fire."

"A song like that goes on forever," Cash told me, in 2002, and it did . . . and it does.

He also appeared at the New York Folk Festival in 1965, recorded a Bob Dylan song ("It Ain't Me Babe"), recorded a concept album about the indignities done to Native Americans, and publicly supported the civil rights movement.

"When I was young, I saw my dad speaking out against the Vietnam War, speaking out against the Ku Klux Klan, and that's where my social activism is rooted," Rosanne Cash said. "He never bent. He never even almost bent."

He and Vivian divorced in 1967, with his pill-fueled debauchery finally forcing the hand of a Catholic woman who believed marriage to be sacred, and believed the cessation of marriage to be sinful.

By then, it was clear that he had eyes for June Carter, and it was clear that June was bent on cleaning him up, and righting his path. Late that year, he committed himself to getting off drugs, though commitment is closer aligned with belief than with permanence. Again, as Rosanne Cash wrote, "He believes what he says he believes, but that don't make him a saint."

Cash, June, the Tennessee Three (drummer W.S. Holland joined in 1960, turning the Two into the Three), and other members of Cash's touring outfit went to Folsom State Prison in 1968, and recorded one of country music's most significant albums, At Folsom Prison. Cash delighted prisoners with a humor-and-profanity-laced stage set, complete with songs about egg-sucking dogs and the "Cocaine Blues." He was carnal, wild, and wise, and producer Bob Johnston (who had pushed Columbia Records to green-light the recording) brilliantly captured the performance.

The Folsom Prison shows kicked off a remarkable, joyful, and harrowing year.

In February, he proposed to June onstage, and he married her a month later. In August, longtime guitarist Luther Perkins died. House fire. Sleep and lit cigarettes are uneasy partners. As the success of At Folsom Prison reinvigorated his career, Cash was faced with his friend and musical partner's horrific end.

The moon-shot year of 1969 found Cash navigating in terrains new and studied. In February, he recorded with Bob Dylan on Dylan's *Nashville Skyline* album, and he returned to San Quentin to record a second blockbuster prison album. This time, he arrived with a new song in hand, about the very place that hosted him:

"San Quentin, may you rot and burn in hell," he sang, as his incarcerated audience shouted in appreciation and anguish. If Cash had shouted "Break!" into the microphone, the prisoners would have rioted.

During a rehearsal, photographer Jim Marshall said to Cash, "John, let's do a shot for the warden." Cash quenched up his face, looked right at Marshall and shot his middle finger at the camera. It was the biggest, most potent bird-flip in recorded American history.

At San Quentin was a hit upon its June, 1969 release, and that same month ABC began airing The Johnny Cash Show.

"This is Johnny Cash, coming to you from Music City, USA, home of the Grand Ole Opry," he announced at each show's beginning. Then he'd go on to introduce guest stars from Louis Armstrong to Bob Dylan to Tom T. Hall to Neil Young. The program, which ran for three years, served to broaden Cash's fame among those who hadn't listened to country music, and it served to emphasize the connections between all forms of American roots music.

Cash sold more than six million records in 1969. Vietnam raged. Richard Nixon presided. Neil Armstrong walked on the moon. Johnny Cash, 37, was bigger than the Beatles.

"Where are your mountains to match some men?" he wrote, in tribute to his friend and admirer, Bob Dylan, in liner notes to *Nashville Skyline*. But he could have been writing about himself: "There are those who are beings complete unto themselves/ Whole, undaunted, a source . . . Some souls like stars, and their words, works and songs like strong, quick flashes of light."

Johnny and June Carter Cash had a son, born in March of 1970. Six months later, Cash played the White House. A Richard Nixon aide told Cash that the president would like to hear him sing right-wing country anthems recorded by Merle Haggard—"Okie From Muskogee"—and Guy Drake.

Guy Drake is largely lost to history. But in 1970, he released a noxious one-hit non-wonder called "Welfare Cadillac." The song came from the hypothetical point-of-view of an impoverished father of ten children, who has purchased an expensive car by cashing government checks.

"My kids get free books and all them free lunches at school," Drake sang. "We get peanut butter and cheese, and, man, they give us flour by the sack/ 'Course, them welfare checks, they make the payments on this new Cadillac."

The song is, essentially and repugnantly, a slur.

"The way that I see it, these other folks are the fools/ They're working and paying taxes just to send my young 'uns through school."

Nixon requested this song.

He requested this song be sung by Johnny Cash, who grew up on land paid for by the government. He requested this song be sung by Johnny Cash, who sometimes embodied indignity but who believed in inherent dignity.

He requested this song be sung by Johnny Cash, an unlettered child of poverty who had been invited to perform at the White House, for the leader of the free world.

Cash said "No."

"I'm not an expert on his music," Richard Nixon said, introducing Cash on April 17, 1970. "Incidentally, I found that out when I began to tell him what to sing. He owns a Cadillac, but he won't sing about Cadillacs tonight."

Infant John Carter Cash slept on the White House's third floor, unaware but forever impacted by his father's quiet moral stand.

Johnny Cash was honored to play for the president, but as an artist, not a pawn.

For the most part, the seventies were awful for Johnny Cash. And the eighties were worse.

His television show was cancelled in 1971. His recordings were scattershot: "Since the late '60s, Cash's records have been rather strange—more the recorded evidence of a great artist floundering in confusion than the masterful products of Cash's own unique mold," wrote Patric Carr of Country Music magazine, at the time.

In 1984, Cash entered the Betty Ford Center and was treated for morphine addiction. Two years later, he was released from Columbia Records, the same label that successfully promoted the artful work of his daughter Rosanne. Cash signed with Mercury/Polygram and reunited with his old pal, Cowboy Jack Clement, for some fine but under-appreciated albums, and then he went about trying to secure another record deal.

At one point, Cash went around Music Row with his guitar, taking office meetings in hopes of finding a new record deal. He and his acoustic guitar played for a label boss named Jimmy Bowen—one of country music's most impactful producers and executives—who told Cash something like, "Thanks, I'll give you a call."

No call ever came.

> **For the most part, the seventies were awful for Johnny Cash. And the eighties were worse.**

"Saying goodbye to that game and just working the road, playing with my friends and family, for people who really wanted to hear us seemed very much like the thing to do," Cash wrote.

He was ready to give up. It had been a good run, as commemorated by his 1992 induction into the Rock and Roll Hall of Fame. We would all revere him. We would all understand that he had done great and indelible things in his limited time.

Rick Rubin was a producer of rock and hip-hop music.
He had produced Run-DMC, and the Beastie Boys, the Public Enemy.
He adored Johnny Cash.

He asked Cash what he'd like to do, and what he'd never done. Cash said that these things were one and the same: He's like to record with his guitar, his strumming thumb, and his voice, just as he'd done in Jimmy Bowen's office.

Rubin said, "Sure."

The result was *American Recordings*, a solo/acoustic album that rescued Cash from creative quicksand.

The album was brilliant and simple. Simply brilliant. It included two songs performed in December of 1993 at hip West Hollywood venue the Viper Room, where actor River Phoenix had died months before.

"It's odd to be in a place like the Viper Room, which is a small but loud nightclub,

> **"I think I'm more proud of it than anything I've ever done in my life,"** he said. **"This is me. Whatever I've got to offer as an artist, it's here."**

and have it be so quiet," Rubin told writer Nick Tosches. "It's nothing you could imagine happening, that kind of silence and awe in an audience in that particular kind of place."

Upon the release of *American Recordings*, Cash addressed the silence and awe of much younger audiences. At a 1994 Austin, Texas concert, he told the crowd, "I hope you enjoy the show, grandchildren."

American Recordings brought Cash to the forefront, yet again. A Time magazine review proclaimed that he was had "reasserted himself as one of the greats of popular music."

Cash was as pleased as punch. He had ceased any trend-battling, recording in a timeless fashion, with only an acoustic guitar and his canyon-deep voice.

"I think I'm more proud of it than anything I've ever done in my life," he said. "This is me. Whatever I've got to offer as an artist, it's here."

American Recordings won a Grammy for best contemporary folk album. After years of decline, Cash was cool again. He was in the mainstream media. He was at a show celebrating the opening of the Rock and Roll Hall of Fame. He was appearing onstage and in the studio with Tom Petty and the Heartbreakers.

He was back, if not from the dead then if from the missing-and-assumed-dead.

Cash's second Rubin-produced album, *Unchained*, came out in 1996. That one featured Petty and other contemporary favorites, and it included selections such as "Rusty Cage," from alternative rock band Soundgarden. The resurgence contained with a Kennedy Center Honor in December of 2006: Vice President Al Gore recommended Cash for the honor, asserting that Cash's music examined "the entire range of existence, failure and recovery, entrapment and escape, weakness and strength, loss and redemption, life and death."

Kris Kristofferson, Emmylou Harris, Lyle Lovett, Robert Duvall, and others joined Rosanne Cash in the Kennedy Center tribute to Johnny Cash, and the Man In Black wiped tears upon hearing his daughter.

The day after, as Johnny Cash wrote, the adulation turned to examination.

"My daughters got together with me and voiced some very deep feelings they'd had for a very long time—told me things, that is, about the lives of girls whose daddy abandoned them for a drug," he wrote.

It was less than a year after the Kennedy Center Honors that Cash just about fell during a concert in Michigan. He told the audience that he was suffering from Parkinson's disease, and they laughed at first.

"It ain't funny," he said. "It's all right. I refuse to give it some ground in my life."

Cash cancelled concerts and book promotions through 2007, though he later claimed that the culprit was not Parkinson's. Years later, we don't know what the actual medical condition was that burdened Cash, that palsied him, that turned solid and formidable into shaky and temporal.

In 1998, Cash won a best country album for Unchained. He's received nothing in the way of attention from country radio programmers or from the industry establishment, yet his work was judged as the best of anyone in the genre.

As he reeled from illness, Cash's pugnacious spirit made waves. He approved an advertisement in *Billboard* magazine in March of 1998: "American Recordings and Johnny Cash would like to acknowledge the Nashville music industry and country radio for your support," the copy read.

The accompanying photograph was of Cash raising a riotous middle finger at San Quentin, in 1969.

"Johnny Cash and I are as close as two men can be," Merle Haggard told me. "He's able to laugh and sing and joke, but he's in a lot of pain. He lives in pain and chooses between pain and pain pills. The only way he can enjoy life is to put up with the pain and not have any pills."

Around that time, Cash and Rick Rubin released an album called *American III: Solitary Man*. On it, Cash recorded a song called "One," popularized by internationally prominent rock band U2.

"I think he's really talking about a love affair," Cash said to me. ""He says at one point, 'We hurt each other, and we're doing it again.' A good love affair gone wrong needs some good work on it. I'm speaking from experience. June and I have done that. We've accomplished that. That song hit home to me solidly, from personal experience."

I asked it his illness had tested their marriage, or if had been a strengthening factor.

"The fighting June and I did and the love affair gone wrong was years ago," he said. "Nobody could ever have a truer companion through the sickness as June was. We're closer now than we've ever been in our lives. We've seen a lot of them die and fall . . . but she and I have fought together and fought for each other, and we're one."

I asked him what scared him. He answered addiction and God.

June Carter Cash died on May 15, 2003. At her funeral, Johnny Cash sat in the front pew and was lifted to his feet at the end of the service. He leaned over his wife's casket, then was aided back to his chair and was wheeled out of the church.

In the following weeks, he returned to recording, out of duty and sorrow.

That spring, he sang at the Carter Family Fold, in Maces Springs, Virginia, within walking distance of where June had grown up. He was hoarse and weak.

"I don't know hardly what to say tonight about being up here without her," he said. "The pain is so severe, there is no way of describing it."

Johnny Cash was reminiscent of no one.

No one as a singer.

No one as a songwriter.

No one as a person.

He was a singular force, communally received.

I've told you all that already.

I saw him in a casket adorned with a wreath of roses, potatoes, figs, and cotton bolls.

I saw him there, three months after June died.

He was only seventy-three.

He was, as Kris Kristofferson said, "The best of America."

He was, as Kristofferson also said. "A holy terror."

Accent on holy.

AN ASIDE: IRISH BAR, JACKSONVILLE, FLORIDA

Four hours before a gig with my brother-of-the-road, Eric Brace.

We were in an Irish bar.

I was typing this book.

Eric was watching a European soccer game, because he fashions himself an international type.

Ireland was playing somebody-or-another in the soccer game, which was cause for interest and enthusiasm in our bar.

Ireland lost. I'm sure the score was 1-0, because all soccer games end in scores of 1-0.

When the game was over, people left, because they were pissed.

I typed, because I had a book to turn in.

Eric listened to announcers pontificate about the game, because, like I said, he fashions himself an international type, and some of the broadcasters had European accents.

I told Eric that the game ended the way it ended because the team that wasn't Ireland had kicked a ball into the goal, whereas Ireland had not.

Then i got back to typing, with the game over and the bar cleared.

Since they had nothing else to do, the waitresses began talking with each other about superheroes.

One of the waitresses said her favorite superhero was Batman, because Batman was a regular guy who had great tools and used them to his advantage.

The other waitress said she liked Batman just fine.

The first waitress said, "Is he your favorite?"

The second waitress said, "My favorite superhero?"

"Yes."

"My favorite superhero is Johnny Cash. He makes Batman look like a little bitch."

CHAPTER
18

GEORGE JONES: WALK THROUGH THIS WORLD WITH ME

Writing is pretty easy, as long as there's a delete key and enough time to use it.

You can write anything you want, and then get rid of it if it isn't right. And no one will ever know the difference. You can take it back, and you don't even have to say, "I was only kidding."

People sometimes ask me, "What was your toughest writing assignment," and I always had trouble answering.

Then, in May of 2013, I got my toughest writing assignment.

"Would you please write George Jones's gravestone?"

Search an acre of marble and you won't find one delete key.

"The King of Broken hearts doesn't know he's the king," wrote Jim Lauderdale. "He's trying to forget other things/ Like some old chilly scenes he's walking through alone."

Jones never forgot those scenes. Even the ones he was too drunk or high or sad to experience in real time—car wrecks, arrests, fist fights, and other indecencies—came back to him in woeful remembrances, recounted in barrooms, bedrooms, and court rooms.

He treated his talent with reckless abandon that bordered on scorn.

"I messed up my life way back there, drinking and boozing and all that kind of stuff," he told me in 2008. "And you wish you could just erase it all. You can't do that, though. You just have to live it down the best you can."

He said that as he was preparing to accept a Kennedy Center Honor from the president of the United States, at the nation's most prominent arts celebration. Days later, $15,000 dresses would rise from $4,000 seats so that their inhabitants could applaud the astonishing life of George Glenn Jones. The most important people in America were celebrating the very thing Jones was trying to live down the best he could.

He used to have to get drunk to sing that way . . . to communicate unblinking emotional truth . . . to convey the powerful terror of betrayal, desperation, and hopelessness, and to walk alone again through the old chilly scenes.

There is no best, no greatest, in music. It's all subjective, all shaded.

But if there was a best or a greatest singer of country songs . . . it's tough to listen to "Walk Through This World With Me," "The Window Up Above," or "He Stopped Loving Her Today" and not say what Patrick Carr wrote in *The Village Voice*: "Jones is definitely, unequivocally, the best there ever was or will be, period." It's tough to hear him slide towards sorrow on the first line of "These Days (I Barely Get By)"—"I woke up this morning, aching with pain"—and not say what Cowboy Jack Clement said when he called Jones "The greatest country singer who ever lived . . . The music just flows out of him. It's the most natural thing."

What a burden he shouldered, to be the most natural conduit for despair in the history of a musical form that dwells so often in sadness. In essence, George Jones cried, and every time we heard him weep we applauded and begged him to bawl some more. Then we wondered aloud why he drank so much.

Born in 1931.
Depression times.
Saratoga, Texas.
Alcoholic, angry father.
Chilly scenes too dark even for sad songs.

But there was a catalog guitar that served as a connection to some vague better place. He took that guitar with him on the way to school, hiding it in the woods and covering it with leaves during the awful hours of arithmetic and book learning.

"If a big rain came and it got wet, I'd pour the water out of it," he said. "Them guitars never warped."

He took that guitar with him to the streets of Beaumont when he was twelve, seeking and receiving things in short supply at home: approval and pocket change.

"A lot of them started throwing change down in front of me, down on the concrete," he said. "When I was done, I counted it and it was $24 and something, and that was more money than I'd ever seen in my life."

That money bought candy and pinball games at a penny archive. He was a kid, drawn to childish things but also to the adult-minded music of his hero, Hank Williams. His love for Williams abided into adulthood, when Jones joined the U.S. Marine Corps, still searching for some vague better place. On the first day of 1953, he celebrated a brand new year. Two days later, a fellow marine passed him a newspaper, with a headline that said Hank Williams had turned up dead in Oak Hill, West Virginia. Jones cried, with no one applauding, in disbelief that someone so dear to him had died, as he later put it, "in such a distant land."

Jones got out of the service in 1954, and he began recording for an independent record label called Starday, based in Beaumont. He moved from there to Nashville's Mercury Records, where he recorded his first Number One hit, a raucous up-tempo song called "White Lightning." Jones was already in the habit of nipping during his sessions, and at the time the only way to make a record was to record the vocals and the instruments at the same time. If anyone made a mistake, they had to start the song over. It took 83 runs through "White Lightning" before the song was recorded to satisfaction.

In the 1960s, Jones moved through record labels and wives, and he recorded classic songs, including "She Thinks I Still Care," the devastating "A Good Year for the Roses," and the rollicking "The Race is On." (On the latter, you can hear him drunkenly slur the lyric that was supposed to be "break right down and bawl" into "ray right down and bawl.") Usually, you couldn't hear the extent to which Jones was inebriated in the studio. His singing voice sounded sober when his speaking voice was tragi-comedically drunk. This was problematic when there was a spoken-word piece within a song, but otherwise the alcohol seemed to allow him the comfort to sing what was profoundly uncomfortable, and the expression to reveal feelings that the rest of us work to mask.

The drinking was a way of life, though, not an artistic intent. Jones' second wife, Shirley, was disgusted with him after he'd been drunk for several days, and she decided to hide every car key in the house, so that Jones couldn't make it to the nearest liquor store, eight miles away. She neglected, though, to hide the keys to the riding lawn mower. An hour and a half later, George Jones had another bottle of booze.

> **The alcohol seemed to allow him the comfort to sing what was profoundly uncomfortable, and the expression to reveal feelings that the rest of us work to mask.**

"There are those who'd like to change the way I'm living," he sang. "It seems they just don't like me the way I am/ Tomorrow, I may live the way they're thinking/ Oh, but tonight I just don't give a damn."

Not shockingly, Jones' marriage to Shirley didn't last. Neither did his next partnership, to the country singing star Tammy Wynette, though that pair recorded memorable music both during and after their legal union. George and Tammy were known to fans as "Mr. & Mrs. Country Music," and they recorded together for producer Billy Sherrill, who Jones called "The Little Genius." The Little Genius wasn't able to figure out how to make Jones straighten up, though. A padded-cell detox didn't help, and neither did the initial threat and eventual certainty of another failed marriage. Neither did lawsuits over the shows he missed, or cold, hard handcuffs that cut into his wrists. Neither did the lyrics of the songs he sang: "I've Aged Twenty Years in Five," or "A Drunk Can't Be a Man."

"I got to my lowest point, where I knew in my thinking that there was no way back at all for me," he told me. "I'd thrown everything away . . . I tried to put puzzles together to make some way out that could turn out positive, and there was nothing."

Nothing. Not the music, for certain. The songs he sang seemed to help the people who heard them, yet they drove the singer to further misery. Music played the same role for him as liquor plays for an alcoholic bartender.

Sherrill thought he might have an answer in the form of "He Stopped Loving Her Today," a ballad written by Bobby Braddock and Curly Putman. The song is about a man who pledges his devotion to a departed lover: "He said 'I'll love you 'til I die'/ She told him 'You'll forget in time.'"

He doesn't forget. The "today" in "He Stopped Loving Her Today" was the day he died.

Sad song, then, about a love both eternal and unrequited. It reminded Sherrill of Jones' feelings about Tammy Wynette. He showed it to Jones in 1978, and Jones paid it little mind. He thought it was unduly long, and unnecessarily depressing. It took more than a year before Sherrill convinced Jones to record it.

"'He Stopped Loving Her Today' took a year to make, and ten years off my life," said Sherrill, who died in 2015, at the age of 78. "That's the *Twilight Zone* of all records. That song destroyed me. I knew someone was going to hit with it, and I thought Jones could be the one."

Jones didn't think so, but eventually Sherrill wore him down. But making George Jones do something and making George Jones do something properly . . . those were separate initiatives.

"I couldn't get him to sing it right," Sherrill said. "He sang it with the melody of Kris Kristofferson's 'Help Me Make It Through the Night.' I called him on that, and he said, 'That's a better melody.' I said, 'I'm sure Kris Kristofferson would think so . . . it's his.'"

Then there was the issue of the song's spoken word portion, made difficult because Jones could sing sober when he spoke drunken. But Sherrill finally got what he wanted, and he was convinced that "He Stopped Loving Her Today" would revive Jones' flagging career.

The men gathered in the studio control room to listen to the playback of the finished recording. Sherrill, the Little Genius, heard a classic. Jones heard irredeemable anguish.

"You know what Jones said?" Sherrill asked me, and I didn't. So he told me. "He said, 'Mark my words. I know you're all excited about this record. Nobody's gonna buy that morbid son of a bitch.'"

They bought it. They loved it. "He Stopped Loving Her Today" won Grammy, Country Music Association, and Academy of Country Music Awards. Many times, it has ranked atop lists of all-time greatest country songs and singles. In three minutes and seventeen seconds, Jones salvaged what would be a fifty-nine year career.

Did it end his misery? No, of course not.

In 2001, I walked George Jones and his fourth wife, Nancy, through the Country Music Hall of Fame and Museum's exhibit halls, and George told me stories about the objects on display. He got emotional when he saw a Gene Autry-model catalog guitar on display, because it reminded him of his first guitar, the one he played on the streets of Beaumont. He lingered long enough at a dress worn by Connie Smith to make me believe he once had quite a personal admiration for Connie Smith. And then he spotted his own stage suit on display.

Nancy pretended to read from a sign next to the suit.

"It says, 'George Jones was the meanest little thing,'" she "read." "'He has now outgrown all his meanness and is married to the sweetest woman in the world.'"

Jones didn't realize she was joking. He thought the text was plausible. He thought it sounded like the God's honest truth.

Nancy Jones, George's fourth and last and best wife, was the one who calmed his agitations, rounded his edges, and led him to something ultimately approaching sobriety and happiness. She did this by force of will and by sense of mission. She did this in fits and starts, and in between setbacks that others would have considered final straws. She did this by loving him unconditionally and by riding his ass constantly.

They married in 1983, at a time when Jones was strung out, dogged by federal agents of various varieties, dodging lawsuits and mafia bad guys. No job pays less by the hour than the job of keeping George Jones straight in 1983, but Nancy did her damndest. Over time, with the help of open-heart surgery and a horrific car wreck, she wore him down.

His surgery came in 1994, two years after his induction into the Country Music Hall of Fame, and nine years after he recorded a song called "Who's Gonna Fill Their Shoes," which is about legacy. The song, which was a major hit, name-checked Merle Haggard, Elvis Presley, Hank Williams, and many others, wondering who could possibly take the place of such icons. Listeners made the natural leap, pondered who could fill Jones's shoes, and decided no one could.

Jones's heart scare turned out to be a fairly small bump. He and his scarred chest recovered from the wounds of healing blades, and he set about recording more sad songs to make the rest of us feel better. He was working on his first album for Asylum Records, *The Cold, Hard Truth*, when his crashed his sport-utility vehicle into a bridge near his home.

He was almost home.

He'd been drinking from a vodka bottle.

They rushed him to the hospital, and treated his collapsed lung, which changed his voice for the worse.

He nearly died.

Then there was the shame, and the DUI admission, and, finally, the fear of God and the love of Nancy.

After the crash, Jones was never the singer he was before the crash.

Before the crash, Jones was never the person he was after the crash.

"The King of Broken Hearts is so sad and wise," Jim Lauderdale wrote. "He can smile while he's crying inside." That was true for years, as Jones swilled mean bottles while raising cackling hell.

"I don't feel that way, not now," he told me after the crash. "Maybe wiser. But not sad."

I never knew the George Jones who was, as Hank Williams Jr. wrote, "cuffed on dirt roads" and "sued over no-shows." I knew a nice old man, who loved children, who rooted for the Tennessee Titans unless he'd placed a bet against them, and who bitched about young country singers who steered the music in non-traditional directions. I knew a man who endured the degradation of the thing that most of us thought to be his greatest attribute—his singing voice—with the help of the thing that turned out to be his greatest attribute, steadfast love. Hundreds of nights, he stood onstage and presented a pale approximation of his past mastery, wincing a little and pointing to his throat, in a gesture of gentle apology.

"It gets into your bronchial tubes, and, Lord, it's just a mess," he said, of yet another respiratory infection.

Every member of Jones' audience knew what he had been, and they knew they'd paid money to hear someone reduced of his powers, and yet they stood and cheered and encouraged. Music no longer flowed from him. He had to fight for every note. In some ways, watching Jones in his last decade was more powerful than hearing him in his glory years, though each experience presented lessons in humanity.

When George Jones died at age 81—thirty years later than expected— there was a visitation at the funeral home.

It was just like any visitation you've ever been to, just more crowded.

We all waited in line to pay our respects. The place was full of famous people, of course, but famous people are just like the rest of us when they're mourning. They stand, powerless in the face of death. They sign the guest register, and they scratch at tight collars, and they hug without smiling, because smiling is unthinkable in the weight of such gloom.

Then came the funeral, which was probably not much like any funerals you've been to.

Four thousand people crowded into the Grand Ole Opry House, and many more gathered outside, or held handmade signs along the route that his hearse took to the funeral home. The music was, of course, marvelous. The mood was sorrowful, with a side of triumph: This was, after all, a man who pissed away what should have been his grandest years but who ultimately found some measure of peace.

Brad Paisley sang the essence of Jones' religion, in the form of "Me and Jesus," written by Tom T. Hall: "I know a man who once was a sinner, I know a man who once was a drunk/ I know a man who once was a loser/ He went out one day and made an altar out of a stump."

Vince Gill sang his own "Go Rest High On That Mountain" through choked tears: "I know your life on earth was troubled, and only you could know the pain/ You weren't afraid to face the devil/ You were no stranger to the rain."

Travis Tritt sang Kris Kristofferson's "Why Me, Lord?": "Maybe Lord, I can show someone else what I've been through myself, on my way back to you."

And Alan Jackson sang that morbid son of a bitch: "Soon they'll carry him away/ He stopped loving her today."

Nancy sat in the front row, beaming love and fear, sadness and triumph.

After the funeral, Nancy asked if I would write the words that would be etched in perpetuity on George's gravestone.

I told her I would, though I had no idea what to write.

I thought of Johnny Cash's question, "Where are your mountains to match some men?" But Cash wrote that about Bob Dylan, not about George Jones. And in some ways, you'd need valleys, not mountains, to match George Jones.

Nancy needed these words in short order, and I fretted over them.

Late one night in early May of 2013, I played a bunch of George Jones records, and I played them loud. Then I sat at my desk, ignored my delete key, and wrote the first things that came to mind:

George Glenn Jones is the king of broken hearts. He sang of life's hardships and struggles, in a way that somehow lightened our own. His voice was effortless and unforgettable. He brought unsurpassed emotional eloquence to every song that he sang. He was the soul of country music, and he remains the soul of country music. No one will fill his shoes. He is at rest, but his music is alive and ageless: He gifted it to all of us, to the joyful and the broken. "Walk Through This World With Me," he sang, and we do.

CODA:
A FEW CLOSING THOUGHTS

An often-quoted axiom:

"Writing about music is like dancing about architecture: It's a really stupid thing to want to do."

Some people say musician Elvis Costello came up with that, though Elvis said it was humorist Martin Mull.

I don't care who came up with the "dancing about architecture thing." It is both funny and untrue.

If you do it correctly, writing about music doesn't distract, it informs. Writing about music invariably becomes writing about musicians, and musicians are among the world's most intriguing people. Musicians can conjure laughter or regret from tone and melody, which is a hell of a trick.

Songwriters sit down with nothing at all, and, on occasion, come up with something that moves people to act, to cry, or to care. People are impermanent, but music people create artful permanence. Writing about that isn't a really stupid thing to want to do, it's a noble thing to want to do.

I suppose I have now ascribed nobility to my endeavors within this book. What a jackass. Yet, there you have it. I've spent many years writing about country music, helping point people to art and artists who might enrich their everyday understanding. I'm not dancing about architecture, I'm hoping to tell you something you'll want to know. (I don't dance about anything, even about music: I learned to play and sing so I wouldn't have to dance.)

On occasion, after a concert or upon hearing a recording, people have attempted to compliment the music that I make by saying, "You're too good to be writing about other people."

I appreciate the sentiment, but deny the implication that writing about music is necessarily of lesser value than making music. The baseball equivalent would be broadcasters, and Vin Scully spent fifty-nine years as the broadcast voice of the Los Angeles Dodgers. He was poignant and hilarious and wise. He fostered understanding and community. He was an absolute delight. He was the poet laureate of baseball. He was more important to the Dodgers than any player other than Jackie Robinson, who broke the major league's color barrier in 1947.

I can't claim to be country music's Vin Scully, but that's a righteous and worthy goal. Peter Guralnick is the only writer who has ever reached it, and it was his *Lost Highway: Journeys and Arrivals of American Musicians*—along with Frye Gaillard's *Watermelon Wine: The Spirit of Country Music*—that convinced me of the art and worth of writing about music, and that assured that I'd be a little pissed off every time someone rattles off the "dancing about architecture" line.

Of course, Vin Scully is the rarest of broadcasters. Plenty of them are blowhards and gasbags who criticize without empathy or comprehension. Lots of music journalists are like that, as well. They're out there foxtrotting around buildings, spewing snark and invectives, posing as taste-makers and acting as if music is valueless if it is not to their preference.

Every mistake I've made in writing about music has come in situations where I did not approach the subject with respect and some measure of sensitivity. Most times I've chuckled at a "gotcha" line upon creation, I've regretted the same line when I saw it staring back at me in print. A gotcha line doesn't only cast judgment on the music in question, it casts judgment on the people who find worth and use and joy from the music in question. To cast judgment is to reject the examples of Tom T. Hall and Kris Kristofferson, and rejecting the examples of Tom T. Hall and Kris Kristofferson is a lousy-making endeavor for anyone seeking to write about music and musicians.

Chet Atkins was a country music shape-shifter. He was as respected as anyone in the music business, for his prodigious skills as a guitarist, for his acumen as a music executive, and for his standing as one of the producers who created the "Nashville Sound" that expanded country music's popularity and accessibility.

One of the enduring talents Chet brought to Nashville was Waylon Jennings, the full-voiced singer from Texas, by way of Arizona. Chet signed Waylon to an RCA Records contract in 1965, and Waylon went on to become a musical renegade and a sure-fire star. Waylon was one of the principal forces in country music's Outlaw Movement, in which musicians wrested creative control from producers and executives, rather than working within prescribed systems to obtain predictable sonic results.

Chet Atkins was one of the producers and executives who developed those prescribed systems, and who believed there were good reasons to seek predictable sonic results. Yet he and Waylon were great friends. They each made history on their own terms, and they are bound as compatriots, as innovators, and as Country Music Hall of Famers.

When Chet died, I wrote his obituary. In doing so, I called Waylon, who was emotional in describing the depth and breadth of Chet's artistry, and in relating Chet's uncommon humanity.

At the end of the conversation, Waylon issued a commandment:

"Write him up good, Hoss," he said. "You can't write him as good as he was."

I couldn't write him as good as he was. But I gave it a shot.

INDEX

Note: The following list contains names used in *Johnny's Cash & Charley's Pride* that may be registered with the United States Copyright Office:

"(My Friends Are Gonna Be) Strangers"; "(Old Dogs, Children, and) Watermelon Wine"; "(Pardon Me) I've Got Someone to Kill"; "1917"; "A Boy Named Sue"; "A Drunk Can't Be a Man"; "A Good Year for the Roses"; "A Week in a Country Jail"; "Ballad of Forty Dollars"; "Best of All Possible Worlds"; "Big River"; "Big Steve"; "Blowin' in the Wind"; "Blue Moon of Kentucky"; "Blue Suede Shoes"; "Blue Yodel No. 1 (T for Texas)"; "Branded Man"; "Bury Me Under the Weeping Willow"; "Cheatham Street Warehouse"; "Cheeseburger in Paradise"; "Coal Miner's Daughter"; "Cocaine Blues"; "Come Monday"; "Cowboy"; "Crazy Arms"; "Crazy Man, Crazy"; "Crescent City Blues"; "Cry! Cry! Cry!"; "Darby's Castle"; "Deeper Well"; "Desperadoes Waiting for a Train"; "D-I-V-O-R-C-E"; "Don't Come Home A'Drinkin' (With Lovin' on Your Mind)"; "Don't Take Your Guns to Town"; "Don't Tempt Me"; "Dreaming with Tears in My Eyes"; "Duvalier's Dream"; "Floptop Beer"; "Folsom Prison Blues"; "For The Good Times"; "From Sad Street to Lonely Road"; "From the Bottle to the Bottom"; "From the Bottle to the Bottom"; "Go Home"; "Go Rest High on That Mountain"; "Great Speckle Bird"; "Harper Valley P.T.A."; "He Stopped Loving Her Today"; "He'll Have to Go"; "Heart of Gold"; "Help Me Make It Through the Night"; "Hey Loretta"; "Hey Porter!"; "Hole in My Pocket"; "Homecoming"; "Honky Tonk Girl"; "I Can Help"; "I Love You Because"; "I Love"; "I May Hate Myself in the Morning"; "I Started Loving You Again"; "I Walk the Line"; "I Will Always Love You"; "I Wonder Do You Think of Me"; "I'll Have a New Body (I'll Have a New Life)"; "I'm a Lonesome Fugitive"; "I'm No Stranger to the Rain"; "I've Aged Twenty Years in Five"; "I've Got a Tiger by the Tail"; "If You Want to Be My Woman"; "Irma Jackson"; "It Ain't Me Babe"; "Jerusalem Tomorrow"; "Jimmy Martin's Life Story"; "Jody and the Kid"; "Joseph Cross"; "Junior's Farm"; "Kern River Blues"; "Leonard"; "Little Bitty"; "Live Like You Were Living"; "Lloyd's of Nashville"; "Long Black Veil"; "Look at Us"; "Louisiana Man"; "Love Insurance"; "Mama Bake a Pie (Daddy Kill a Chicken)"; "Mama Tried"; "Margaritaville"; "May the Bird of Paradise Fly Up Your Nose"; "Maybe You Heard"; "Me & Bobby McGee"; "Me and Jesus"; "Memories of Mother and Dad"; "Million Miles to the City"; "Murder on Music Row"; "My Happiness"; "My Head Hurts, My Feet Stink, and I Don't Love Jesus"; "National Everybody Hate Me Week"; "Near You"; "Nobody to Blame"; "Ocean of Diamonds"; "Oil Tanker Train"; "Okie from Muskogee"; "On the Other Hand"; "Once a Day"; "One's on the Way"; "One"; "Opal, You Asked Me"; "Pan American Blues"; "Pencil Thin Mustache"; "Portland, Oregon"; "Rainy Day Women #12 & 35"; "Real Rock 'n' Roll Don't Come from New York"; "Red River Valley"; "Remember When"; "Rex's Blues"; "Ring of Fire"; "Rock Around the Clock"; "Rocket '88"; "Rusty Cage"; "Sallie Gooden"; "Sally G"; "Saphronie"; "She Thinks I Still Care"; "Silver Wings"; "Sing a Sad Song"; "Sing Me Back Home"; "Single Girl"; "Souvenirs"; "Suffer a Fool"; "Sunday Morning Coming Down"; "Sunny Side of the Mountain"; "Teenage Boogie"; "That's All Right, Mama"; "The Ballad of Jed Clampett"; "The Bridge Washed Out"; "The End of the World"; "The Fightin' Side of Me"; "The Gambler"; "The Grand Ole Opry Song"; "The Great Filling Station Holdup"; "The Heart"; "The Man Who Hated Freckles"; "The Prisoner's Song"; "The Race Is On"; "The Silver Tongued Devil"; "The Three Bells"; "The Window Up Above"; "The Winner"; "The Year Clayton Delaney Died"; "These Days (I Barely Get By)"; "Thunderhead Hawkins"; "Titanic"; "To Beat The Devil"; "Traveller"; "Trip to Hyden"; "Two Wrongs Won't Make a Right"; "Uncle Pen"; "Viet Nam Blues"; "Wabash Cannonball"; "Walk Through This World with Me"; "Walking the Floor Over You"; "Waterloo"; "Welfare Cadillac"; "What Is Truth"; "When the Golden Leaves Begin to Fall"; "When You Say Nothing at All"; "Whispering Sea"; "White Lightning"; "Who's Gonna Fill Their Shoes"; "Who's on First"; "Why Me, Lord?"; "Why You Been Gone So Long"; "Widow Maker"; "Wildwood Flower"; "Will the Circle Be Unbroken"; "Wine"; "Without You"; "Workin' Man Blues"; "Workin' Man Blues"; "You Are My Sunshine"; "Young Love"; *A Good Natured Riot: The Birth of the Grand Ole Opry*; *A Hard Act to Follow*; *A Story of the Grand Ole Opry*; ABC; ABC Records; *Air Castle of the South: WSM and the Making of Music City*; *All I Want To Do In Life*; *American Beauty*; *American III: Solitary Man*; *American Recordings*; Amusement Business; Andrew Johnson Hotel; Applebee's; Arthur Murray; Asylum Records; *At Folsom Prison*; *At San Quentin*; Atlantic Records; Auburn University; Batman; Belcourt Theatre; BellSouth; Betty Ford Center; Bighorn Publishing; *Billboard*; Birchmere; Bistro; *Black Cadillac*; *Blonde on Blonde*; Bluebird Café; Bluefield Cab Company; *Bluegrass Unlimited*; *Bobby Bare Sings Lullabys, Legends and Lies*; Bon Bon's; Bridgestone Arena; Budweiser; Burger Bar; Cadillac; Capitol Records; *Cash*; CBS; Cellar Door; *Changes in Latitudes, Changes in Attitudes*; Chart Room; Chevy; Chicago Cubs; Chiclets; Chisca Hotel; *Coal Miner's Daughter*; Coca-Cola; Columbia Records; Commander's Palace; *Country Music*; Country Music Association; Country Music Hall of Fame; Cowboy Arms Hotel & Recording Spa; Crown Electric; D&D Lounge; *Dear Dead Delilah*; Decca Records; Dixie Tabernacle; *Don't Bump the Glump!*; Dough Boy Lunch; *Dreaming My Dreams*; Duke University; *Encyclopedia of Country Music*; ESPN; Falstaff Beer; Fender; *Flatt & Scruggs—Recorded Live at Vanderbilt University*; *For Once and For All*; Gibson; Gone; *Gone Girl*; Google; Gospel Music Association; Grammy; Grand Ole Opry; *Guess Things Happen That Way*; Guinness World Records; Harley Davidson; Harvard University; *High Noon Roundup*; Hohner; *Hub City Music Makers*; I.R.S. Records; *In Person*; *In Search of a Song*; *Inside Folsom Prison*; iPod; John Prine; Kay Guitars; Keegan School of Broadcasting; Kennedy Center; *Kristofferson*; *Last of the True Believers*; *Late Night with David Letterman*; Lee Street Taxi Company; Linebaugh's Restaurant; *Live at the Old Quarter*; *Live at the Philharmonic*; Los Angeles Dodgers; *Lost Highway: Journeys and Arrivals of American Musicians*; *Louisiana Hayride*; Major League Baseball; *Man in Black*; *Mark Twang*; Martha White Flour; *Meeting Jimmie Rodgers*; Mercury Nashville; Mercury/Polygram; Merriam-Webster; MexiMelt; Mighty Mouse; Milwaukee Braves; Modesto Garden; Monument Records; *Mountain X-Press*; Music Appreciation Hour; MusiCares; *Nashville Skyline*; National Association of College Talent Buyers; National Life and Accident Insurance Company; NBC; Neely Auditorium; New York Knicks; *New York Times*; New York Yankees; Nine-O-One Club; *Old No. 1*; Oxford University; Pete Burdette's Pure Oil; *Pieces of the Sky*; *Playboy*; Poligrip; Pomona College; *Porter Wagoner Show*; Prednisone; Professional Club; Quad Studios; Quiet Night; *Rattle and Hum*; RCA; *Recorded Live at Panther Hall*; *Repossessed*; Rock and Roll Hall of Fame; *Rolling Stone*; *Roots*; Roxy; Ryman Auditorium; Sandista; *Serving 190 Proof*; *Shakespeare Was a Big George Jones Fan: 'Cowboy' Jack Clement's Home Movies*; Silverado; SportsCenter; Staples Center; Starday; Station Inn; Stella Guitars; Styrofoam; Summer Records; Sun Records; Super Bowl; *Sweetheart of the Rodeo*; Syracuse University; Taco Bell; Tally Ho Tavern; Tally Records; Taylor-Christian Hat Company; Telecaster; Tennessee Titans; Texas World Speedway; *The Beverly Hillbillies*; *The Cold, Hard Truth*; *The Devil and Billy Markham*; The Ernest Tubb Record Shop; *The Fabulous Johnny Cash*; *The Giving Tree*; *The Godfather*; *The Johnny Cash Show*; *The Lady or the Tiger*; *The Lloyd Green Album*; *The Oxford American*; *The Silver Tongued Devil and I*; *The Tennessean*; *The Tonight Show*; *The Village Voice*; *There's More Where That Came From*; *Third World Warrior*; *Time*; Tootsie's Orchid Lounge; Top Rank Records; *Traveller*; Trayer's; *Twilight Zone*; *Unchained*; United States Air Force; United States Marine Corps; University of Alabama Crimson Tide; *Van Lear Rose*; Vanderbilt University; Victor Talking Machine Company; Viper Room; Wagon Wheel; War Memorial Auditorium; *Washington Post*; *Watermelon Wine: The Spirit of Country Music*; West Point; WHBQ; *Where the Sidewalk Ends*; *Will the Circle Be Unbroken*; *Will You Miss Me When I'm Gone: The Carter Family & Their Legacy in American Music*; WMPS; Wollensak; *Workingman's Dead*; World Series; *Wrecking Ball*; WSM; Zero Records.

ABOUT PETER GURALNICK

PETER GURALNICK has been called "a national resource" by critic Nat Hentoff for work that has argued passionately and persuasively for the vitality of this country's intertwined black and white musical traditions. His books include the prize-winning two-volume biography of Elvis Presley, *Last Train to Memphis* and *Careless Love*; *Sweet Soul Music*; and *Dream Boogie: The Triumph of Sam Cooke*. His latest work, *Sam Phillips: The Man Who Invented Rock 'n' Roll*, was a finalist for the Plutarch Award for Best Biography of the Year, awarded by the Biographers International Organization.

ABOUT THE AUTHOR

An award-winning musician and respected music journalist, **PETER COOPER** is the Country Music Hall of Fame and Museum's Senior Director, Producer, and Writer, and a senior

 lecturer in country music at Vanderbilt's Blair School of Music. He is a Grammy-nominated music producer, and a songwriter whose works have been recorded by John Prine, Bobby Bare, Jim Lauderdale, and others. He has appeared on *The Tonight Show* and *The Late Show with David Letterman* and has had the honor of being named one of Nashville's "10 Most Interesting People" by *Nashville Arts & Entertainment* magazine.

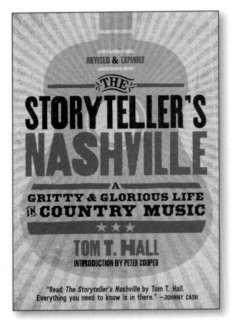

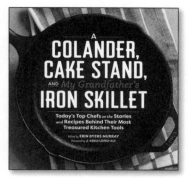
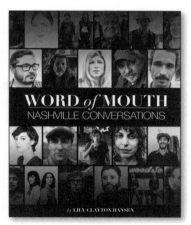